Perpetual Wealth™

Five Entrepreneurial Truths to Rig the Legal, Tax, and Financial Systems, Increase Revenue & Expand Your Freedom

Other Books by the Author

The Florida Estate Planning Guide
Selecting Your Trustee
Asset Alignment and Your Estate Plan
Common Cents Estate Planning: Practical Advice You Should
Consider With Your Attorney, CPA, and Financial Advisor
Common Cents Estate Planning II
Legal Matters When a Loved One Dies

Perpetual Wealth™

Five Entrepreneurial Truths to Rig the Legal, Tax, and Financial Systems, Increase Revenue & Expand Your Freedom

CRAIG R. HERSCH

ethos
collective

Printed in the United States of America

Published by Igniting Souls
PO Box 43, Powell, OH 43065
IgnitingSouls.com

LCCN: 2025903046
Paperback ISBN: 978-1-63680-477-4
Hardback ISBN: 978-1-63680-478-1
eBook ISBN: 978-1-63680-479-8

Available in paperback, hardcover, e-book, and audiobook.

Any Internet addresses (websites, blogs, etc.) and telephone numbers printed in this book are offered as a resource. They are not intended in any way to be or imply an endorsement by Igniting Souls, nor does Igniting Souls vouch for the content of these sites and numbers for the life of this book.

Some names and identifying details may have been changed to protect the privacy of individuals.

TABLE OF CONTENTS

Legal Stuff You Can't Ignore (Even If You'd Like To)

Let's get this out of the way so my compliance folks can sleep at night.

This book is for educational and informational purposes only. It's designed to make you think, not to give you specific legal, tax, or financial advice. Why not? Because I don't know your situation, goals, income statement, balance sheet, or mother-in-law. And trust me, all of those matter.

So don't take what you read here and run with it before talking to real, licensed professionals who understand your unique circumstances. Laws change. Tax rules shift. And what's true today might not be true tomorrow—especially if Congress tries solving one problem and, in doing so, creates three more.

This book does **not** create an attorney-client, CPA-client, or fiduciary relationship. If you want one of those, hire someone. Ideally, someone good. Preferably someone who isn't your brother-in-law who once watched a Suze Orman special.

You've been officially disclaimed.

INTRODUCTION

Confronting a Rigged System

> I've never seen a white male billionaire
> scream at the top of his lungs,
> "I know the system is rigged because I use it!"
>
> —*Comedian Dave Chappelle parodying
> Donald Trump's response to Hillary Clinton's
> debate accusation that he doesn't pay taxes*

Regardless of whether you admire or abhor President Trump, it's remarkable that he chose not to deny or defend the accusation. Instead, he turned it into a mic-drop moment. As bold as it was polarizing, the statement pulled back the curtain on a harsh reality—our legal, tax, and financial systems are rigged. But they're only rigged against you if you don't know how to play the game.

Plenty of great books exist about building wealth through real estate, dividend investing, or monetizing intellectual property. Some of them are excellent; if that's where you are in your journey, they're worth your time.

But this isn't that book.

We're not focused on creating income. We're focused on what happens after—or better yet, what should happen *while* you're building it. Whether you've already scaled a successful business or are just stepping onto the entrepreneurial path, how you structure ownership from the outset can determine whether your hard work compounds or leaks. Trusts, entities, and estate strategies aren't just for the ultra-wealthy or the nearly retired. They're how serious entrepreneurs reduce taxes, protect what they're building, and lay a foundation that grows with them.

What you'll find here is a blueprint for how to structure the things you're already pouring your time, energy, and capital into—or may have already built with blood, sweat, and spreadsheets. Because what you create is only as strong as how you own it. If your legal and financial framework is haphazard or reactive, you'll feel it—sometimes painfully—when life or business throws a curveball. But when you structure with intention? You create a system that minimizes taxes, shields assets, and supports the exponential growth most entrepreneurs dream about but few ever reach.

So no, this isn't about getting rich quick. It's about getting rich *intelligently*—and staying that way. It's about designing or refining your enterprises with foresight, so what you build works for you today and is fortified to last through challenges, transitions, and even generations. Think of it like framing a house: no one sees the beams, but they keep the roof on when the storm comes.

Entrepreneurs like you are uniquely positioned to engineer the system in your favor. Trump wasn't inventing loopholes or breaking the law; he was playing the game as it was designed, better, and with the knowledge that the rules weren't built for the uninformed.

If you pay too much in taxes, are exposed to lawsuits, or struggle to systematize exponential growth within the rules, this book will teach you how to flip that script.

It's not just about manipulating the legal, tax, and financial systems. It's about uncovering the Five Entrepreneurial Truths™ that lead to soaring revenues, expanding freedoms, and a legacy of perpetual, accumulating wealth. These truths aren't theoretical—they're actionable. They're the principles that transform hard work into an empire, creativity into exponential growth, and risk into generational opportunity.

Who This Book Is For

This book is for entrepreneurs—builders, doers, and those who've taken the risk and poured everything into a business, practice, or idea bigger than themselves. You've generated revenue, built a team, and created momentum. You're not wondering *how* to grow but how to protect, scale, and keep what you've built working for you instead of against you.

If you're like most entrepreneurs, you've figured out how to generate income but not how to *structure* it. Your ownership model, tax exposure, legal strategy, and liquidity position may not work harmoniously. Instead of fueling your next growth stage, they may slow it down, leak opportunity, or leave you vulnerable.

That's where this book comes in.

Perpetual Wealth™ isn't about death. It's about *design.*

It's about rigging the rules—legally, intentionally, and with precision—so the structures holding your wealth work as hard as you do. It's learning how trusts, entities, tax laws, and liquidity tools can become a *system* that protects and multiplies what you've already built.

This book is for entrepreneurs ready to stop reacting to advice in silos and creating a cohesive plan. It's for those willing to challenge traditional thinking, rethink what ownership means, and build a strategy designed to outlast the business itself.

If you're looking for tactical ways to play the game differently—*and win*—you're in the right place.

The Five Entrepreneurial Truths: Foundations of Perpetual Wealth™

This book is anchored by Five Entrepreneurial Truths—principles that will revolutionize your thinking about business ownership, structure, tax, and liquidity strategies. Here's a sneak peek:

1. Man-Made Rules Are Just That

Let's not pretend the rules of wealth—tax law, lending standards, liability traps—were handed down from Mount Sinai on stone tablets. These weren't divine revelations; they were drafted in back rooms and boardrooms by fallible people who may have never signed a paycheck. These aren't laws of nature—they're man-made frameworks. And like most things man-made, they're flawed, negotiable, and—if you understand how they work—navigable. Once you see how these rules decide who gets taxed, who gets sued, and who gets access, you stop playing the game with your eyes closed. You stop asking, "What are the rules?" and start asking, "Who wrote them—and who wins from them?"

2. Seven Entrepreneurial Mindsets Build Systemic Success

Most entrepreneurs chase strategies—growth hacks, tax tricks, shiny blueprints. But a plan without the right mindset crumbles under pressure. After decades of working with business owners, I've discovered one truth stands tall: those who build enduring wealth don't just think differently—they think systemically. Seven specific mindsets form the internal operating system that drives better decisions, sparks innovation, and protects freedom as

wealth grows. Master these, and you won't just suc-
ceed—you'll do it on your terms, in a system built
to serve you.

3. Winning Mandates: Flip the Script

The legal, tax, and banking systems weren't built
to grow your wealth but to feed off it. High taxes,
liability exposure, and rigid lending rules weren't
designed with entrepreneurs in mind. But here's
the twist: the structures meant to limit you can be
turned into tools that protect assets, reduce taxes,
and unlock opportunity. The game doesn't change
when you hustle harder—it changes when you stop
playing by rules never written for you and start living by the ones you wrote to win.

4. Freedom Requires a Tax-Free War Chest

Cash is only as valuable as its availability—and
its immunity from taxation. Liquidity isn't just about
having money; it's about having the *right kind* of
money. The kind Uncle Sam doesn't get to share in.
Tax-free liquidity, by contrast, is nimble and resilient. That financial fuel lets you seize opportunities
and sidestep the IRS or your banker when their grip
gets too tight. In an uncertain world, a reservoir of
tax-free capital doesn't just offer options; it delivers
peace of mind and a strategic advantage. True freedom requires capital that answers to you alone.

5. Great Advisors Aren't Enough

No matter your success, if your legal, tax, financial, and liquidity strategies were built separately,
you'll eventually hit a ceiling. Freedom doesn't come
from one-off solutions—it comes from a unified
team of external experts operating from a single,
coordinated blueprint. When your advisors operate

in silos, you face rising taxes, missed opportunities, and conflicting recommendations. Perpetual Wealth isn't built with isolated advice. It's engineered by a coordinated team that can rig the rules in your favor.

Mastering these Five Entrepreneurial Truths isn't about passive learning; it's about taking action. But action requires the right mindset. If you're not ready to challenge outdated beliefs, rethink strategies, and commit to intentional wealth-building, you may find what follows uncomfortable. However, that discomfort is the price of transformation.

Who This Book Is Not For

This book isn't for the passive entrepreneur. It's not for those waiting on a "perfect plan," a market trend, or a government program to make things easier. It's not for business owners who believe more hustle will solve structural problems, or that a generic tax and estate plan from a "we do any business that walks in the door" law firm will somehow protect what they've spent decades building.

If you're hunting for a checklist, shortcut, or plug-and-play template, this book will frustrate you.

And if comfort, certainty, and doing things "the way they've always been done" sound like a solid plan, put this book down now. We're not talking about tweaking around the edges. We're rethinking the system entirely.

This book demands more than curiosity. It asks for engagement, discipline, and willingness to challenge traditional business ownership, protection, and transfer strategies. These changes won't fit if your legal and tax structures are too ingrained to rethink. Don't read further if you think lawyers, CPAs, and liquidity specialists are fungible.

But if you're still reading, you may have felt a gut-level sense that what got you here won't take you where you're going. That your current team means well, but plays it too safe. That your planning is solid, but not strategic. You're chasing *freedom*. Freedom built from a system to expand with you, not contain you.

If that's what you're after, you're exactly where you need to be.

The Shift from Estate Planning to Perpetual Wealth Engineering

This book is less about financial planning and more about the structures in which you house your entrepreneurial ventures. Traditionally, entity selection, establishing trusts, and creating internal transactions between those trusts and entities are filed under the banner of "estate planning." And yet, for most people, that phrase still triggers dusty images of death, division, and final wishes.

That definition isn't just incomplete—it's dangerous. Because while the clock's still ticking, your planning shouldn't be about dividing the pie. It should be about growing, protecting, and designing it to work for you now. Trusts, partnerships, LLCs, and corporations aren't tombstones. They're tools. Used properly, they create leverage while you're alive and thriving—and set the stage for everything that follows.

But before you can engineer something new, you must first understand why the old models fail.

This book is about engineering a Perpetual Wealth Program. This proactive, dynamic approach integrates tax strategy, financial freedom, asset protection, and family governance into a single living system that evolves with you.

Why Most Structures Don't Maximize

Entrepreneurial ownership and management structures don't maximize value; instead, they reveal a sobering reality: Most entrepreneurs pay too much in taxes and expose too many assets to liability. Why? Most are reactive, not proactive. Their advisory teams aren't coordinated, and are likely to make these five mistakes:

- **Ignoring the First Truth**: Everything is made up. Most people operate within the constraints of outdated systems without questioning whether they can reimagine those systems.

- **Overlooking Tax Opportunities**: Tax codes are riddled with hidden opportunities. Without advanced planning, you're leaving money on the table.

- **Failing to Protect Assets**: Lawsuits, creditors, and even family conflict constantly threaten wealth. Without a robust protection system, it's a sitting target.

- **Forgetting the Power of Liquidity**: Without accessible cash flow, even successful systems crumble under unexpected demands.

- **Limiting Thinking**: It's easy to rely on decades-old traditional ownership and legal structures. But have you ever thought there could be more creative solutions to your problems? *When an innovative solution is offered, does your legal, tax, and financial team shut it down because they didn't first suggest it, don't understand it, and won't profit from its implementation?*

A vital truth is that most entrepreneurial organizations lack a proactive, cohesive design. But the good news is that just as poor strategies leave wealth vulnerable, the right strategies can make it resilient and perpetual.

This book isn't here to lament failures but to help you to imagine possibilities.

You'll discover how to turn obstacles into opportunities in the pages ahead. Using proven principles, you'll build systems that protect your wealth and empower it to grow. Let's move from the flaws of the old approach to the strengths of a new paradigm—one where your legacy is secure, developing, and inspiring for generations.

What You'll Learn in This Book

- **Rig the System in Your Favor**: From tax laws to entity and trust integration, you'll learn strategies to minimize taxes, protect assets, and create opportunities others miss.

- **Employ Strategies for Perpetual Wealth**: Discover how to turn your balance sheet into a self-sustaining machine that compounds assets over time.

- **Integrate Asset Protection**: Build an impenetrable fortress around your wealth, shielding it from legal and financial risks.

- **Overcome Outdated Thinking**: Find innovative, tradition-busting approaches you'll be eager to implement and adapt to your organization.

- **Build an Enduring Enterprise**: Create a governance framework that aligns your values, goals, and resources for future generations.

Armed with these insights, you'll have the tools to transform your wealth-building approach from reactive to revolutionary. But having tools isn't enough—you need the commitment, courage, and mindset to implement them. That's where the real work begins.

As you turn the page to consider your journey, reflect on what you've built so far, what it can achieve for you today, and how it can pave the way for enduring success tomorrow. The next step is yours to take, and it begins with a single, powerful decision: to embrace the challenge of unlocking your full wealth and freedom potential.

How This Book Is Structured

This book is divided into four parts, each dedicated to one of the Five Entrepreneurial Truths that form the foundation of the Perpetual Wealth Program. These truths aren't just abstract ideas; they provide practical, actionable frameworks for navigating estate planning structures, taxes, asset protection, and family governance in a way that positions you for long-term success.

This book is organized around four central structural truths, with an essential mindset woven into every chapter as a continuous foundation.

Each section will explore a core entrepreneurial truth, breaking down advanced strategies designed to help you rig the system in your favor. However, one truth—Mindset Unlocks Exponential Growth—is so fundamental that I haven't confined it to a single part. Instead, every chapter presents a challenge to reassess your mindset, encouraging you to adopt a new perspective on your entrepreneurial journey.

At the end of each chapter, you'll find a **Mindset Shift** section, allowing you to reflect on how the lessons apply to your unique situation. Even the most potent strategies are meaningless if you don't have the right mindset to implement them.

Your Challenge

You've worked hard to get to where you are today. The sleepless nights, the risks you took, and the sacrifices you made all add to the wealth, business, and influence you now control.

But what happens next? Have you maximized what you've built? Is there a better way? Will your success endure? Will it empower your family for generations, or will it eventually erode?

The Five Entrepreneurial Truths aren't just concepts—they're the tools to ensure your wealth survives but also thrives. Tools to turn knowledge into power, strategies into compounding growth, and your vision into a lasting legacy.

The question isn't whether you can create a new future.

The question is: Are you ready to take the first step?

Let's get to work.

TRUTH #1

Man-Made Rules Are Just That

The deck is stacked, but most entrepreneurs don't realize it until it's too late. The First Entrepreneurial Truth reveals that legal, tax, banking, and financial man-made rules aren't unbreakable laws—they're constructs to understand, navigate, and then turn to your advantage.

Chapter 1 reveals a hard truth entrepreneurs instinctively feel but rarely articulate: the tax, legal, and financial systems aren't broken—they were never designed with you in mind. Through real-world examples and unvarnished history, this chapter reveals how laws and incentives have been shaped to reward certain behaviors, often benefiting insiders while penalizing those who build through effort, not influence. You'll begin to see the system not as an impartial referee, but as a game with rules that favor those who know how to read them. Understanding that truth is the first step to changing how you play.

Chapter 2 reveals the hidden cost of success: a growing tax burden that scales with your income and never lets up. Most entrepreneurial structures weren't designed to withstand the four major tax forces—income, capital gains, self-employment, and transfer taxes—exposing your hard-earned wealth. Through real examples and overlooked dynamics, this chapter reframes taxes not as a line item but as a strategic force that quietly shapes outcomes. Before building a tax-efficient system, you must see the whole terrain and understand how many ways the system is wired to take advantage.

Chapter 3 sheds light on the biggest dangers to your wealth—the obvious threats and those hiding in plain sight. They range from customers, clients, and patients to vendors, partners, employees, regulators, and even a divorcing spouse. Success doesn't just invite attention—it attracts attacks. In a lawsuit economy, where litigation is a business model and perception equals liability, having assets makes you a target. This chapter sheds light on productivity as well as how the system incentivizes plunder, from billboard attorneys to bitter ex-partners. It's not about fear—it's about clearly seeing the landscape. If you think good intentions and LLC paperwork will protect you, you haven't met the wolves.

Chapter 4 confronts a truth most entrepreneurs only discover when it's too late: success without cash access is a trap. When markets crash, banks retreat, or conversely, when opportunity appears, your ability to act comes down to liquidity. But not just any liquidity. Liquidity that's accessible, on your terms, and beyond the reach of taxes or gatekeepers. Through the lens of an oak tree moment—when hustle and heart weren't enough—you'll see how traditional finance keeps you dependent, while tax-free capital becomes the quiet force separating those who survive from those who scale. When the money's locked, so are you. But when you structure it right, it unlocks everything.

Finally, Chapter 5 reveals the false security of traditional estate plans—those polished binders filled with impressive documents that do little to serve the living. Most estate plans are built for death, not life. They focus on dividing wealth instead of expanding it, transferring assets instead of protecting or multiplying them. This chapter reframes estate planning as more than a static set of documents—it asks whether your current plan works for you now, while you're still building, growing, and making decisions. Because if your wealth strategy only activates after you're gone, you're not planning. You're preserving. And preservation without optimization isn't what you're interested in.

Each chapter weaves aspects of the Second Truth—Success is Built on Seven Entrepreneurial Mindsets—preparing you to move beyond understanding the system to mastering it.

TRUTH #2

Seven Entrepreneurial Mindsets Build Systemic Success

As you progress through this book, you'll learn to upend the system and discover the importance of the *Mindset Shifts*. These aren't motivational quotes or surface-level tips. They're candid, self-reflective prompts, grounded in decades of experience guiding driven entrepreneurs.

In each chapter, you'll evaluate yourself across the seven distinct mindsets below that high-performing entrepreneurs consistently embody.

Growth-Oriented

The worst growth mindset avoids change like the flu, clinging to old methods, fearing competition, and thinking, "What I've built is enough." However, the best entrepreneurs see growth as a process, not a finish line. They invest in themselves and others, seek partnerships with complementary skill sets, and understand that exponential results demand exponential thinking. They don't just scale their businesses; they scale themselves.

Strategic Humility

At the bottom, ego rules. Advice is dismissed, expertise is undervalued, and professionals are treated as fungible. That mindset is fragile, not confident. However, the strongest entrepreneurs lead with strategic humility. They ask sharp questions, invite challenges, and collaborate with advisors not to delegate thinking but to expand it. They're not looking for lackeys—they're building intellectual leverage.

System-Oriented

Some entrepreneurs run everything on instinct. No structure, no coordination, only hustle and hope. That approach works until it doesn't. The best, however, know that structure beats speed. They build systems that scale legally, financially, and operationally. They don't just add entities when needed but design frameworks that evolve with their ventures, giving them control without chaos.

Tax-Aware

The tax-oblivious entrepreneur wakes up every April to surprises—and not the good kind. They overpay, understructure, and assume their CPA will "handle it." On the other hand, there are those who understand the tax code is a toolbox. The best tax-aware entrepreneurs engage experts who build coordinated strategies. They design income, move assets intentionally, and collaborate with cross-disciplinary teams to create lasting efficiency.

Liquidity Conscious

The worst liquidity mindset is reactive because there's no plan, and panic sets in when the bank says no. Liquidity is an afterthought—until it's not. But elite entrepreneurs are Liquidity Conscious. They design their systems to move fast and flexibly, with access to tax-free capital that puts them in control. They don't scramble for cash—they're ready for opportunity or crisis at a moment's notice.

Contrarian Curious

Conventional thinkers seek confirmation. They hire advisors to reinforce what they already believe. But the Contrarian Curious entrepreneur questions the default, challenges the assumptions, and explores the edges. They're not reckless— they're rigorous. While others follow outdated playbooks, they uncover overlooked ideas that unlock real advantage. Curiosity isn't a trait—it's a tool for freedom.

Risk Vigilant

The least prepared entrepreneurs are the most optimistic until something breaks. They skip protection, assume the best, and build on sand. But Risk Vigilant entrepreneurs know that downside protection sustains the upside. They structure purposefully, anticipate threats, and treat lawsuits, taxes, and family conflict as inevitable friction points, not remote possibilities. They don't eliminate risk; they engineer for it.

A Mindset Mirror

These mindset check-ins aren't fillers—they're your mirror. Because no strategy, no matter how powerful, works without the right thinking behind it. And when does the right mindset meet the proper structure? That's when entrepreneurs build enduring, perpetual wealth.

CHAPTER 1

The System Isn't Broken, It's Just Not Built for You

> That tax laws have any degree of fairness or logic is one of life's huge fictions.
>
> *—James J. Freeland, Co-Founder of the Graduate Tax Program at the University of Florida Levin College of Law, and Craig Hersch's Income Taxation of Estates & Trusts Professor.*

In 2021, *ProPublica* dropped a bombshell.

Reporters had obtained confidential IRS records showing that some of the wealthiest Americans—Jeff Bezos, Elon Musk, and Warren Buffett—had legally paid little to no federal income tax in multiple years. Bezos paid nothing in 2007 and again in 2011. Elon Musk managed the same feat in 2018. Warren Buffett, who has long criticized the tax code's inequities, paid a tax rate of just 0.1 percent on the wealth he accumulated between 2014 and 2018.[1]

These weren't illegal tax dodges. There was no offshore laundering or backroom bribery. They followed the rules, as written. But those rules weren't written with average business

---

1   ProPublica. "2021 Annual Report." ProPublica. Accessed July 8, 2025. https://assets-c3.propublica.org/pdf/reports/2021AnnualReportFinal2.pdf.

owners or wage earners in mind. They were constructed to encourage specific behaviors, such as investing in appreciating assets, borrowing instead of earning, giving to charity, and sheltering wealth in carefully designed entities and trusts. And who helped write those rules? Lobbyists, special interest groups, and lawmakers with campaign contributions on the line.

The report confirmed what many entrepreneurs already feel in their gut: the system isn't just complicated; it's tilted. For every small business owner writing checks to the IRS each quarter, there's a billionaire borrowing against stock gains tax-free, using insurance strategies you've never heard of, or locking assets behind fortress-like trusts. The real scandal isn't that they're breaking the law. It's that the law was built for them.

Let's not sugarcoat it: the legal, tax, and financial systems are rigged. Legislators draft and pass rules and laws. They are political beings who desire reelection every cycle to retain more and more power. Who mandates these laws? Lobbyists and other influencers who fund the legislators' campaigns. We know how the system works. Yet, at the same time, the government needs money to operate. Who pays?

For most, this means sacrificing significant wealth to taxes, navigating a maze of legal complexities, and scrambling to protect what they've built from lawsuits, creditors, and market risks. It feels unfair—because it is. These systems weren't designed to create an even playing field; those with power and influence built them for their use. Even as a wealthy entrepreneur, you may rightly feel the system is rigged against you until you understand the hidden rules.

But here's the twist: the same rules that can feel stacked against you are the very ones you can use to your advantage. Most people never realize it's not illegal to be smarter than the system; it's rare. The smarter ones build freedom on top of the rules designed to restrain them. The difference between those who struggle and those who thrive isn't luck or effort; it's knowledge and strategy. This book is your guide to shifting from being at the mercy of these systems to mastering them.

How the Game Is Rigged

At first glance, the tax code's complexity seems overwhelming, but don't be fooled—it's deliberate. The system rewards specific behaviors while penalizing other legitimate activities.

Legislators and lobbyists rarely start with a blank slate when writing laws. Instead, they inherit a system designed to favor the activities and assets of particular groups. These incentives are baked into the tax code, making it less of a rulebook and more of a map of behaviors the government wants to encourage.

Consider these examples:

- **Inescapable Wage Earner Taxes:** Salaried employees lose a substantial portion of their income to taxes, while business owners can shelter their earnings through deductions, depreciation, and retirement accounts.

- **Asset Protection Gaps:** If you hold assets in your name, they're exposed to creditors, lawsuits, and even family disputes. The best systems layer tax-favored trusts with entities like LLCs to protect wealth.

- **Liquidity Blind Spots:** Many people lack access to liquid capital, making it challenging to handle emergencies or seize opportunities. Those who understand the system create pools of tax-free liquidity, ensuring flexibility and security.

- **Inheritance Inefficiencies:** Without proper planning, wealth dissipates quickly—the second generation loses 70 percent of family fortunes and the third, 90 percent.

These aren't isolated quirks of the system; they're its defining features. The game may be rigged, but it's not unbeatable. Entrepreneurs who understand these dynamics can turn the system into an ally rather than an adversary.

Entrepreneurs Are Built to Win

Here's the good news: as an entrepreneur, you're already playing the game on a different level. You've built something remarkable, pouring creativity, perseverance, and vision into your business. You may have already taken steps to protect what you've built by creating LLCs, S corporations, limited partnerships, and other legal entities, owning your interests through revocable and irrevocable trusts.

But let's take a closer look.

Has your business and wealth structure evolved as part of a cohesive plan, or has it expanded reactively, piece by piece, over the years? If you're like many entrepreneurs, your framework has likely grown organically, with each new LLC or trust being created to solve an immediate problem rather than fitting into a more comprehensive framework.

For example, your S corporation might provide asset protection and pass-through tax advantages, but disallow the types of trusts used to own and transfer wealth outside the transfer (gift, estate, and generation-skipping transfer) tax systems. Your trusts may focus on an estate tax issue but can create unresolved income tax problems. Your LLCs may address the S corporation dilemma discussed above, but they can still create self-employment tax issues.

Your succession, estate, and tax plans may not consider the differences between entities wholly owned by you or within your family against those you share with third parties.

What began as a way to manage growth and protect wealth may now feel disjointed, leaving inefficiencies and vulnerabilities that could undermine your success and your family's future.

From Patchwork to Symphony

This isn't about starting over; it's about optimization. Your next step is transforming what you've built into a well-orchestrated machine: a *Perpetual Wealth Program* that protects what you've earned and multiplies it for future growth.

Think of your wealth structure like a symphony orchestra. Each instrument—your trusts, entities, tax strategies, and investments—has its role, and when played independently, each can create beautiful music. But without a conductor to bring these elements into harmony, the result isn't a symphony—it's noise.

Your S corporation might be like a powerful brass section, providing bold asset protection and tax advantages. Meanwhile, your LLCs act as the string section, creating a delicate balance of flexibility and growth potential. Your trusts could represent the woodwinds, offering rich, nuanced estate planning benefits. But if these instruments aren't aligned, they compete rather than complement.

A Perpetual Wealth Program is the conductor, ensuring that each part of your financial "orchestra" works harmoniously. When everything is synchronized, the result is a masterpiece—a wealth structure that protects what you've built and amplifies it for future generations.

Mindset Shift: Strategic Humility and the Contrarian Curious

After reading "The Tax and Financial Systems Are Rigged, But You Can Win," you've likely realized that success isn't just about understanding the rules; it's about how you position yourself within the system. To truly gain an edge, you must cultivate two essential qualities: Strategic Humility and a Contrarian Curious Mindset.

Strategic Humility isn't about doubting yourself. It's about recognizing that achieving your fullest potential requires assembling the right team and being open to insights beyond your own experience. True strategic leaders aren't driven by ego. They seek perspectives that challenge their thinking, sharpen their strategies, and reveal hidden opportunities. But they're also discerning: they don't follow advice blindly. They seek out advisors who think differently, see beyond conventional wisdom, and align with their higher goals.

In parallel, a *Contrarian Curious Mindset* pushes you to question the obvious and explore the unconventional. Accepting traditional advice at face value is not enough; you must be willing to dig deeper, ask better questions, and uncover paths others miss. Curiosity and a healthy skepticism of the status quo unlock advantages rigid thinkers never discover.

Reflect for a moment:

- Are you seeking advice that expands your thinking or reinforces your beliefs?
- Do you engage advisors as strategic partners or service providers who check boxes?
- When new strategies are proposed, do you explore them with curiosity or reject them reflexively?

Imagine a shift: Before making major decisions, you don't just seek advice—you interrogate the advisors. You recognize that traditional advisors' conventional wisdom is outdated, generic, or designed for someone else's goals. With Strategic Humility and curiosity, you ask better questions, pressure-test assumptions, and co-create strategies customized to your vision, not someone else's playbook.

This isn't about blind trust. It's about building an ecosystem of expertise that aligns with your vision and amplifies your strengths.

The game may be rigged. But with Strategic Humility and a Contrarian Curious Mindset, you become the conductor of your own financial symphony, setting the tempo, choosing the instruments, and leading the performance toward a crescendo of success.

Are you ready to play at a higher level?

Next Up—The Not-So-Hidden Cost of Success: Taxes

Ivan was 39, running a booming e-commerce business and working with an aggressive CPA. That year, he cleared $3.6 million in net income. When he saw his Q4 tax estimate, he texted me a screenshot with just two words:

"Is this legal?"

He wasn't joking. He was furious.

He'd maxed out his SEP IRA. Bought the SUV. Ran his bonuses through payroll. He thought he was playing the game right.

What he didn't realize was that he was playing Wall Street's game, not his own. His CPA was reacting, not designing. No pre-funded opportunity. No structured access to capital. No tax-free liquidity. No real system.

By the time Ivan found me, the damage was done. But the next year?

We rigged it differently.

Before I show you how, you need to understand the five tax systems that hit entrepreneurs harder than a UFC elbow to the jaw when you're already on the mat. And you'll see exactly why "just doing what your CPA says" is usually the most expensive strategy of all.

CHAPTER 2

The Silent Partner You Can't Fire: Taxing Authorities

> The taxpayer—that's someone who works for
> the federal government but doesn't have
> to take a civil service exam.
>
> —*Ronald Reagan,*
> *40th President of the United States of America*

In 2008, actor Wesley Snipes—action star, martial arts expert, and multimillionaire—was convicted on three misdemeanor counts of willfully failing to file federal income tax returns. His sentence? Three years in federal prison.

Not house arrest. Not probation. Prison.

Snipes had earned tens of millions from hits like *Blade* and *White Men Can't Jump*. Yet during the early 2000s, he bought into the popular "tax protester" argument circulating in fringe circles: income taxes were unconstitutional, the IRS had no jurisdiction over citizens, and filing tax returns was optional. Armed with this "advice," he stopped filing and submitted $11 million in bogus refund claims.

The government wasn't amused.

Despite his celebrity status—or perhaps *because* of it—Snipes became a public example of what happens when you treat taxes as optional. During sentencing, prosecutors clarified that this wasn't just about unpaid taxes. It was about deterrence. About reminding Americans, particularly those with significant income, that they have a silent partner in every financial success story: the IRS.

Even after his release, the IRS wasn't done. They pursued civil penalties and back taxes, filing liens and collection actions to recover what he owed.

Now, you may not believe in fringe tax theories. You probably file your returns on time, hire CPAs, and sign off on what looks right. But here's the takeaway: it's not enough to play by the rules. You must understand how the rules work—and, more importantly, how they work *against* you if you don't plan.

The tax code is vast, complex, and designed to benefit a specific kind of taxpayer. Unfortunately, that kind isn't usually working twelve-hour days running a business. It's the one who structures strategically—who plays offense, not just defense.

Consider the following:

You don't just have a tax bill if you're a successful entrepreneur. You have a target on your back. This brings us to the part most entrepreneurs avoid until it's too late: how much taxes are really costing you, how to stop treating them like a line item, and how to start treating them like a strategy.

You've probably approached taxes deal-by-deal: a little strategy here, a quick deduction there. And sure, that works—for a while. However, one of the core takeaways from this book is that you're not just building a business. You're building a system. A Perpetual Wealth Program. And that system must be designed to handle whatever opportunities the future throws your way—before Uncle Sam shows up with a fork and a napkin.

So let's break down the layers of the tax system that quietly eat away at your earnings, starting with the one that hits the hardest and most often.

Ordinary Income: The Meat Grinder of Wealth

Let's start with ordinary income. This is the government's favorite flavor of money because it's easy to collect and hard to avoid. It includes wages, salaries, business profits, tips, commissions, and any income that comes from actually doing work. You know, the kind that requires effort.

Businesses withhold most Americans' taxes on this income before their paycheck hits the bank. It's a system that works great—if you're the IRS.

But here's the twist: as your income increases, the percentage you owe does too. That's the joy of a progressive tax system. The more you earn, the more they take, like a weird punishment for being productive.

And if you're an entrepreneur? Buckle up. You don't just pay ordinary income tax—you often pay self-employment tax too. That's right. The tax code looks at your hustle and says, "Double it."

Which brings us to...

Self-Employment Taxes: The Silent Killer

Self-employment tax is like the appendix of the tax world— mostly ignored until it explodes.

This tax covers Social Security and Medicare; when you're self-employed, you pay both the employee and employer portions. Because, hey, you're the boss now—congratulations! Here's the bill.

In a regular job, your employer picks up half of this tab. But when you work for yourself, you get to treat yourself to the entire 15.3 percent rate on the first $168,600 of income (based on 2025 figures). And if you earn more? You still owe 2.9 percent in Medicare tax, with no cap. Ouch.

And unlike ordinary income tax, self-employment tax is regressive. This means that the more you earn, the smaller percentage you will pay on the total. So, if you're a high roller, congratulations—you've outgrown the tax. But for entrepreneurs just grinding to hit their stride? This one bites. Hard.

Innovative entrepreneurs often use S corporations or management companies to reduce their exposure. Why not pay yourself a "reasonable" salary and flow the rest of the profits out as distributions, which are not subject to this tax?

Think of it like replacing a flood with a leaky faucet. Still wet but manageable.

Capital Gains: The Government's Love Letter to Investors

Now, let's talk about capital gains—Uncle Sam's gentle way of saying, "Thanks for not working too hard."

These taxes apply when you sell something—stocks, real estate, businesses—for more than you paid. And if you hold it long enough, you get rewarded with lower tax rates than you'd pay on regular income. That's right: the tax code rewards people for sitting on their hands.

And let's be honest: this system was not built for middle-class salary earners. It's custom-designed for entrepreneurs and investors who make money while sleeping. Long-term capital gains are taxed at 0, 15, or 20 percent—plus that little 3.8 percent Medicare surcharge, if you're lucky enough to be "wealthy" by government standards.

In the 1980s, Congress briefly tried taxing capital gains like ordinary income. That idea went about as well as New Coke. The structure for preferential treatment was never actually deleted from the tax code. They just turned it off temporarily—like the idea was on vacation, not gone for good. And sure enough, the minute political winds changed, capital gains got their discount back.

So, if you're building and eventually selling a business, the lesson is obvious: structure it for capital gains treatment, not ordinary income. It's not just a difference in rates; it's a difference in lifestyle.

> One very large foreshadowing—there are several ways to tap the resource but not pay capital gains! Keep reading. You'll see that later!

State Taxes: Same Income, Different Pain

Where you live matters more than you think. A lot more.

Do you live in California, New York, or Massachusetts? Congrats—you get to pay some of the highest state income taxes in the country. Florida, Texas, or Nevada? None. Nada. Zero.

These aren't small potatoes. For high earners, the difference can be hundreds of thousands of dollars per year.

Unsurprisingly, entrepreneurs are flocking to low-tax states like they're heading to a music festival with free VIP passes. And they're not just buying second homes—they're changing their residency. Why? Because residency drives the tax bill. Move your legal and economic home base to a no-income-tax state, and suddenly, your world looks friendlier.

I'm a Florida estate planning attorney. Many of my clients keep two homes—one here in Florida, where they wisely declare their primary residence, and another somewhere up north (let's be honest, from here *everything* is north). Usually, that second home is in a tax-hungry state that would love nothing more than to claim them for residency. I even own a place in North Carolina—not because I'm sentimental about the state, but because I enjoy outdoor activities like biking the mountains, white water rafting, and hiking, especially when it's summer, and the temperature in Florida reads "surface of the sun until a Category 5 hurricane hits."

You don't necessarily have to move yourself. Sometimes, moving your structures is enough. States like South Dakota and Nevada have trust laws practically written in gold leaf for entrepreneurs.

Case in point: community property opt-in trusts. States like Florida, Alaska, and Tennessee now let couples opt into community property treatment, even if they don't live in a community property state. Why does that matter? Because community property enjoys a 100 percent step-up in basis at the first spouse's death.

Translation: You eliminate capital gains taxes when selling appreciated assets after your spouse dies. Plus, you get to re-depreciate those same assets. It's like winning the tax lottery twice.

Why the IRS Makes a Terrible Wedding Guest: Understanding the Transfer Tax Trifecta

Imagine you're throwing a lavish wedding with shrimp towers, monogrammed champagne flutes, and a 12-piece band. Now picture the IRS showing up uninvited, ordering top-shelf bourbon—on your tab. He doesn't stop at one drink, either. Before long, he's ordering rounds for his buddies at the Treasury and running up a bill big enough to make your accountant blush. That's how transfer taxes feel.

Most entrepreneurs are familiar with income tax. Some even have a love-hate relationship with capital gains tax (love the gains, hate the tax). But transfer taxes? That's the dark art of taxation, luring in the estate planner's playbook like a Marvel flick villain. We're talking about the Gift Tax, the Estate Tax, and—cue ominous music—the Generation-Skipping Transfer Tax, or GSTT, which I'm convinced was created just to test how many acronyms a single estate plan can hold.

The Gift Tax: Generosity with Strings Attached

You might assume you're allowed to give away your own money. Seems fair, right? You earned it and paid tax on it, and now you just want to pass it along to your kids, grandkids, or maybe that niece who runs a kombucha truck and is still "finding herself."

Not so fast! The IRS has a rulebook thicker than a wedding registry. You can gift up to $19,000 per person annually (2025) without triggering anything more than a thank-you card. But go over that, and you start dipping into your lifetime gift and estate exemption, $15 million in 2026.

Congratulations if you exceed that exemption during your life; you're now in 40 percent estate and gift tax territory. And no, that doesn't come with a commemorative plaque.

Oh, and don't assume the exemption itself is permanent. It's tied to the estate tax, which has a history of disappearing and reappearing like a magician's rabbit. Just ask the Steinbrenners. (More on that in a minute.)

The Estate Tax: Death and Dollars

Now, let's talk about the final send-off: the estate tax. Think of it as a goodbye hug from the IRS—except they pat down your pockets on the way out.

Anything you own at death over that same lifetime exemption could be taxed up to 40 percent. Homes, businesses, investment accounts, that weird antique watch collection; everything is fair game.

And if you're married, your unused exemption can roll over to your spouse, but only if your executor promptly files the right paperwork after you die. Miss that deadline, and the rollover disappears like a best man's speech after three bourbons.

The GSTT: Because Skipping a Generation Is Cheating

Then, there's the generation-skipping transfer tax, or GSTT—which might be the only tax in the code that punishes you for being *too generous* to your grandkids.

Let's say you want to leave money directly to the grandkids, bypassing your adult children (who, let's be honest, probably have enough of your stuff already). The IRS sees that and says, "Nice try. That'll be an extra 40 percent."

And here's the kicker: *that's in addition to* any estate or gift tax already owed.

The original goal was to stop the rise of American aristocracies, or at least prevent the IRS from waiting patiently for a second bite when your children die.

But in practice? It's a double whammy: a 40 percent GSTT stacked on top of a 40 percent estate tax: same dollars, two taxes. Skip a generation, and the IRS skips the courtesy.

The State Death Tax Trap

Remember our friends at the state department of revenue from earlier—when we talked about income taxes? Well, they're back. And this time, they're bringing transfer taxes. While most of the estate planning conversation focuses on the federal estate tax, many states have their own estate or inheritance taxes, with *exemptions that are dramatically lower* than the federal level. And if you're not paying attention, your estate, or even just a piece of it, could end up triggering a tax bill you never saw coming.

And here's the kicker: you don't have to live in that state to be taxed by it. If you own real estate or tangible property in one of those states, they can—and will—want their piece.

Let's say you're a Florida resident with no state income or estate tax. Great. But you also own a $2 million home in Boston. Massachusetts, unlike Florida, has a state estate tax and a $2 million exemption. So, you might think that since your residence there is equal to or less than the exemption, you won't pay the state death tax. But here's what most people don't realize:

The Massachusetts estate tax isn't just on the property in Massachusetts.

It's on *your entire estate*—if your entire estate exceeds the Massachusetts threshold.

So, if your total estate is $10 million, even though only $2 million of it is located in Massachusetts, that $2 million may get taxed as part of a *proportionate share* of your estate's exposure. You've now triggered a state death tax even though you don't live there, and even though the bulk of your assets are outside the state.

Here's what this example looks like:

Step	Description	Amount ($)
1	Total Value of Estate - FL Resident	10,000,000
2	Value of Massachusetts situs property (Boston residence)	2,000,000
3	Value of Total Estate exceeds Massachusetts exemption?	Yes

4	Tax Calculation if entire estate subject to MA Estate Tax	1,070,080
5	FL Resident pays pro-rata share of MA estate to Total Estate	20%
6	Massachusetts Estate Tax Due (20% of $1,070,080)	214,160

Figure 2-A

Sucks, doesn't it? And that's not the only trap. Most states that impose a state-level estate or inheritance tax do so in a similar fashion.

When "Free of Tax" Isn't Really Free

Many older trusts—or even recent ones drafted without state-specific estate planning—use *standard formula clauses* to divide a couple's estate when one spouse dies. These formulas are often set to maximize federal tax savings and include phrases like:

- Credit Shelter Amount
- Applicable Exclusion
- Amount that can pass free of estate tax

They sound harmless. And for federal purposes, they usually do their job.

But here's the problem: those clauses typically only consider the *federal* estate tax exemption, not your state's exemption, which can be much lower.

Take our Massachusetts couple as an example. The federal exemption in 2025 is $13.99 million. But Massachusetts only exempts $2 million. That's not a rounding error; that's a tax time bomb.

If the trust is written to fully fund the credit shelter trust with the entire $13.99 million at the first spouse's death, here's what happens:

- From a federal perspective, you've done smart planning.
- From Massachusetts's perspective, you've just triggered a large state estate tax on everything above $2 million.

And here's the kicker: even though the credit shelter trust is often designed to benefit the surviving spouse, it's not considered theirs for tax purposes. So, while they might still receive income—or be able to access principal—they don't get a *deduction* for state estate tax purposes. The trust can be doing everything it was built to do, and the state still gets a check.

You know what's scary? A well-meaning estate plan that quietly detonates your financial future—because someone overlooked how a state's tax laws interact with your trust's formula clause. These clauses are often designed to minimize the federal estate tax, which sounds smart in theory. But if they ignore state-specific exemptions? You could be looking at a six- or even seven-figure surprise bill. And the worst part? No one sees it coming until the tax bill shows up—often long after you can do anything about it.

A formula clause is the language in your trust or will that governs how assets are divided when one spouse dies. It typically creates two shares: a Credit Shelter Trust (which uses the federal exemption) and a Marital Trust (for the surviving spouse). Sometimes, these are

---

referred to as an A/B Trust. Sounds straightforward, right? Yet, for most families, the language might as well be written in Sanskrit. You could read it ten times and still not understand how it functions or what traps might be buried inside.

That's why hiring a qualified estate planning attorney isn't just a formality. It's protection, the kind of protection you don't know you need until it's too late. Cutting corners on your estate plan doesn't save you money; it just shifts the cost—and the mess—to your loved ones.

What Could Have Been Done Instead?

The trust could be written to take advantage of the marital deduction not just for federal transfer taxes but for state transfer taxes. For example, anything up to the *state exemption* ($2 million) could go into the credit shelter trust, while anything above that could go into a marital trust. That would

- delay the state-level estate tax until the second spouse dies;
- allow the surviving spouse to continue to access those funds; and
- preserve flexibility while keeping the long-term plan intact.

It's a small change. But in the right estate, it can save hundreds of thousands—and avoid frustration, confusion, and unnecessary cash crunches for your family.

You didn't mean to cause the problem. Your documents didn't mean to cause the problem. But the state's revenue department doesn't care.

Why Does All This Matter?

Most entrepreneurs don't plan to fail; they just fail to plan. They're too busy scaling businesses, launching projects, and dodging flaming arrows from regulators to pay attention to something that won't hit them until after they're gone.

But here's the kicker: The wealthy rarely pay transfer taxes. Why? Because they structure their assets. They build trusts. They use strategies like GRATs, SLATs, IDGTs, and Dynasty Trusts that sound like rejected *Star Wars* characters but are brilliant planning tools.

Meanwhile, those who ignore the rules? They leave behind a beautiful estate, only for their heirs to hand 40 percent of it to the IRS in cash. And trust me, the IRS and the state department of revenues don't even send a thank-you card.

The Year the Estate Tax Vanished

Let's rewind to 2010. Under the Bush administration, Congress had passed legislation temporarily repealing the federal estate tax, and 2010 was the year it vanished.

No estate tax. At all. None.

Now, most people didn't notice because, well, most people didn't die that year. However, one person who *did* was George Steinbrenner, the legendary owner of the New York Yankees.

Steinbrenner's estate? Worth billions. Yankees. YES network. Tampa shipyard. All George's. Under normal tax laws, his heirs would have owed hundreds of millions in estate taxes.

But in 2010? They paid nothing. Zero. Zilch. Nada.

It was the tax planning equivalent of winning the lottery—only the ticket was death, and the prize was of full value passed to heirs, untouched by the IRS.

There was a catch, of course. No estate tax also meant no automatic step-up in basis, so capital gains taxes became more complex. But given the scale of Steinbrenner's estate, the family came out way ahead.

The estate tax returned in 2011, but here's what's essential: the infrastructure was never dismantled. Just like capital gains, it wasn't deleted from the tax code but paused. The system was ready to spring back into action when Congress decided to bring it back.

And they did.

Could it vanish again in the future? Absolutely. The estate tax is a political football—passed, repealed, revived, rebranded. If you're counting on consistency, you're in the wrong game.

If you think tax laws are set in stone, you haven't spent enough time watching Congress break its chisel.

The Federal Tax Disappeared— But the States Didn't Get the Memo

Now, when the federal estate tax briefly vanished, many assumed the entire game was paused. It wasn't.

Even in 2010, when the federal estate tax dropped to zero for a single year, state death taxes didn't go anywhere. The states didn't say, "Let's sit this one out." They kept their tax codes in place, and families continued to get hit by estate taxes they didn't see coming—simply because of where they owned assets.

So, while the federal landscape may shift depending on Congress and the political winds, state-level taxation remains a persistent, often-overlooked threat. Savvy entrepreneurs don't just ask what the federal law says; they ask, "What happens if I die owning property in Massachusetts? Or New York? Or Oregon?"

Because when it comes to death and taxes, it's not always where you live that matters.

It's where your stuff lives.

Using Tax Loopholes to Build Perpetual Wealth

Let's talk loopholes.

These aren't bugs in the system. They're incentives. The tax code says, "Hey, if you do X, we'll reward you with Y."

Use an irrevocable trust to remove assets from your estate? Great. But with some planning, you can still pay the income taxes yourself, further reducing your estate without using up your gift exemption.

And by controlling how and when income is distributed, you turn the income faucet on or off as needed. Want to drip income to your kids during a low-income year? You can do that. Want the trust to grow tax-free while you foot the bill? That's possible, too.

It's like playing Monopoly, but you're writing the house rules.

Mindset Shift: Flipping the Script on Taxes

If reading this chapter made you wince a little, good. That's the point.

Taxes aren't just about what you owe; they're about what you *allow*. And for most entrepreneurs, what's costing them isn't the IRS—it's inertia.

So, let's start with a few tough questions:

- Have you built a tax strategy, or have you simply accumulated tax habits?

- Are your entities and trusts aligned under a master plan, or just scattered, one-off moves from past advisors?

- When was the last time you reviewed how your tax, legal, and financial systems interact, not just individually, but as a whole?

If your answer is "not recently" or "not really," you're not alone. Most entrepreneurs are too busy solving today's problems to notice tomorrow's traps. But here's the truth: the IRS doesn't wait for you to get organized. And neither does Congress.

The tax-aware entrepreneur doesn't just look for deductions. He or she orchestrates income. They don't "keep it simple" to avoid complexity; they build smart complexity so their structure can carry exponential growth. They know that simplicity without coordination is just another word for fragility.

And here's where structural soundness comes in. Having a few LLCs and a trust with a poetic name is not enough. Is your business built inside a blueprint that anticipates growth, taxes, exits, and generational transfer? Or are you hoping the pieces will magically fit together when the time comes?

Because they won't.

The best structures evolve. They flex with your ventures, protect your family, and leverage laws that most people never even hear about. And they're not built by one professional working in isolation—they're designed by a team, working in harmony, from the same score.

Finally, we can't ignore the elephant in the tax code: risk.

If you're not risk vigilant, your upside is always vulnerable. The right structure doesn't just reduce taxes; it guards against lawsuits, protects liquidity during downturns, and keeps the government from becoming your largest beneficiary. Risk isn't some imaginary future event. It's woven into the very laws you think you understand. But once you know how to read between the lines, you stop reacting and start engineering.

This chapter isn't about filing better tax returns. It's about flipping the script and turning the system in your favor. Using the same rules, forms, and statutes but with a different playbook. One that doesn't end in April with a bill but begins every January with a plan.

Because here's the truth: The IRS might be your silent partner, but your silence is optional.

The Hidden Risk: The World Wants a Piece of You

We've talked about how taxes chip away at your wealth. But here's the next layer of the onion: lawsuits, regulators, business partners, clients, ex-spouses, and sometimes your family.

Wealth makes you a target.

That's why in the next chapter, we won't dive into legal shields just yet but we will shine a spotlight on the risks that come with being successful.

Because you can't build an empire if you don't know where the landmines are buried.

Stay tuned.

CHAPTER 3

The Bull's-Eye on Entrepreneurs

> There are two ways to acquire the niceties of life: to produce them or to plunder them. When plunder becomes a way of life... they create for themselves... a legal system that authorizes it and a moral code that glorifies it.
>
> —*Frédéric Bastiat, French Economist*

Well, Frédéric, welcome to America.

Let's start with someone who's cracked the code on the modern "take from the rich and give to the poor"—John Morgan. You've seen him. Heard him. You've driven past five of his billboards on your way to the gym. His firm, Morgan & Morgan, didn't grow into a 1,000-attorney, 49-state legal empire on sheer goodwill. It was marketing—$350 million annually of it, on $2 billion of annual revenue, according to a *Forbes* article in December 2024. And behind all those "For The People" taglines, there's a subtler message:

"Isn't there *someone* we can sue for you?"

You, dear entrepreneur? You're *that* someone. You've worked hard, built something valuable, and now you look like a walking, talking target.

The Legal Battlefield for Entrepreneurs

When you start a business, your greatest fears usually center on payroll, cash flow, and whether that new hire is actually who they claim to be on LinkedIn. But the game changes once the world knows your name or sees your brand on a building.

Now, your mere visibility becomes a liability.

Lawsuits aren't reserved for the corrupt or the careless anymore. These days, all it takes is *perceived* success. Having assets makes you a target. And the people taking aim at you? They've built entire business models around finding folks like you.

Plaintiff attorneys often work on contingency. They frequently have little to no skin in the game—until they win. If they lose? They walk away. If they win or settle? They feast. So, who do they come for?

You.
With your equity.
Your reputation.
Your headlines.
You're a human jackpot!

And no, this isn't paranoia. It's pattern recognition. In my career, I've worked with dozens of clients whose mistakes weren't arrogance or bad faith; they were successful.

Lawsuits Are a Business Model

Here's the hard truth most entrepreneurs only discover once in the courtroom: *the legal system isn't built to keep you out of trouble but to process you once you're in it.*

- Depositions drain your time.
- Defense fees drain your profits.
- Stress drains your relationships.

And the scariest part? The lawsuit itself may not even be strong. It doesn't have to be. The process is the punishment. Many attorneys know they don't need to win; they just need to make you bleed long enough that you'll write a check to make them go away.

It's like playing poker where they get to look at your hand and bluff anyway.

Personal Insight: Why Florida Still Has No DAPT

Want proof of how stacked the system is?

I served three years on the Florida Bar's Asset Protection Committee, part of the Real Property, Probate & Trust Law Section. We aimed to pass a Domestic Asset Protection Trust (DAPT) statute—something several other states had already done to protect entrepreneurs from frivolous lawsuits.

We had a Republican governor and majority in the legislature, which is theoretically pro-business. You'd think it would have been easy.

It wasn't.

We drafted, lobbied, and debated, but the legislation never reached a House floor vote. Why?

Because the trial bar, the family law bar, and the banking lobby lined up to kill the bill. It seems plaintiff, divorce, and banking lawyers hold sway even in a state known for no income tax and sunshine conservatism.

So, the next time someone tells you Florida is "business-friendly," just remember that it depends on what kind of business you're in. Are you in the business of building, growing, and protecting wealth? You're on your own liability-wise (that is, until you create a Perpetual Wealth system!). If you're in the business of suing people who build wealth, the state practically rolls out the red carpet.

And it's not just Florida, by the way; thirty-three states still haven't enacted a DAPT statute, and in many of the ones that have, the laws are so diluted they offer little real protection.

Litigation: The Middle-Class Jackpot

Lawsuits have become the scratch-off tickets of the disenchanted.

"Injured? Call now!"

"Get the compensation you deserve!"

Translation? "Find someone with money and shake the tree."

Contingency fees mean that anyone can sue without putting a single dollar at risk. A semi-plausible claim, a few exaggerated emails, maybe an awkward conversation replayed out of context—and suddenly, you're the villain in someone else's payday script.

And while you're in your office trying to grow something valuable, the plaintiff is in a conference room with his billboard lawyer whose favorite word is "settlement."

The Politics of Plunder

You might think the law is about justice. It's not. It's about leverage, and that leverage is reweighted every election cycle.

Laws created to protect consumers and employees, while good in theory, have morphed into tools for targeting opportunities. You're not just a business owner. You're a defendant-in-waiting.

Over forty million lawsuits are filed annually in the US—more than the population of California. And a disproportionate number are aimed at entrepreneurs. Why? Because we've built a lawsuit economy, and you're the liquidity event.

Welcome to the Lawsuit Economy

This isn't fearmongering. It's arithmetic.

The more successful you are, the more likely someone will come for what you've built. And not with a handshake, but with a subpoena.

You don't just need a good attorney. You need a structure—a system—that discourages lawsuits from the start. Most of these cases aren't filed because of wrongdoing. They're filed because you look like someone who can afford to settle.

That's how the game works. Your best protection is not to be the biggest or boldest—it's to be the most challenging target.

Who's Gunning for You?

Clients and Customers

What used to be "the customer is always right" has become "the customer is always armed." A botched invoice. A missed deadline. A sharp word in an email—suddenly they're offended, and your attorney's on speed dial.

Vendors and Suppliers

Partnerships sour. Contracts get weaponized. They miss their obligation and still blame you. Now, you're not just their customer; you're their scapegoat.

Employees

Even the best HR policies are no match for a plaintiff's attorney who smells blood. Harassment, discrimination, and wage violations require only one complaint. And whether it's true? That's not the point. The process itself becomes punishment.

Business Partners

Breakups between founders feel like divorces with a legal team. The people you once trusted to help you build are now using your operating agreement against you.

Regulators

The IRS, OSHA, and the EPA don't need to prove guilt to ruin your week. The alphabet agencies act first, audit second, and assume guilt third.

Divorce Court

Family court is where logic goes to die. And equity law? It laughs at your prenup.

It doesn't matter if you built the business before you got married. A judge can still divide it like leftover wedding cake. The legal standard is "whatever's fair." Fair is often defined by who cries louder.

Judges can assign ownership, divide future profits, or force you to buy out your ex at inflated valuations. They can assign phantom equity based on "emotional support," even if your spouse never stepped foot in your office.

This is not an exaggeration. Equity law is a legal system in which emotions are evidence and outcomes are often dictated by narrative over numbers.

Divorce isn't just a personal crisis; it's a business threat. And for many entrepreneurs, it's the most expensive lawsuit of their lives.

The Misguided Faith in Tenants by the Entirety (TBE)

Not everyone reading this is worried about divorce court. Some of you have strong marriages, full of trust, respect, and the occasional good-natured debate over the thermostat. If that's you, congratulations. You've cleared one significant risk.

And if you've gone the extra mile to title assets jointly under Tenancy by the Entirety (TBE), you've built another layer of protection, or at least, it feels that way at first. Some advisors pitch TBE ownership as a legal force field, claiming that state law shields assets from creditors chasing only one spouse. And sometimes, it does.

But like most things legal, the devil hides in the details. In many states, TBE protection only applies to real estate, not your brokerage accounts, business interests, and indeed not anything held inside a revocable trust, even if it's a joint trust. Beneficial interests in trusts usually don't qualify for TBE protection at all. So, while TBE can look like a fortress, it often turns out to be just a picket fence—sturdy enough against rabbits but not much good against a wolf.

And there's more. TBE has a few fatal weaknesses that no one seems to mention when they're handing you the pen to sign:

- Your spouse dies → You become the sole owner. Now, everything's exposed.
- You get divorced → TBE evaporates faster than your wedding DJ's deposit.
- You're jointly sued → Like in a car accident caused by your teenager. TBE doesn't apply when both of you are on the hook.

- You try to retitle accounts post-lawsuit → Congrat-ulations, you've just entered the realm of fraudulent transfers. Cue the court orders.

In other words, TBE isn't a strategy. It's a happy accident that works — until the real storm comes. If Tenancy by the Entirety is a picket fence, trusts are the start of real stone walls. They're stronger, smarter, and can seriously frustrate would-be creditors. But that doesn't mean they're foolproof. In fact, depending on how and where they're built, even the strongest-looking fortress can have hidden cracks. Let's take a closer look at what trusts can do—and just as importantly, where they can still let you down.

Married couples: Don't title your autos in joint name! Title each car in the name of the spouse who drives it the most. That way, you minimize the likelihood that an accident leads to your joint assets. Do, however, name each other as insured on your solely owned vehicles. Better yet—pur-chase a healthy umbrella policy!

Trust the Trust—But Not Blindly
Foreign Asset Protection Trusts (FAPTs)

Imagine if Fort Knox had a beach view and a legal system that couldn't care less about US court orders. That's essen-tially what you get with offshore asset protection trusts in places like the Cook Islands or Nevis.

These jurisdictions have been specifically engineered to make life miserable for US creditors. A judgment from a US court? Worthless. The burden of proof? Higher than Everest. The timeline? Longer than glaciers are old.

It's about as bulletproof as it gets in terms of legal armor. Even so, it's not exactly a walk on the beach.

FAPTs come with high setup costs, annual maintenance fees, and complexity that makes most entrepreneurs break out in hives. You must also hand over control of your assets to a trustee in a jurisdiction you likely can't find on a map—to someone you've never met, who lives twelve time zones away and isn't returning your calls if you're panicking.

Don't forget the IRS. It monitors foreign trusts like a hawk on a caffeine bender. Fail to report your income correctly, and the penalties can make the trust itself feel like a bargain.

My experience? Most entrepreneurs blanch at giving up that kind of control, especially to someone they've never met and will probably never visit. So, unless you've got an extra $100 million lying around, earmarked for the "just in case the whole world collapses" fund, FAPTs are probably not your first move.

Effective? Absolutely.

Comfortable? Not even a little.

Essential? Only if you're playing at the ultra-high-stakes table.

Domestic Asset Protection Trusts (DAPTs)

If FAPTs are the offshore armored bunker with palm trees, **DAPTs** are the friendly neighborhood fortress—less intimidating, easier to access, and with less chance of triggering an IRS audit that makes your CPA sweat through his blazer.

States like Nevada, South Dakota, Delaware, and a handful of others have passed laws that allow you to create asset protection trusts right here on US soil. These trusts are designed to shield your assets from future creditors while enabling you to retain some control, directly or through people you know and trust.

Sounds too good to be true? That's because sometimes it is.

However, there's a catch: Not all states play nicely together.

Let's say you set up a DAPT in Nevada. The structure is perfectly legal under Nevada law. You appoint a Nevada trustee. You cross your T's and dot your I's. Everything is wrapped up in a tidy trust with all the proper disclaimers, asset schedules, and indemnity clauses.

Then someone sues you in California—a state that doesn't recognize DAPTs, and frankly, treats them with the same level of reverence as expired yogurt. That California judge? They may ignore your Nevada trust and allow the plaintiff to go straight for the assets.

Why? Because interstate comity—the idea that one state respects another's laws—is more of a *suggestion* than a rule in litigation. Especially when the judge thinks you're hiding assets.

This is the legal equivalent of trying to use Monopoly money at a poker table. You're playing by one state's rules, but the dealer—and the house—don't follow those rules.

While DAPTs are growing in popularity, and states like Nevada have invested considerable time in making them attractive, their effectiveness is directly tied to the geography of the courtroom. If your legal problems land in the wrong jurisdiction, your fancy trust may be nothing more than a stack of expensive paper.

Now, does that mean DAPTs are useless? Not at all. I use them for my clients when appropriate. DAPTs offer substantial protection when used thoughtfully, especially in multi-layered structures with entity structuring and situs planning. But they work best as part of a larger asset protection framework, not your sole defense strategy.

In other words, DAPTs are a great wall, as long as you're not solely relying on it.

Why Incorporation Isn't a Get-Out-of-Jail-Free Card

When most entrepreneurs start their first company, they treat forming an LLC or corporation like installing a three-step home security system.

1. File the paperwork.
2. Pay the fee.
3. Protection guaranteed.

Well, yes, it can be that simple if you treat it like a business and not like a hobby with a logo.

Too many entrepreneurs think that their assets are forever insulated once they've set up a company. And on paper, that's true. Corporations and LLCs are liability shields—a legal wall between your business dealings and your personal bank account.

But that wall? It has rules. And if you don't respect them, the courts won't either.

Did you forget to file your annual report? Did you use your company debit card to book a Hawaiian getaway for your anniversary? Did you co-mingle funds between your business and personal accounts like a big family picnic?

If so, you've just opened yourself up to a piercing of your corporate veil. And in legal terms, that means the judge may treat your company like it never existed.

Suddenly, your residence, your brokerage accounts, and even that fishing boat you told your spouse was a "marketing expense," are now fair game for creditors.

And if you're relying on a single-member LLC for protection in a state that doesn't offer robust charging order protections? You've got a problem.

A *charging order* is supposed to be a creditor's only remedy. They can take your distributions, but can't force the company to liquidate assets or hand over control. It's the legal version of waiting at the mailbox for a check.

But in some states—especially if your LLC only has one member—*those protections don't apply*. The court may grant the creditor the keys to the kingdom, including voting rights, control over operations, and access to the underlying assets.

So, if you're operating a single-member LLC in the wrong jurisdiction, you might as well have written your company name in sidewalk chalk before a thunderstorm.

Yes, incorporation is valuable. But only if you treat the entity with the formal respect the courts expect. File your reports. Maintain separate accounts. Don't blur the lines between personal and professional, because the judge won't just see paperwork when things go sideways. They'll uncover patterns.

Timing Is Everything: Fraudulent Transfers

Of all the missteps an entrepreneur can make when it comes to asset protection, this is the granddaddy of them all: They wait too long.

Here's the typical scenario: Things have been going well. Business is humming. Maybe you're even riding a bit high. Then suddenly, there's a problem. A client gets aggressive. A partner gets petty. An employee gets litigious. And now the heat is on.

That's when panic sets in, and the frantic Google search begins:

"How to protect assets from a lawsuit that hasn't technically been filed yet."

Too late.

You can't just start retitling your home, moving cash offshore, or transferring your Tesla to your cousin Vinny three weeks after receiving a demand letter and expect the court to smile and nod.

Because here's what you've just done: You've triggered a fraudulent transfer.

And while many legal principles are murky, this one is crystal clear: *you can't hide the money once you hear the footsteps.*

Courts don't just dislike fraudulent transfers. They *relish* the opportunity to unwind them. To freeze accounts. To claw back funds. To humiliate you in the process, especially if you were sloppy about it, which, let's face it, people in a panic usually are.

Here's how it plays out in a courtroom:

- A sudden flurry of asset transfers occurs just days after legal trouble appeared on the horizon.
- Assets are transferred between family members or shell entities, often conveniently just outside your name.
- Entities spring up like mushrooms after rain, with your spouse, child, or poker buddy listed as the new "owner."

To the judge, it's like you're sneaking the hotel's monogrammed bathrobe into your bag at checkout—only to be stopped in the lobby by the manager, who unzips your suitcase in front of everyone. That's what a court does when it unwinds a fraudulent transfer.

And the law is unambiguous on this: Intent matters—but not as much as *timing*. If you transferred the asset when the writing was already on the wall, even if it was "technically legal," the court can still undo it—and possibly sanction you for trying to get cute with the rules.

Let's be blunt: This is not the time to channel your inner Houdini.

The best asset protection plans don't rely on sleight of hand. They don't come together overnight. And they never start *after* you've already stepped on the landmine.

The best plans are boring. Quiet. Intentional.

They're put in place years in advance, long before there's even a whiff of trouble. That's what gives them strength. That's what gives them legitimacy.

Because when a judge sees a structure that's been in place for five, ten, or fifteen years—well before any legal issue arose—they don't see deception.

They see design.
They see discipline.
They see someone who plans like an adult.

But what happens when they see a last-minute scramble?
They see **panic.**
And panic doesn't win in court. It bleeds.

So, remember:
Don't wait for the smoke to install the fire alarm.
And you don't wait for a lawsuit to install the shield.

Plan early. Sleep well. Stay protected—more on that in upcoming chapters.

Mindset Shift: Risk Vigilance

If your blood pressure crept up while reading this chapter, that's not bad. It means you're waking up to a reality many successful entrepreneurs miss until it's too late.

Most estate and business planning revolves around growth and legacy. Rarely does it confront what can dismantle all of it in a single stroke: legal vulnerability.

And make no mistake—you don't have to do something wrong to be sued. You merely have to look like someone who can afford to settle.

The Perpetual Wealth mindset doesn't view lawsuits as unlikely events. It sees them as *inevitable friction points* in a life of success. If you're building, expanding, hiring, signing deals—you're in the arena. And the arena has spectators and attackers.

So, let's step back and ask the hard questions:

- **Do you have a system or a set of documents?**

    Many entrepreneurs believe their estate plan protects them. But a will doesn't protect you from a lawsuit. A revocable trust doesn't shield assets. And a dusty binder in your safe isn't a plan; it's paperwork. Do you have a system behind the scenes to protect what you've built?

- **Are your entities doing more than filing taxes?**

    Did your LLCs and S-Corps come with real strategy, or were they just the default option from your CPA ten years ago? Are they structured not just for efficiency but for insulation? Or are you unintentionally mingling personal and business accounts, piercing the veil you thought would protect you?

- **Have you created layers, or just a thin outer shell?**

  Think about your trust structures, your insurance policies, and your corporate governance. Do they form a cohesive defense strategy? Or are they like armor pieces from different suits—none quite fit together? The most successful entrepreneurs don't just accumulate legal documents. They **orchestrate** them.

Because here's what the truly vigilant understand:
Success attracts attention. And attention brings attack.

You can't build in today's environment and expect to be invisible. That's not how the world works anymore. Plaintiff attorneys advertise more than car dealerships. Regulators are more aggressive than ever. And bitterness often travels faster than reason.

A Perpetual Wealth system anticipates this. It's not reactive. It's proactive, coordinated, and continuously evolving with your business and life.

So, where are you today?

Are you trusting that your good intentions will protect you?

Or are you structuring your assets like someone who knows the wolves are coming and plans to be five steps ahead when they do?

Remember:
You can't stop the world from taking shots.
But you can make damn sure they don't land.

Next up: financial danger. You've seen how legal threats put a bull's-eye on your back. But what about the silent killer of growth—lack of liquidity?

Let's talk about how to stop scrambling for cash and start building your bank.

CHAPTER 4

When the Money's Locked, So Are You: The Case for Liquidity

> It's not a problem if you can
> easily write a check to solve it.
>
> —*Dan Sullivan, Co-Founder, Strategic Coach®*

The Oak Tree Moment

It was the spring of my junior year at the University of Florida, and I was in a financial tailspin. My old jalopy, with zero functioning air conditioning, awful for Florida, had eaten the last of my summer internship savings. I was juggling two part-time jobs at $3.50 an hour, grinding through a full-time accounting course load, and even with student loans, I was living on fumes.

My parents had no money to spare. So when tuition loomed, I had nowhere to turn.

Determined not to quit, I showed up at the campus financial aid office at 6 a.m., three hours before it opened, hoping to plead my case for more aid. I figured they'd see my hustle and help.

When I finally sat down with the loan officer, she didn't even lift her head.

"Nothing for you. Next."

"There has to be something," I said. "I'm already working two jobs—"

She glanced at her screen, shook her head, and repeated it. "Nope. Next."

I walked outside and collapsed under a giant oak tree. Head in my hands, heart in my shoes, tears in my eyes. That was my *oak tree moment*.

Two fraternity brothers passed by and invited me to breakfast. They noticed my red, swollen eyes and asked if I'd been crying. I muttered something about allergies and waved them off. I was too embarrassed to admit that I might have to drop out because I couldn't pay for school.

Instead, I wandered into the Hillel House, where they offered free bagels and coffee. Rabbi Friedman noticed I wasn't myself. I told him the story.

He made a phone call.

I received an interest-free loan from Jewish Welfare Services; this program is now known as the Jewish Educational Loan Fund. There was no co-signer, no red tape, just trust and timing. They supported me through undergrad and law school. I paid back every penny and have donated to JELF annually ever since.

That oak tree moment didn't just teach me about survival. It taught me about the power of liquidity—what it means to have access to the right resources at the right time. Grit isn't enough.

Success: A Double-Edged Sword

There's a saying in the financial world:

Bankers hand you an umbrella when the sun is shining and take it away when the storm rolls in.

In 2008, that wasn't just a metaphor—it was a brutal reality. Fort Myers, Florida, was one of the hottest real estate markets in the country. And then, seemingly overnight, it turned into a financial disaster zone. Foreclosures piled up. Construction projects stalled. Banks panicked.

Jim, a developer from Fort Myers, had been on a roll. He leveraged his resources heavily—buying land, launching projects, and stretching his reach. On paper, he looked bulletproof.

However, when the crash occurred, his lack of liquidity was exposed. His over-leveraged position offered no cushion, no room to breathe. Banks pulled funding, properties were foreclosed, and his empire crumbled.

Now, meet Robert—another developer who is also aggressive in growth, but with a radically different approach. Robert understands liquidity. He built *tax-free cash reserves*, used asset protection strategies, and structured his business to withstand economic chaos.

When the crash came, Robert's banks didn't foreclose. They extended the terms. They trusted him.

Why? Because he had cash. And cash makes people *a lot* more agreeable.

Robert didn't just survive; he *thrived*. He bought prime land at rock-bottom prices and rode the recovery to even greater wealth.

Same economy. Same city. Very different outcomes.

Preparing for the Unexpected

Economic shocks aren't rare events; they're recurring guests. One decade, they're subprime mortgages; the next, a global pandemic or a sudden spike in interest rates.

Robert's story proves the power of liquidity, not just as a survival mechanism, but as a tool for leverage. When the world panics, liquid entrepreneurs pounce. They don't freeze; they *buy*.

A Perpetual Wealth Program isn't just about saving money. It's about building flexibility. It's about having dry powder when the rest of the market is underwater.

Lenders Aren't Lifeguards

Let's be honest—banks aren't your safety net. They're lenders, not lifeguards.

Following the 2008 financial crisis, the Dodd-Frank Act introduced sweeping reforms to stabilize the financial system. However, like many government interventions, Bank of America, Wells Fargo, Chase, and Citibank didn't feel the fallout. The regional and community banks felt it—the ones entrepreneurs like you commonly deal with.

Compliance costs soared, and paperwork grew mountainous. Between 1985 and 2010, over 50 percent of community banks with assets under $10 billion disappeared.

The result? You, the entrepreneur, while trying to get credit, now face higher hurdles, slower approvals, and far stricter underwriting, especially when you need cash the most.

That's why the ultimate move isn't just being bankable.

It's becoming your own bank.

Debunking the Tax-Free Liquidity Myth

Ask a traditional financial planner about using life insurance for liquidity, and you'll usually get a lecture about "low returns" and "high fees."

They're looking at it like a standalone investment, not a system component.

Robert wasn't buying a product. He was building a strategy.

His life insurance wasn't for the death benefit (although that's nice to have). It was for tax-free access to cash. When the real estate market tanked and banks froze credit, Robert tapped into his policy's cash value—quickly, privately, and without asking permission.

While his competitors filed for bankruptcy, Robert bought up assets at a discount.

Liquidity, when appropriately structured, doesn't just provide a safety net. It provides a launchpad.

Asset Protection: Guarding the Castle Before the Siege

Another thing Robert got right? He didn't commingle his assets like a plate of spaghetti.

Jim's business and personal assets were tangled together. When the crash came, everything was exposed. Robert had the opposite experience. His trusts and entities acted like silos—firewalled, independent, protected.

Asset protection isn't just about shielding yourself from lawsuits. It's about ensuring your wealth survives economic, legal, or personal disruption.

The Black Hole and a New Trust Company

Twelve years into practicing law, I had a referral relationship with a national bank and trust company. Clients went both ways, and on paper, it looked perfect.

In practice? Not so much.

Whenever I named them as trustees in a client's trust, I'd send the documents to their legal department. But those documents didn't come back; they disappeared into a black hole.

Weeks would go by. No communication. Clients got nervous. I started looking like the slowpoke.

I didn't want to throw the bank under the bus, but their bureaucracy made it tough.

So, I sat down with my friend Charles Idelson, the bank's regional president.

"I love your team," I said. "But I hate your bank. We should start our own trust company."

He laughed. "Craig, I've got golden handcuffs. Not happening."

Two years later, Charles got fired on the Page Field municipal airport tarmac. No joke. A corporate exec flew in, handed him a pink slip without exiting a private jet, then took off.

Charles called me right after he called his wife. "How long would it take to build that trust company?"

"A year," I said.

"That's perfect. That's how long my non-compete severance lasts."

We raised $4 million in capital. My contribution came from the cash value in my life insurance policy. I didn't ask a bank, I didn't fill out paperwork, and, like Nike says, I just did it.

We launched, hired talent, and gained many clients. The trust company thrived, paid dividends for eighteen years, and sold for a healthy profit to a regional bank.

And it all happened because I controlled my *liquidity*.

Liquidity Is Leverage

Most entrepreneurs live in "borrower mode." Something breaks? Call the bank. Need capital? Beg, explain, wait.

But what if you didn't have to ask? What if you could move decisively because you were your own banker?

When you've built tax-free liquidity reserves, you stop reacting and start *directing*.

You borrow when it makes sense, not when someone else says you're "creditworthy." You invest when the opportunity is hot, not when a loan committee gets around to it.

Liquidity is leverage. But only when you own it.

Why You Should Become Your Own Creditor

Let's go even further: *become your own creditor*.

Think about what that means.

You create an ecosystem. One of your trusts loans money to a related entity to do a business deal; your IP company loans to your operating company, and your family trust lends to your holding company.

You control the terms. You earn the interest. And you keep the capital *within* your wealth structure.

Now, you're not just self-financing—you're also self-profiting.

Because it's internal, you can structure it to enhance *asset protection*, *estate planning*, and *tax efficiency*.

This isn't a theory. The ultra-wealthy do it all the time. You should, too.

Building a Tax-Free Bank

So, how do you build your own bank?

Start with cash-value life insurance—but not the kind they pitch in airport lounges. Structured correctly, it becomes your private liquidity vault.

Then, layer in *irrevocable trusts*, *entities*, and *inter-company loan structures*. Suddenly, your money is protected, growing tax-advantaged, and ready to deploy when you need it most.

In the coming chapters, I'll show you how to

- structure life insurance for tax-free growth and access;
- use trusts for funding and flexibility; and
- lend across entities without weakening protection.

It's not about having more money. It's about structuring what you have to work harder, smarter, and forever.

Mindset Shift: Liquidity Isn't a Luxury—It's Leverage

Let's call it what it is: most entrepreneurs only think about liquidity when they don't have it.

They live like success means being all-in, fully deployed, capital committed, and resources optimized. But that "optimized" feeling vanishes when the bank changes its mind, the market turns on a dime, or opportunity knocks with an expiration date.

The Perpetual Wealth mindset flips that default on its head.

This mindset knows liquidity isn't waste. It's not idle. It's *a weapon*. The entrepreneurs who rise in downturns—the ones who buy when others sell, who launch when others retract—aren't lucky. They're liquid. And they're structured to stay that way.

So let's get painfully specific. Ask yourself:

- Do you treat cash like fuel—tax-advantaged, easily accessible, and internally directed—or is it still a dusty balance line on your bank statement, vulnerable to someone else's underwriting?

- Can you fund a deal, acquire a competitor, or pivot your business *without* asking permission from a lender, or do you still live in borrower mode?

- Have you designed your entities and trusts to allow inter-company lending, tax-efficient movement of capital, and internal control, or are you still writing checks between personal and business accounts and hoping it all "balances out"?

- Suppose your liquidity is tied up in real estate or business assets. Do you have the structure to free it up *without* selling, panicking, or paying outrageous taxes?

- Have you run a stress test on your liquidity? This is not simply asking, "Can I cover payroll?"—but "Can I capitalize when others collapse?"

- Is your life insurance just a death benefit, or have you structured it as your tax-free private vault, available on demand, without a credit pull or bank meeting?

- Are you thinking like a borrower or like a banker?

Liquidity Conscious entrepreneurs don't just survive volatility; they *convert* it. They don't wait for conditions to improve; they deploy when others hesitate. And they do it confidently because they built the system before the storm.

Being **Structurally Sound** means your liquidity isn't just "available"—it's protected. It's tax-advantaged. It's mobile. You don't wait for approval; rather, you write your terms. That's the benefit of interlocking trusts, intelligent life insurance, and internal lending. They turn your money into a machine.

And **Risk Vigilance**? That's the firewall. It keeps your liquidity from becoming someone else's opportunity in court. Because money that's not protected is money that's already halfway gone. Robert's story didn't just highlight access—it showed *resilience*. His system wasn't just liquid. It was built to last.

So, have you built a liquidity system? Or are you still chasing cash like a spectator, hoping the banks, markets, or regulators give you a window to act?

Because in the Perpetual Wealth mindset, *freedom doesn't come from what you earn but from what you can move.*

CHAPTER 5

Dead Man's Plan: Why Traditional Estate Planning Leaves the Living Powerless

The difficulty lies not so much in developing new ideas as in escaping from old ones.

—*John Maynard Keynes,*
English economist and philosopher

The Binder That Did Everything—Except the Important Stuff

I practice law in Southwest Florida, where many new clients of my firm arrive with estate plans already in place, usually created by an attorney from their former home state. These plans often come wrapped in leather binders, embossed with gold foil, and with an air of finality.

They look impressive.

They check all the technical boxes for what happens *after* you die. Revocable trust? Check. Pour-Over Will? Check. Health Care Directives? Double check. But most of them fail spectacularly at what matters *most while you're alive*: building wealth, protecting it, and accessing it tax-efficiently.

Take Mark, a self-made entrepreneur who recently moved to Florida. He walked into my office with a binder the size of a Manhattan phone book and placed it on the table as if it held the nuclear launch codes.

"I've got everything set," he said proudly. "Revocable trust, pour-over will, durable power of attorney, healthcare directives—the works. Chicago's best estate attorney put it together."

I flipped through it. Technically sound. Thorough. Designed to do one thing exceptionally well: distribute assets once Mark had shuffled off this mortal coil.

"Mark," I said gently, "this plan takes care of your family after you're gone, but what's your plan for protecting your wealth while you're still here?"

He blinked. "What do you mean?"

"Structuring your assets so you can invest without getting hammered by taxes. Accessing capital without triggering gains. Reducing your income taxes, protecting assets from lawsuits…"

Mark gave me the look people typically reserve for calculus or cryptocurrency. "I just use my personal bank accounts for that. And my CPA handles the taxes."

Exactly as I thought.

"Mark, your binder is designed for your absence. But *you're here now*. Where's the plan that works for you while you're still living, breathing, and looking for the next opportunity?"

That's when it hit him. His estate plan wasn't a wealth plan. It was a "what happens when I'm dead" plan.

And that's the flaw with most estate plans—even the expensive, three-ring-binder, "best-attorney-in-Chicago" variety. They focus on death while completely ignoring life.

Revocable Trusts: The Illusion of Being "All Set"

The biggest myth in estate planning is that a *revocable living trust* makes you "all set."

Avoids probate? Yes. Smooths out wealth transfer? Sure. Helps your family after you're gone? Definitely.

But a revocable trust won't:

- reduce your income tax burden while you're alive;
- build wealth outside your taxable estate;
- give you tax-free liquidity; or
- shield your assets from lawsuits, creditors, or your kid's third divorce.

It's *reactive*. It works when something terrible happens.

On the other hand, a *Perpetual Wealth Program* is *proactive*. It helps you while you're still in the game, building, and living. It protects, multiplies, and gives you access to wealth now, not just after you're gone.

The Perpetual Wealth Strategy: A Lifetime Playbook

If a revocable trust is a seatbelt, a Perpetual Wealth Program is a race car tuned for performance.

Let's look at the key plays:

1. Stop Overpaying Taxes

Mark was wildly successful—and like many entrepreneurs, he was also unknowingly subsidizing the IRS.

There are dozens of ways to legally reduce income taxes. Which strategy to use depends on what you want your money to do. We explored

- **shifting income to lower-taxed entities.** Rather than taking everything through personal income, Mark could have flowed profits through an S-corp, a family LLC, or even a trust structure.

- **utilizing tax-free loans.** Instead of paying himself a taxable salary or dividend, he could borrow against tax-favored assets.
- **giving strategically to charities.** Donating appreciated assets (not cash) allowed deductions *and* control through a family foundation.

No two clients are the same. But here's the universal truth: If you don't plan proactively, you're writing Uncle Sam a bigger check than necessary.

2. Get Assets Out While Retaining Control

Entrepreneurs often think, "Estate taxes won't affect me—I'm under the exemption limit."

Until they're not.

Here's the kicker: a *revocable trust doesn't remove assets from your estate*. It just holds them in a pretty binder.

A Perpetual Wealth Program, on the other hand, helps you move assets out *while maintaining access and control.* Options include:

- **Spousal Lifetime Access Trusts (SLATs).** Get assets out of your estate while still being able to access them through your spouse.
- **Intentionally Defective Grantor Trusts (IDGTs).** Move appreciating assets outside your estate, while still paying income taxes yourself (which reduces your taxable estate even further).
- **Perpetual Wealth Family Bank Trusts™ (PWFBTs).** Create a tax-free bank from which your family can borrow to fund new business ventures, professional

practices, and other investment opportunities. The bank is "repaid" through tax-free insurance policies on each beneficiary's life.

You don't have to give up control; you just have to plan for how you want it.

3. Access Capital Without Tax Consequences

Entrepreneurs hate waiting.

So when an opportunity comes up, they want to move. But if your capital is tied up in taxable structures, your options are painful:

- sell something (hello, capital gains taxes);
- take a taxable distribution; or
- beg a bank.

A Perpetual Wealth plan sidesteps all three. It gives you access to tax-free liquidity through:

- **Private Family Bank Trusts.** As mentioned above, your family's private lending institution. Skip the loan committee.
- **Cash Value Life Insurance.** This is not for the death benefit but for tax-free borrowing power.
- **Structured Private Loans.** Lending between your own entities, with terms you control.

This isn't about beating the tax code. It's about working with it smarter.

4. Keep Wealth Unreachable to Predators

Mark didn't realize it, but he was one lawsuit away from a very bad day.

If he chose a revocable trust, he'd have zero protection. Judges could reach right in.

But with a Perpetual Wealth Program, he's protected because it's built to *repel* lawsuits, creditors, and even nosy in-laws. Depending on your risk level, it might include:

- **Domestic or Offshore Asset Protection Trusts**
- **LLCs and Partnerships,** where you control assets but technically don't "own" them.
- **Irrevocable Dynasty Trusts.** Keep wealth protected *and* growing across generations. Think of this as a vault that holds your family's wealth and stays protected from divorce, debt, or dumb decisions for decades.

You don't need a moat. You need a legal structure that functions like one.

Build a Plan That Works Now, Not Later

Mark arrived with a plan covering what happens after he dies.

We built a plan while he's still very much alive.

Because while it's great to leave something behind for your heirs, wouldn't you rather build something that lets you thrive now *and* leave a legacy later?

A revocable trust is a will with window dressing. A Perpetual Wealth Program is an engine. One keeps your affairs tidy when you're gone. The other helps you win while you're still playing.

Mindset Shift: Does Your Plan Serve You— Or Just Your Heirs?

Let's be honest.

Most estate plans are focused on death: who gets what, when, and how much. Necessary? Yes.

But if that's *all* your plan does, you're missing the most valuable part—**what it can do for you while you're still here.**

Let's shift the frame:

1. Are You Stuck with a Static Plan, Or Do You Have a Living, Breathing Wealth Strategy? (Structurally Sound and Tax-Aware)

When was the last time you updated your estate plan? More importantly, has it *evolved* with your wealth?

A Perpetual Wealth strategy isn't a binder residing in a fireproof safe. It's a living, breathing structure that adapts as your business grows and your goals change.

Ask yourself:

- Does your plan minimize income, capital gains, *and* estate taxes?
- Can you legally grow assets *outside* your estate while keeping access?
- Could you fund an investment tomorrow *without* tax consequences?

If not, your plan is just legal window dressing.

2. Are You in Control of Your Capital—Or at the Mercy of Banks and Taxes? (Liquidity Conscious)

Where do you turn when opportunity strikes?

If your answer is "sell something" or "call the bank," you're playing defense.

Ask yourself:

- Do you have *tax-free* liquidity ready for deployment?
- Can you invest without needing outside approval?
- If lending froze tomorrow, could you still strike deals?

Real control isn't about how much cash you have; it's about how fast and tax-efficiently you can *use it.*

3. Are You Overpaying Taxes Because You Haven't Engineered Your Income? (Tax-Aware)

Most entrepreneurs pay more tax than they need to, not because they lack a CPA but because they *lack a plan.*

Think about it.

- Are you shifting income to lower-taxed entities or family members?
- Are you using loans instead of taxable distributions?
- Are you thinking about *effective tax rates*, not just top-line numbers?

If you're just reacting each April, you're not planning. You're *settling.*

4. Is Your Wealth Protected, Or Just Waiting to Be Attacked? (Risk Vigilant)

You've built something valuable. But if it's not protected, you're vulnerable to

- Lawsuits.
- Creditors.
- Opportunists.
- Even your own family.

Ask yourself:

- If someone sued you tomorrow, how much of your business would be exposed?
- Do you have *real* protection in place, or just good intentions?
- Is your wealth legally siloed, or is it all in your name?

If it's not protected, it's not secure. Period.

5. Are You the Bottleneck, Or Have You Built a Team That Thinks With You? (Growth Oriented and Contrarian Curious)

Consider this a hard truth: even the best structure won't save you from flawed thinking or from going it alone.

Estate planning isn't a solo project. And yet, most entrepreneurs treat it like one. They avoid deep collaboration because they fear giving up control. They tolerate surface-level advisors who file forms instead of challenging assumptions.

A proper Perpetual Wealth strategy isn't just technical. It's collaborative by design.

Ask yourself:

- Do your legal, tax, and financial advisors talk to each other—or are they solving problems in isolation?
- Do you invite thoughtful questions and challenges from your team, or do you want quick answers and silence?
- Are you treating your planning meetings like strategy sessions or dental appointments you'd rather reschedule?

You're already losing if you're the only thinker in the room.

Freedom doesn't come from being the most intelligent person at the table. It comes from building the right table and being willing to let others sharpen your vision.

Is Your Wealth Working for You—Or Just Preserved for the Next Generation?

It's time to reframe what estate planning means.

You don't need a plan for what happens when you're gone. You need a strategy for how to maximize your wealth *while you're still here.*

So, ask yourself:

- Can I access capital without triggering taxes or begging a bank?
- Am I minimizing my taxes across *income, capital gains,* and *estate categories?*
- Have I structured my wealth for growth *and* protection?

The difference between a traditional estate plan and a Perpetual Wealth strategy is simple:

One prepares for your absence. The other maximizes your life.

Which one do you have?

TRUTH #3

Flipping the Script:
Turning the System in Your Favor

The Flip Begins: When the System Isn't Built for You, Build a Better One

If you've made it through Chapter 5, you already know the truth: Most estate plans are built to distribute wealth, not grow it. They preserve, divide, and wrap things up in a tidy bow. This is fine—if your goal is to pass on a modest estate net of taxes and avoid probate.

But for entrepreneurs? That kind of planning falls short. You're not looking to check a few boxes and "be done." You're building, evolving, and investing. You don't just want your plan to work—you want it to work for you. To grow with you. To protect what you've built and position it to multiply.

That's where the real fun begins.

The following five chapters are about flipping the script and taking structures meant to limit you—like tax laws, trust codes, and corporate regulations—and using them to your advantage. These aren't loopholes in the shady sense of the word. They're engineered openings in the system, often born from congressional overreach or unintended side effects of legislation. And when you know where to look? They're game-changing.

Chapter 6 starts with a glitch in the tax code that became a gift for the savvy entrepreneur. The Intentionally Defective

Grantor Trust (IDGT) may sound like something you'd want to avoid. However, it's one of the most powerful ways to move appreciating assets out of your estate while keeping control and cash flow. It's the tax version of discovering your broken hammer is a Swiss Army knife.

Then, in Chapter 7, we introduce a twist: what if you're not paying the taxes? What if your beneficiary is in a lower bracket or lives in a zero-income-tax state? Enter the PWBDOT™ (Perpetual Wealth Beneficiary Deemed Owned Trust™) structures that keep assets protected inside a trust while assigning the tax burden to someone more favorable. You'll see how to preserve compound growth and keep the IRS from siphoning your momentum.

Chapter 8 confronts us with a role most estate plans neglect: the Trust Protector. This is the silent sentinel of your Perpetual Wealth™ plan—the person who can course-correct your structure when life throws a curveball, family dynamics shift, or Congress decides to rewrite the playbook (again). Batman references may or may not appear.

In Chapter 9, we take flexibility to another level. Using strategic powers of appointment, you'll see how to design trusts that adapt over time. Want to add new beneficiaries? Shift the inheritance split? Optimize for tax treatment based on future laws? A properly built trust lets you do all of that, without starting from scratch.

Finally, in Chapter 10, we show you how all these moving parts come together. You'll see real-world case studies of families who've built Perpetual Wealth™ systems—not to hoard money but to sustain freedom—freedom from taxes, lawsuits, forced sales, family drama, and planning fatigue.

Because once you understand the system, you can do more than survive it. You can bend it. Reshape it. Rewrite the rules entirely.

And that's what the following chapters are all about.

CHAPTER 6

Flawed by Design: How Tax Loopholes Become Family Wealth Engines

> If you want to understand the future, study the past.
>
> —*Confucius, Chinese teacher,*
> *philosopher, and political theorist*

The Accidental Breakthrough That Changed Everything

In the early 1970s, a scientist named Spencer Silver was working in a lab at 3M, trying to develop a super-strong adhesive. The goal was to create a glue that could permanently bond materials—something powerful and unyielding. But Silver's formula didn't work as expected. Instead of super glue, he ended up with a low-tack adhesive that stuck to surfaces but could be easily peeled away without leaving a residue. By all traditional standards, he had *failed*. The adhesive was *defective* for its intended purpose.

For years, the discovery sat unused. It wasn't until another 3M scientist, Art Fry, grew frustrated with his bookmark constantly falling out of his church hymnal that an idea struck—what if this "failed" adhesive could be used to create a removable note? Instead of trying to make something permanent, they could flip the script and use it for *temporary* sticking. And just like that, the Post-it Note was born.

Today, Post-it Notes are a billion-dollar product. What started as a *defect* became an *advantage*—a tool that revolutionized office communication and organization worldwide. But it only happened because someone saw past the original intent and realized that *weakness* could actually be a *strength*.

And that's exactly how savvy entrepreneurs approach tax and wealth structuring. Some of the most powerful wealth-building strategies weren't originally designed to benefit you—they were designed to take more from you. But once you understand the mechanics of these rules, you can flip them in your favor.

Like the Post-it Note, an *intentionally defective* structure can be the key to something far more useful than what it was initially designed for. Let's look at how a so-called "flaw" in the tax code can become one of the most potent tools for transferring wealth, minimizing taxes, and controlling where it belongs—with you.

Flipping the Tax Law

Traditional estate planning, as we explored in the last chapter, focuses on avoiding probate and minimizing transfer taxes. It's a sound approach on paper. But when you dig deeper, it becomes clear that many traditional methods divide wealth among heirs rather than position it for growth.

A revocable trust ensures that your assets transfer smoothly but doesn't prevent them from dissipating. A basic estate tax plan may shield some of your wealth from taxation, but it doesn't do much to create tax efficiencies during your lifetime that allow it to compound over time.

For entrepreneurs and high-net-worth individuals, wealth isn't something to distribute—it's something to perpetuate, requiring more than a traditional approach.

In the following chapters, I will demonstrate how advanced strategies can transform a traditional plan into a Perpetual Wealth Program. We'll explore key concepts beyond simple wealth transfer—strategies that *minimize taxes, protect assets,* and *amplify growth across generations.* These techniques aren't just theoretical; they're practical tools that, when structured correctly, allow you to maintain control while leveraging the tax code to your advantage.

Of course, estate planning isn't a paint-by-numbers exercise. Every family's financial picture, business structure, and long-term goals are unique. There's no way to cover every strategy because the most effective solutions depend on individual circumstances. My goal isn't to provide a rigid formula but to give you a *framework* for strategically thinking about estate planning. By understanding how these creative planning strategies work, you'll gain insight into how working with a team of highly knowledgeable professionals can create a system that aligns with your own Perpetual Wealth vision.

Revocable vs. Irrevocable

This chapter explores two estate planning strategies based on irrevocable grantor trusts. If you're familiar with revocable trusts, you know they can be changed at will. They're great for probate avoidance, but don't offer much regarding tax planning or asset protection. Irrevocable trusts, on the other hand, serve a different purpose. When properly structured, they move assets out of your estate for tax purposes and can protect those assets from creditors.

Real Life Application: Kendall's Creditor Problem

Kendall had a revocable trust and thought she was protected. But when a contractor sued, her trust assets were fair game. One correctly structured irrevocable trust later, those same assets became invisible to future lawsuits—without losing access or control.

A revocable trust is, by definition, a grantor trust during the grantor's lifetime. That means any income earned by the trust is reported on the grantor's personal tax return, just like any other income they receive. Irrevocable trusts, however, are different. The assets they hold typically aren't counted as part of the grantor's estate, and the trust itself (or its beneficiaries) pays the income taxes, not the grantor.

But here's where things get interesting. An irrevocable grantor trust is a unique hybrid. The grantor permanently transfers assets to the trust but still pays the income taxes those assets generate! That might sound like a bad deal—why pay taxes on money you don't personally benefit from? In the eyes of the IRS, covering those taxes is like making another gift to your beneficiaries, *but without triggering any gift tax or using up your gift or estate tax exemption*. It's a little-known way to transfer wealth efficiently.

The grantor trust rules were initially designed to prevent people from dodging taxes. Ironically, over time, savvy estate planners have figured out how to use them to a family's advantage. Now, these rules open up powerful planning opportunities instead of acting as a barrier. That's where two strategies—the Intentionally Defective Grantor Trust (IDGT) and the Sale to an Intentionally Defective Grantor Trust (IDGT)—come into play. Before diving into these strategies' mechanics, let's examine how grantor trust laws evolved. Once you understand their history, you'll see precisely how we can flip the tax code in your favor.

Tax Law—A Puzzle Constructed Over Decades

Our tax system wasn't built from the ground up as a perfectly designed structure; it evolved piecemeal over decades, shaped by political compromises, shifting economic priorities, and the realities of each era. New laws were introduced at every turn to close perceived loopholes, only to create new ones. What emerges isn't a clean, logical framework but a complex web of intersecting rules, exceptions, and incentives. Those who understand these nuances and how to align them with their goals gain significant advantages.

For example, while irrevocable trusts remove assets from your taxable estate, with the right planning, they can still be structured so that their income is attributed to you. This quirk results in a greater transfer of wealth without further reducing your lifetime or death tax exemption. Even better, while assets are moved out of your taxable estate, layering different strategies allows you to retain control and income streams over the overarching business or investments, adjusting the income spigot to match your needs and goals.

The Origins of Grantor Trusts: When Congress Cracked Down on Income Shifting

Understanding how irrevocable grantor trusts came to exist is important for fully appreciating why they are so powerful today.

In the 1950s and 1960s, the top marginal federal income tax rate was a staggering 91 percent (dropping to *only* 70 percent in 1965!). To minimize exposure to these punishing rates, attorneys developed a strategy using *multiple trusts* to distribute income across lower tax brackets. Each trust was treated as a separate taxpayer, meaning it had its *own marginal tax bracket*, just like an individual taxpayer.

High-net-worth individuals would establish multiple trusts, each holding a different type of asset. But they would retain control and the trust's income. For example, one trust might own investment accounts, another might hold commercial real estate, and another could own shares in a family business. By *spreading income across these trusts,* each trust's taxable income remained within lower tax brackets, significantly reducing the owner's overall tax burden.

Figure 6-A

Concerned that taxpayers were exploiting trusts to dodge taxes, Congress cracked down in the Internal Revenue Code overhaul of 1954. That's when the grantor trust rules were born. The goal? To stop people from setting up multiple trusts they still controlled, just to spread income around and snag lower tax rates in each one. Under the new rules, if the trust's creator (the "grantor") kept certain powers—like the ability to swap assets, control investments, or tap into income—the IRS would simply ignore the trust for tax purposes and slap all the income back onto the grantor's personal return.

In 1969 and 1982, legislative enhancements tightened the screws even further, pushing individuals into higher income tax brackets even when income flowed from multiple trusts. Seeing the writing on the wall, estate planners largely abandoned the multiple trust strategy.

But if you've learned anything from reading this far, you already know that the law never stays still.

The Clinton Administration Flipped the Script

By the 1990s, minimizing estate taxes had become the holy grail of trust planning for the wealthy. The federal estate tax exemption was just $600,000—peanuts compared to the value of growing businesses, real estate, and investment portfolios. Wealthy families needed ways to shield those assets from the taxman.

One of the most popular moves? Placing fast-appreciating assets into irrevocable trusts, keeping them outside the taxable estate. Income taxes weren't the big worry back then; thanks to Reagan-era tax cuts and relatively low rates under Clinton, the estate tax could gut a fortune.

In other words, wealthy families weren't sweating income taxes. They were focused on growing their assets quietly, safely, and outside of their taxable estates.

Congress, however, wasn't blind to what was happening. Under the Clinton administration, lawmakers decided to close the loophole. They collapsed the income tax brackets for trusts, meaning trusts would now slam into the highest tax rates after earning just a few thousand dollars. The goal was simple: make it expensive to accumulate wealth inside a trust and force more assets to stay within taxable estates.

The plan worked, and it still works today.

In 2025, a non-grantor (mostly irrevocable) trust will be subject to the highest federal income tax bracket (37 percent) after earning just $15,650. By comparison, an individual won't hit that same 37 percent bracket until they earn $609,350, and married couples filing jointly have to clear $720,000 to get there. That's not just a gap—it's a canyon.

Here's why it matters: Imagine a trust owns a business that earns $400,000 in a year. If the trust pays the taxes, it will owe about $146,000. But if a married couple earned that same $400,000, their tax bill would be around $82,000. That's a $64,000 tax penalty—*a 43 percent haircut*—just for letting income stay trapped inside the trust.

Estate planners saw the danger and, true to form, flipped the script. If irrevocable trusts could be structured so that the grantor, not the trust, paid the income taxes, the assets would still escape estate taxation, but the income tax hit would be dramatically lower.

And just like that, the Intentionally Defective Grantor Trust (IDGT) was born—a strategy still crucial to smart estate planning today. The name's clunky, but the strategy is pure gold, and once you see how an IDGT works, you'll never look at trust planning the same way again.

What Is an IDGT, and Why Is It "Defective"?

Only in the world of tax planning could something called "defective" be a good thing. But when it comes to the Intentionally Defective Grantor Trust (IDGT), the so-called "defect" is precisely what makes it so powerful. The IRS sees the grantor as the owner for income tax purposes, meaning the trust's assets grow outside the estate, while the grantor keeps footing the tax bill.

In plain English, that means the trust grows untouched by the estate tax—while you, the entrepreneur, get to pay the income tax bill without it counting as a gift. Strange? Yes. Smart? Definitely!

Here's how it works.

As we learned, the grantor trust rules made decades ago were designed to stop wealthy individuals from dodging income taxes by shifting earnings into separate trusts. If the person who set up the trust—the grantor—kept certain powers over income, investments, or principal, the IRS said, "Nice try, but you're still paying the taxes." This was a weapon against tax avoidance at the time, ensuring the rich couldn't stash income in lower-bracket trusts while still controlling the cash flow.

Fast-forward to today, and that old safeguard has been flipped on its head. Estate planners realized a clever loophole:

A grantor who retains certain rights must pay income taxes on trust earnings, *but* those same rights don't necessarily drag the trust's assets back into the grantor's estate for estate tax purposes.

That's the magic behind the IDGT and why the "defect" is no defect.

Now, you might be wondering why anyone would volunteer to pay taxes on money they don't receive.

Fair question. After all, most people are trying to lower their tax bills, not happily signing up to cover someone else's.

But this is where smart wealth transfer comes into play. When grantors pay the trust's income taxes out of their pocket, they give their beneficiaries a tax-free gift. The key is *paying someone else's debt normally counts as a gift*, reducing your lifetime gift exemption.

But when you pay the income taxes on a grantor trust? The IRS doesn't count it as a gift at all. Not one dime comes off your exemption.

It's a silent gift the IRS blesses without blinking, allowing the trust to grow tax-free, the grantor's estate to shrink for estate tax purposes, and the family's overall tax burden to drop through the floor.

In short, while paying taxes on the income you never touch might sound crazy initially, it's one of the savviest moves a wealthy entrepreneur can make. It's using a restriction from decades ago—written for a completely different world—as a weapon for building Perpetual Wealth today.

And we're just getting started.

Now, let's layer the IDGT with a sale of assets and take things to an even higher level.

The IDGT Strategy in Action: Selling Assets to the Trust

One of the most powerful ways to use an Intentionally Defective Grantor Trust (IDGT) is to sell highly appreciating assets to it in exchange for a promissory note.

Done right, this strategy freezes the asset's value for estate tax purposes, shifts future growth out of your taxable estate, and dodges capital gains taxes—all without giving up control.

Let's break it down with a real-world story.

Meet Sarah. Sarah owns a business currently valued at $10 million. She expects it to explode in value over the next decade, but she knows that if she leaves it inside her estate, her heirs could face a brutal estate tax bill. Instead, Sarah uses an IDGT to shift that future growth to her children tax-free.

To structure the deal, Sarah first sets up an IDGT and funds it with $1 million in seed capital—approximately 10 percent of the transaction value—to give the trust a solid financial foundation. She files a Federal Gift Tax Return (Form 709), using a slice of her lifetime exemption for the gift.

Next, Sarah gets a formal business valuation. Instead of transferring the business outright, she slices the ownership into multiple non-controlling minority interests. Why? Because by doing so, she can legitimately apply valuation discounts:

- Lack of control (because the interest can't dictate operations)
- Lack of marketability (because it's difficult to sell private company shares)

Put simply, she's getting a legal discount on the value of her own business for estate tax purposes. The IRS lets her pretend it's worth less, so the tax hit is less too. These discounts total 35 percent, slashing the value for transfer purposes from $10 million to $6.5 million.

Sarah then sells these discounted interests to the IDGT for a $6.5 million promissory note. No extra gift tax is triggered; this is a fair market sale, not a gift.

Because the IRS treats Sarah and the IDGT as the same for income tax purposes, the sale does not trigger capital gains tax, even though the asset has appreciated.

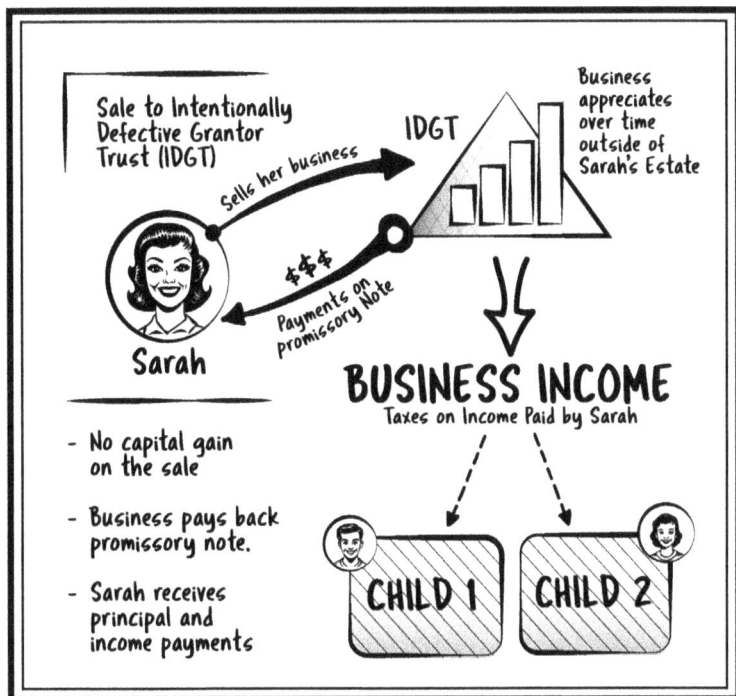

Figure 6-B

Over the next ten years, the trust will use business cash flow to pay Sarah back under the note, along with interest at the Applicable Federal Rate (AFR)—a rate often far lower than the business's growth rate.

The result? The business appreciates the trust, far outpacing the small interest payments Sarah receives. Meanwhile, Sarah pays the trust's income taxes personally, allowing the trust assets to grow tax-free.

By the end of ten years, Sarah's business had grown from $10 million to $30 million—but because the IDGT owns it, that $30 million escapes estate tax entirely. Had she kept the business inside her estate, her heirs would have faced a $12 million tax bill. Instead, they inherit the full value tax-free.

Bonus Benefits: Control and Asset Protection

Even though Sarah transferred ownership, she retained control by serving as the managing member of the LLC. That means she still makes business decisions day-to-day, without pulling the asset back into her estate.

Because the business is now locked inside an irrevocable trust, it gains a crucial layer of protection against lawsuits, creditors, and even future divorce claims. We'll explore this topic further in subsequent chapters.

Mindset Shift: See the Flaws—Then Use Them

You've just learned how something "defective" can become the most effective way to build and preserve wealth. You've seen how tax law, designed to *stop* you from avoiding taxes, can be legally rerouted to *accelerate* your family's future.

This isn't a strategy. It's a mindset.

Most people see flaws in the tax code as a danger. Entrepreneurs with the Perpetual Wealth mindset? They see flaws as leverage.

Take a step back and ask yourself:

- Are you seeing tax rules as obstacles or invitations to create something smarter?

- When your advisors say "you can't do that," do you push deeper—or take it at face value?

- Are your trusts, entities, and structures designed to passively hold wealth or actively grow it, shield it, and multiply it across generations?

- Are you relying on your advisor's intent or verifying their understanding of the IRS's intent and how to flip it in your favor?

- Is your wealth architecture still using twentieth-century logic in a twenty-first-century environment?
- Do you own structures that feel sophisticated, or do you understand how they work, why they work, and what happens when they don't?

The more profound truth is that being *Tax-Aware* isn't just about deductions or exemptions. It's about understanding that Congress never meant to help you, but they wrote the rules in a way that lets you help yourself.

Being *Structurally Sound* means you're not putting your faith in surface-level planning. You're aligning entity design, trust provisions, cash flow systems, and tax positioning to work in concert, not just in theory, but in pressure-tested reality.

And being *Risk Vigilant?* Knowing that every plan eventually meets friction—death, downturns, divorces, and regulations. But if you've flipped the code in advance, the cracks don't cause collapse. They redirect pressure away from your core.

The Perpetual Wealth mindset doesn't just react to new laws. It predicts what others will miss and designs structures to capitalize before knowing the rules have changed.

So now that you've seen how an "intentional defect" can build unstoppable strength...

Are you still afraid of complexity—or are you ready to command it?

Understanding these strategies is essential. But *executing* them with precision, foresight, and creativity is how the ultra-wealthy stay ahead.

And that's the direction we're heading next.

What Happens When the Grantor Stops Paying the Bill?

The Intentionally Defective Grantor Trust (IDGT) is a powerful tool for building tax-free growth and shrinking a taxable estate.

But like any strategy, it's not bulletproof. There are real-world situations where the plan can crack:

1. The grantor dies.

When that happens, the trust immediately loses its grantor status. It's now a standalone taxpayer and gets hammered by the compressed trust tax brackets. Remember, trusts hit the top 37 percent federal rate after just $15,650 of income (based on 2025 rates). Compare that to married individuals, who don't hit the same rate until $720,000. The difference is staggering.

2. The grantor can't afford to keep paying.

Life happens. Businesses wobble. Cash flow dries up. Medical expenses arise. If Sarah, our entrepreneur from earlier, hits a rough patch, she may no longer have the liquidity to cover the trust's tax obligations out of pocket. If that happens, the trust becomes the taxpayer, and again, it bleeds under the brutal trust tax brackets.

3. The beneficiary ends up wealthier than the grantor.

Imagine Sarah's child becoming a wildly successful entrepreneur while Sarah has more modest resources. Forcing Sarah to continue paying the trust's taxes doesn't just cause financial strain—it misses the opportunity to shift income taxation to someone with a potentially lower personal tax rate.

In each of these cases, the burden shifts back to the trust. When that happens, taxes spike dramatically, undermining the very goal of wealth compounding.

But there is good news: Just because an IDGT's initial structure falters doesn't mean the plan has to fail. We can use another tax loophole that shifts the income tax responsibility to the beneficiary when it's strategic, without dragging the assets back into the estate.

The next chapter introduces you to the Perpetual Wealth Beneficiary Deemed Owner Trust (PWBDOT). This structure fixes the vulnerabilities you've just seen and opens the door to even smarter, more flexible wealth compounding across generations.

CHAPTER 7

The Wealth Multiplier Nobody Talks About: Who Pays the Tax— and Why It Matters

The tax code is a roadmap.
Most people never learn how to read it.

—*Judge Learned Hand,*
American jurist, lawyer, and judicial philosopher

Most people think wealth is built by owning more. But the real secret to Perpetual Wealth lies in its structure: who holds the asset, who controls the asset, and most importantly, who pays the tax bill. To see why that matters more, let's start with the story of a struggling milkshake machine salesman who built an empire without ever owning the crown jewels.

How Ray Kroc Built an Empire Without Owning It

Ray Kroc wasn't a visionary chef. He didn't dream up the world's most efficient fast-food operation or even start McDonald's. What he did do—brilliantly—was take control of a business without owning it outright, using financial leverage and legal structuring to create an empire while minimizing risk and maximizing returns.

In 1954, Kroc was a 52-year-old struggling milkshake machine salesman, bouncing from diner to diner, trying to convince restaurant owners to buy his Multimixer—a device that could make five milkshakes simultaneously. Business was tough, and Kroc was barely scraping by. That changed when he heard about a small burger stand in San Bernardino, California, run by two brothers, Dick and Mac McDonald. These two had pioneered a revolutionary system that churned out perfectly cooked burgers, fries, and shakes in record time with assembly-line precision. Unlike the traditional mom-and-pop diners Kroc had been pitching to, this single restaurant had purchased eight of his Multimixers—enough to make forty milkshakes at a time.

Intrigued, Kroc flew to California to see what was happening. He immediately recognized the potential for explosive growth, not as a single restaurant, but as a franchise model that could be replicated nationwide. But there was a problem: the McDonald brothers were content with their one successful location. They didn't have the vision—or the drive—to expand. Kroc, however, saw an empire waiting to be built.

But there was another issue. Kroc didn't have the money to buy out the McDonald brothers or the financial backing to launch a nationwide expansion. So, he did something unconventional: He structured the business so that he could control its most valuable asset without owning it outright. In other words, Kroc did what innovative entrepreneurs do–leverage other people's money.

The Secret Behind McDonald's Expansion: Leveraging Other People's Money

Ray Kroc, working with his financial strategist Harry Sonneborn, founded Franchise Realty Corporation in

1956 to purchase land for new McDonald's locations. They needed substantial capital to acquire properties. But instead of relying on personal wealth or bank loans, he took a three-pronged approach to financing:

1. **Private Investors.** Sonneborn devised a plan to secure financing from institutional investors and banks by using franchisee lease payments as collateral. This meant that the more franchises Kroc opened, the more land Franchise Realty Corporation could acquire, creating a self-sustaining growth cycle.

2. **Franchisee Payments and Rent Model.** Instead of simply charging franchise fees, Kroc's company purchased the land for new locations and leased it to the franchisees at a markup. This provided an ongoing revenue stream, which he used to acquire even more land without needing to put up his capital.

3. **Reinvesting Cash Flow for Expansion.** Kroc didn't extract profits for himself early on. Instead, he reinvested revenue from franchise royalties and rent payments into growth, allowing McDonald's to scale rapidly. This reinvestment strategy helped finance new locations, marketing, and operational improvements, ensuring that expansion remained self-funded and sustainable.

The Hidden Business of McDonald's: Real Estate, Not Hamburgers

We are not basically in the food business.
We are in the real estate business.

—*Harry Sonneborn,*
first CEO of McDonald's Corporation

Owning the land, not just the brand, gave Ray Kroc control, leverage, and unstoppable growth—the same principle innovative entrepreneurs apply when structuring Perpetual Wealth.

Why Kroc's Strategy Was Brilliant—and How It Relates to Trust Planning

Ray Kroc didn't build McDonald's with deep pockets; he built it with deep strategy. Instead of raising massive capital up front, Kroc used his business's future income streams to finance its expansion.

Through Franchise Realty Corporation, Kroc ensured McDonald's didn't just serve burgers; it also owned the dirt underneath the grills. Every franchisee paid rent to Kroc's real estate company, locking them into long-term commitments that gave McDonald's powerful leverage and dependable cash flow.

That structure allowed Kroc to scale exponentially, using predictable rental income to fund new locations, without risking his fortune. By the time he bought out the McDonald brothers in 1961 for $2.7 million, McDonald's wasn't just a fast-food chain. It was a real estate empire disguised as a restaurant, and it was just getting started.

From McDonald's to Modern Trusts: Controlling Wealth Without Owning It

Ray Kroc didn't need a fat inheritance to build an empire, and you don't need one to build Perpetual Wealth. While the legal tools available in the 1950s and 1960s differed from those of today, the underlying strategy remains the same: control the most valuable assets without exposing them to unnecessary taxes, lawsuits, or risks.

Today, that principle is captured in a Perpetual Wealth Beneficiary Deemed Owner's Trust (PWBDOT). Just as Kroc controlled the real estate empire beneath the McDonald's brand without technically owning it, entrepreneurs can control business interests through a properly structured trust, keeping the growth outside their taxable estate while maintaining strategic command.

Even if the trust's grantor isn't a multimillionaire, a relatively modest initial investment, smartly leveraged, can create exponential growth. It's not about how much capital you start with. It's about structuring what you have to unlock maximum opportunity while minimizing exposure.

And that's precisely what the next part of our strategy shows in action.

Why Structure Beats Ownership: Introducing the PWBDOT

By structuring his empire through real estate holdings instead of directly owning every restaurant, Kroc multiplied his growth while minimizing his risks. In the same way, a Perpetual Wealth Beneficiary Deemed Owner Trust lets entrepreneurs control the development of their businesses, without dragging those assets into their taxable estate or exposing them to lawsuits, creditors, or future divorces. (If the acronym PWBDOT makes your eyes glaze over, don't worry—this just means we're giving beneficiaries both protection and power, while locking in tax advantages the IRS can't unwind.)

In today's world, structure often beats ownership.

The previous chapter taught us about the grantor establishing an IDGT. The IDGT estate planning structure has advantages when the grantor is wealthy. While it can be a powerful tool for wealth transfer, it has limitations.

That's why it's essential to compare IDGTs with PWBDOTs and understand how shifting the tax burden to the right person—whether the grantor, trust, or beneficiary—can make the difference between compounding wealth and eroding it through unnecessary taxation.

When It Makes Sense for the Beneficiary to Pay Taxes

Sometimes, shifting the tax burden onto the beneficiary isn't just smart; it's essential for maximizing long-term wealth. Instead of letting punitive compressed tax rates hammer trust income, a properly designed structure enables the beneficiary to pay taxes at their rate, often much lower, while keeping the trust's principal fully protected.

When used strategically, this shift saves taxes, accelerates compounding, protects the principal from creditors, and shrinks the beneficiary's estate—a triple win for any serious wealth-building plan.

The real advantage shows up in:

- **Protecting Trust Assets from Creditors and Divorce.** Keeping assets inside the trust ensures they remain shielded from lawsuits, creditors, and ex-spouses. The principal remains intact, and the beneficiary pays the taxes, rather than the trust, allowing the assets to grow tax-free.

- **Allowing the Trust to Compound Growth**. Trusts that retain their earnings are subject to high tax rates, which can hinder wealth accumulation. By shifting the tax liability to a beneficiary in a lower tax bracket, the trust retains more capital, allowing wealth to grow exponentially rather than being eroded by excessive taxation.

- **Reducing the Beneficiary's Taxable Estate.** When beneficiaries pay taxes on trust income, they reduce their estate while keeping assets inside the trust. This strategy helps families stay below estate tax thresholds and preserves more wealth for future generations.

- **Capital Gains vs. Ordinary Income.** Trusts are subject to high tax rates on ordinary income, often exceeding 50 percent with state taxes. However, capital gains taxes are lower, maxing out at 23.8 percent (including the 3.8 percent Medicare surtax). In some cases, it's more beneficial to let capital gains remain taxable at the trust level while shifting ordinary income to the beneficiary.

Now, let's see the real impact numbers.

When you control who pays the tax bill—the trust, the grantor, or the beneficiary— the difference isn't measured in nickels and dimes. You keep hundreds of thousands of dollars inside the family's wealth system instead of losing it to unnecessary taxes.

Here's how a $400,000 income stream plays out, depending on who holds the tax burden:

Total Federal Tax Liability, Effective Tax Rate, and Net Amount Retained

Taxpayer	Total Federal Tax (Approx. in $)	Effective Tax Rate	Net Amount Retained ($)
Trust (37% compressed rate)	147,500	36.90%	252,500
Grantor (Married, Filing Jointly)	99,700	24.90%	300,300
Beneficiary (Single)	110,000	27.50%	290,000

Figure 7-A

Taxes aren't just a cost; they're a control lever. Shift them the right way, and you don't just keep wealth. You build an engine that outlives you.

Shift Taxes to the Beneficiary

So, how exactly do you move the tax burden from the trust to the beneficiary while keeping the trust's protection intact? Let me introduce you to another acronym: a Beneficiary Deemed Owner Trust (PWBDOT™).

Reducing Trust Taxes Without Losing Protection

A Perpetual Wealth Beneficiary Deemed Owner Trust is all about tax efficiency. It ensures that trust income is taxed at the beneficiary's lower rate instead of the trust's higher rate, keeping assets inside and protected.

How It Works:

- The beneficiary is granted a temporary right to withdraw trust income for a short period each year, typically thirty to sixty days.
- The beneficiary doesn't have to take the money—just having the right amount on hand is enough for the IRS to treat her as a taxpayer.
- The trust principal remains protected, but the tax liability is lowered significantly.

Why This Matters:

- Trusts are taxed at 37 percent on just $15,650 of income (2025 tax table).
- Individuals don't hit that same rate until they earn hundreds of thousands of dollars.
- If a beneficiary is in a lower tax bracket, the total tax bill drops, keeping more money inside the trust.

Let's look at how shifting the tax burden to the beneficiary can lead to significant savings.

A Game-Changing Tool: The PWBDOT

Ray Kroc didn't start with a vast fortune, yet he built one of the most successful business empires by leveraging a structure that gave him control without direct ownership. Instead of trying to fund expansion with personal capital, he created Franchise Realty Corporation, which enabled him to utilize outside financing and franchisee lease payments to acquire real estate while maintaining control of the most valuable part of McDonald's operations.

Now, imagine applying this strategy:

Ray Kroc's Strategy	Entrepreneurial Parent & PWBDOT
Used Franchise Realty Corporation to control McDonald's real estate without owning the brand directly.	The entrepreneur sets up a PWBOT, allowing the child to control a business without personally owning the assets.
Secured outside bank financing using franchisee lease payments as collateral.	The child borrows capital, leveraging the trust's seed assets to secure bank loans for business expansion.
McDonald's business profits flowed into the real estate entity, compounding over time.	Business income is retained inside the trust, compounding outside the estate tax system.
Avoided excessive tax burdens, as real estate holdings offered depreciation and other tax advantages.	Income is taxed at the child's lower rate, avoiding punitive trust tax brackets while protecting assets.

Figure 7-B

The Entrepreneurial Parent and the Next-Gen Business Builder

Let's walk through a real-world example.

John Smith is a successful entrepreneur who has built a thriving real estate and investment business. Now, he wants to help his adult son, Ryan, launch a business of his own.

But John knows better than to simply gift assets outright. A direct transfer could expose the funds to creditors, lawsuits, and future estate taxes, eroding the wealth he worked so hard to build.

Instead, John designs a more innovative strategy. For Ryan's benefit, he establishes a Perpetual Wealth Beneficiary Deemed Owner Trust (PWBDOT).

To structure the test, John seeds the PWBDOT with $1 million in diversified assets—a mix of cash, stocks, and passive real estate holdings. This initial funding stays within gift tax exemption limits, avoiding unnecessary tax triggers.

Ryan doesn't take distributions. Instead, he uses the trust as a financial springboard, just as Ray Kroc used Franchise Realty Corporation to fuel McDonald's explosive growth. Leveraging the trust's assets, Ryan secures $4 million in outside financing to scale his new business.

Fast forward ten years, and Ryan's business is now valued at $20 million. Because it's owned inside the PWBDOT, the entire amount sits safely outside his taxable estate. There is no estate tax exposure, no creditor access, and Ryan retains full control; the trust is also protected.

What's even better is that while Ryan pays income taxes on the business profits at his individual rate—around 27.5 percent—he avoids the punitive compressed trust brackets. Meanwhile, the business continues compounding inside the protected trust structure.

The $8 Million Lesson: Why Ownership Structure Changes Everything

Without the trust, Ryan's family would face a crushing tax bill that could wipe out nearly half of everything he built.

But thanks to the PWBDOT, his business remains safely outside the estate tax system, and the full $20 million stays intact for future generations.

To put this in perspective, let's compare what would happen if Ryan had owned the business personally versus inside the trust:

Scenario	Business Value At Death ($)	Estate Tax (@ 40%) ($)	Net Passed to Heirs ($)
Business Owned Personally	20,000,000	8,000,000	12,000,000
Business Owned in a PWBDOT	20,000,000	0	20,000,000

Figure 7-C

That $8 million saved isn't just a number—it's another generation of opportunity preserved. All $20 million stays inside the family's wealth ecosystem, compounding for future generations.

But the story doesn't end with avoiding estate taxes at death. Wealth preservation also depends on what happens during the entrepreneur's lifetime—how business income is taxed year after year, and how much is retained to fuel future growth. Let's look at how Ryan's structure protects not just the business value, but the profits it generates every year.

Visual Breakdown: The Power of Leveraging a PWBDOT

Scenario 1: Business Owned Personally by Ryan

Taxpayer	Business Income ($)	Federal Tax (@ 27.5%) ($)	Net Retained ($)
Ryan (Ryan as Business Owner)	400,000	110,000	290,000

Figure 7-D

✓ Business profits are taxed at Ryan's individual rate.

✗ However, *all assets remain in his taxable estate*, subject to future transfer taxes.

Scenario 2: Business Owned Inside a PWBDOT

Taxpayer	Business Income ($)	Federal Tax (@ 27.5%) ($)	Net Retained in Trust ($)
PWBDOT (Ryan as Beneficiary)	400,000	110,000 (paid by Ryan)	400,000

Figure 7-E

- Business profits are taxed at Ryan's individual rate, just like in Scenario 1.
- All assets remain outside Ryan's taxable estate, compounding free of transfer taxes.
- If Ryan later sells the business, the proceeds stay inside the trust, protected from estate and creditor risks.

Mindset Shift: Structure Beats Ownership. Always.

This chapter should've rattled a few assumptions loose.

Because you don't need to own the empire to control it; you don't need your name on every title to direct its growth. Ray Kroc didn't. And neither do you.

The Perpetual Wealth mindset understands that structure beats ownership every time. Ownership exposes you to taxes, lawsuits, and estate erosion. When done right, structure puts the power in your hands without putting the liability in your lap.

Let's sharpen the lens. Ask yourself:

- Are you still clinging to ownership when control is what matters?

- Is your business legally structured to outlive you or taxed when you die?

- Do you know *who* pays the tax in your structure, and have you chosen that person strategically?

- Are your entities and trusts engineered to keep income, growth, and assets flowing in the right direction, or are they just paperwork that no one's reviewed in five years?

True wealth isn't about what you own but what you *design.* That's the System-Oriented mindset.

Tax-Aware entrepreneurs don't just minimize taxes. They orchestrate who pays them. They think in brackets, not balances. They don't accept "that's just the way it is"—they ask, "What's possible if I flip the burden?"

Liquidity-conscious entrepreneurs make sure their wealth can move, pivot, and adapt. If you can't access capital without triggering a firestorm of tax or risk, you don't own liquidity. You own friction.

Risk Vigilant entrepreneurs know the real risk isn't market downturns. It's a *poor design*. It's building a $20 million business and forgetting to put it behind a firewall. It's handing your kids a business without shielding it from their in-laws.

And **Contrarian Curious** entrepreneurs are willing to say, "Wait—why *wouldn't* I pay someone else's tax bill if it saves us millions and keeps control in the family?"

That's not *recklessness*. That's *elite thinking*.

The average entrepreneur builds a business. The Perpetual Wealth entrepreneur builds a machine with structures, timing, and tax roles all aligned to protect and multiply across generations.

The question is simple:

Are you chasing ownership? Or are you engineering control?

The first builds net worth. The second builds freedom.

Protecting business profits inside a trust is critical, but genuine Perpetual Wealth planning doesn't stop at building walls. You also need guardians watching those walls. In the next chapter, we'll introduce the role of the Trust Protector: the often-overlooked position that ensures your plan stays flexible, your intentions stay honored, and your wealth stays protected no matter what the future brings.

CHAPTER 8

The Superpower Hidden in Plain Sight: Why Most Trusts Are Weaker Than They Should Be

> You don't need a cape to be a hero.
> Sometimes, you just need a plan.
>
> — *Tony Stark (Iron Man)*

When I was a kid, I wanted to be Batman. I even had a purple cape that my Bubby (Yiddish for *grandma*) made for me. Not because he was the strongest or the fastest—he wasn't. Superman could leap tall buildings. The Flash could outrun a bullet. Batman? He couldn't even fly. But he *did* have something far more interesting: a contingency plan.

Batman never entered a situation without an escape route, a secondary plan, and a backup to the backup, just in case the first two didn't work. He carried smoke bombs, grappling hooks, and—if you believe the old comics—even shark repellent in his utility belt. He had files on every superhero's weakness in case one went rogue. Batman wasn't about brute force. He was about optionality. He was about control. Quiet, behind-the-scenes, *precautionary* control.

That's the part that always stuck with me. He wasn't the guy running into the fire—he was the one who wired the building with exits no one else saw. He didn't flaunt his authority; he only used it when things got messy and needed correcting. Most people missed it. But to me, that was the most powerful guy in the room. Batman was the guardian of the guardians. The protector of the plan. He ensured the system didn't collapse, even when those inside it lost their way.

That's precisely what a *Trust Protector* is. They don't wear a cape or sit at the head of the table. Most trust documents only reference them a few times, often in language only a lawyer would love—limited fiduciary powers, tax-sensitive provisions, and the like. But peel back the legalese, and you'll find your own personal Bruce Wayne: someone in the shadows (who is not the grantor, a trustee, or a beneficiary) who can't be bullied, manipulated, or caught up in family drama. Someone who exists solely to keep the trust running as intended, even if life doesn't go as planned.

And life *never* goes as planned.

The Trust Protector's role isn't to manage money. That's the trustee's job. The Trust Protector does not distribute funds or manage investment accounts. No, their role is more surgical than that. They *fix*, *amend*, *adjust*, and *remove*—discreetly, efficiently, and with a laser focus on preserving the plan's integrity. Their power isn't loud, but it's real. And if you've built a multigenerational wealth structure, you want them in your corner.

Why You Don't Have One in Your Current Trust

Most estate planning attorneys won't touch Trust Protectors with a ten-foot pole. Why? The traditional legal playbook doesn't allow someone to amend a trust document, remove a trustee, or toggle tax-sensitive provisions on and off. It's not something they teach in law school, and it wasn't on the bar exam. It lives in the gray, advanced areas of planning—the intersection of tax law, trust law, and good old-fashioned practical strategy. And let's face it: most lawyers don't feel comfortable operating in the gray.

Many of my colleagues avoid Trust Protectors entirely because they aren't confident in explaining the role to their clients. The nuances are deep. You need to understand how state trust codes interact with federal tax law. You need to anticipate how a court of equity might try to be creative, similar to a divorce or bankruptcy court. Planning takes more than a fill-in-the-blank trust form or a forty-five-minute document signing. It requires vision. More importantly, it requires conviction.

My introduction to Trust Protectors didn't come from a law review article or a CLE seminar. It came from asset protection planning. That's where the real innovation happens because the stakes are higher. We're not just talking about minimizing taxes—we're talking about *keeping the assets from getting wiped out altogether*. Clients facing lawsuits, business liabilities, or messy divorces aren't interested in theories. They want shields. Trust Protectors are one of the strongest shields you can install.

Trust Protectors are often given significant authority in asset protection trusts, particularly those structured offshore or under favorable domestic jurisdictions. They can change the situs (the legal home of the trust), veto distributions, or even rewrite portions of the document to comply with emerging threats. Their job is to react faster than a judge, creditor, or angry ex-spouse can. And when properly designed, they can do so without tipping off the opposition or triggering unintended consequences.

Not long ago, I got a call from a divorce attorney. Her client was the son of one of my deceased clients. The son was both the trustee and the beneficiary of a testamentary trust established under his father's revocable trust, which I drafted—a strategy similar to the one I espouse throughout this book. Everything was going fine until the son's marriage started to unravel.

That's when I saw my Batman signal light up the sky.

His soon-to-be-ex-wife's attorney was sharpening her sword, claiming that the trust assets—technically outside the marital estate—had been used routinely for family purposes. Mortgage payments. Private school tuition. Vacations. She also had the loan and credit card statements to support her claim. Her argument? It should be classified as a marital asset because the trust had always been used as a family piggy bank. She wanted the divorce court judge to order the son to make alimony and child support payments from the trust.

Now, those of you who read Chapter 3 will remember what I've said about divorce courts. They're courts of equity, not strict legal interpretation. That means judges have broad discretion to do what they think is fair, even if it flies in the face of technical legal ownership. And here's the kicker: If a judge tells you to do something in a court of equity and you don't comply, you can be held in contempt. You can be fined. Or worse—you could be stuck in a cell for the night with a guy who insists on giving you unsolicited crypto investment advice and calls himself "The Blockchain Bandit."

The divorce attorney then asked me the million-dollar question: "Should the son resign as trustee, so he can't comply with the court's order?"

I told her flatly, "No."

Why? Because a resignation would look like a stunt. A judge might see it as a bad-faith tactic and order him to resume trusteeship or face contempt anyway. Worse, the son is in a legal gray area with a target painted on his back.

Instead, I offered a different solution.

I told the divorce attorney, "Let's have the Trust Protector remove him as trustee. Not at his request, of course. Against his will, if you catch my drift." She did; lawyers speak in winks more often than we care to admit.

So, that's exactly what we did.

The Trust Protector exercised their authority under the trust document to remove the son as trustee and replace him with a corporate trustee—one with no emotional involvement, one who couldn't be pressured, guilted, or browbeaten into making distributions, and one who wasn't subject to the divorce court's jurisdiction because they weren't even a party to the lawsuit.

Suddenly, the trust became a fortress. The new trustee wouldn't make any distributions unless the trust terms allowed it, and those terms didn't say anything about supporting ex-spouses. The judge couldn't hold the son in contempt because he was no longer the trustee. The court couldn't order the trust to pay because the trustee wasn't under its thumb. And the ex-wife's lawyer had nothing left but smoke.

That, my friend, is the power of the Trust Protector.

It's Batman stepping out of the shadows at just the right moment—not to steal the scene, but to ensure the mission doesn't go sideways. In the next part of this chapter, I'll share a few more real-world stories that show how Trust Protectors can be used in creative, high-stakes situations—from saving family businesses to neutralizing predatory lawsuits.

When the Enemy Isn't an Ex—it's the IRS

Of course, not all threats to your trust come with subpoenas and accusations. Sometimes, the real villain is quieter, harder to detect, and wears a badge that says "Internal Revenue Service." And that's where the Trust Protector appears again—not to block a courtroom ambush this time, but to tip the tax scales back in your favor.

You'll remember from a prior chapter that non-grantor trusts—typically are their own taxpayers—face compressed income tax brackets. While individuals don't hit the top federal tax rate (currently 37 percent) until well into the six-figure range, trusts get there after just a modest amount of accumulated income, around $15,650 (in 2025). That's not a typo. Once a trust earns more than that, it's taxed like a Manhattan hedge fund manager.

You'll remember from the "Beneficiary as the Taxpayer" section that we often include a PWBDOT provision—that's short for *Beneficiary Deemed Owner Trust*. It's a tax-savvy mechanism that shifts the trust's taxable income onto the primary beneficiary's return. Rather than letting the trust pay income taxes at those painful compressed brackets, we attribute the income to the beneficiary's 1040, where we can often take advantage of more favorable individual rates. At the time, we discussed why that's usually a good move—and it is. *Usually.* But like most good strategies, its usefulness depends entirely on the circumstances. And sometimes, circumstances change.

But sometimes—just sometimes—that move backfires.

What if the primary beneficiary is already in the top tax bracket? Or what if they live in a high-tax state like California, New York, or New Jersey? Sure, they might benefit from individual brackets, but they are also subject to high state income taxes. Meanwhile, if the trust is administered in Florida, where there's no state income tax, it might be more efficient for the trust to pay the federal tax and skip it entirely.

Or let's say the trust is a sprinkle trust—meaning it can distribute income to multiple beneficiaries. Maybe a grandchild in college has no other income and would pay zero federal tax on a $10,000 distribution. Why saddle the primary beneficiary with tax on that income just to be "efficient" from a top-down view? Tax law isn't about rules—it's about opportunity.

Here's the kicker: if we've baked the right flexibility into the trust document, the Trust Protector can turn off the PWBDOT provision. That's right—they can flip the switch. They can *unhook* the trust's income from the primary beneficiary and let the trust be taxed independently. If the situation flips again in a few years, the Trust Protector can turn it back *on*.

No court petition. No amendment filed with the clerk. No drama.

Just a carefully crafted provision, triggered by a watchful guardian who understands the bigger picture—not just legally, but strategically. Because what matters most isn't what the trust *could* do, but what it *should* do, given where the tax rates fall, where the beneficiaries live, and what Congress might do next to stir the pot.

This is where the Perpetual Wealth mindset kicks in. Wealth isn't just built through investment returns or real estate appreciation. It's grown quietly and steadily through thousands of small, intelligent decisions. And the ability to switch tax characterization on and off? That's one of the smartest.

So, while some attorneys are still arguing over whether Trust Protectors belong in a domestic trust, those of us playing the long game are already three moves ahead. And yes, we've got Batman sitting quietly in the corner, ready to step in when the game shifts.

Below is an example of a Trust Protector stepping in, not because of litigation or tax consequences, but to preserve family unity and business continuity when a well-meaning but overwhelmed matriarch starts unintentionally steering the family business into troubled waters.

The Family Business and the Matriarch Who Meant Well

Not every Trust Protector moment is filled with legal drama or high-stakes tax strategy. Sometimes, the quiet crisis comes from *within* the family, and it's well-intentioned, familiar, and destabilizing.

A few years ago, I worked with a family who owned a successful third-generation manufacturing company. The matriarch, Elaine, had taken over the trust and voting interest in the business after her husband passed away. Elaine was sharp, generous, and deeply respected by her children and grandchildren. She was also, to be honest, tired.

The business had grown complex—multiple product lines, a warehouse expansion, and a leadership team that needed firm direction. Elaine had promised her late husband she'd "keep the family together," so instead of stepping aside, she dug in. She micromanaged the CEO, second-guessed the board, and began distributing from the family trust to "smooth things over" whenever one of her children complained.

It was all out of love, but it was also slowly unraveling the structure that had been built to last.

Her oldest son, Mark, was the company's de facto leader. He approached me, concerned but careful not to throw his mother under the bus. "She's giving money to my sister to cover her 'consulting' expenses," he said, "but she hasn't worked in the business since college. The employees are confused, and we're losing board control."

This wasn't a lawsuit. It wasn't a tax issue. But it was a *succession failure* in the making.

The trust document, drafted years earlier, had been thoughtfully constructed to give the Trust Protector—not the beneficiaries—the authority to evaluate trustee fitness. If the trustee acted outside of the trust's intent, or in ways that jeopardized its structural integrity, the Trust Protector could remove and replace them.

Mark didn't want to confront his mother. And no one wanted to embarrass or make her feel like she was being pushed out. However, the family recognized that the trust required a fiduciary who would adhere to the rules, not interpret them on the fly. The Trust Protector reviewed the situation and removed Elaine as trustee, citing the potential harm to the business and the misalignment of distributions, and brought in a neutral, experienced, and emotionally detached corporate fiduciary.

What you might find surprising is that Elaine stayed on the board. She remained the family's spiritual and emotional compass. The board still valued her wisdom, but she no longer controlled the checkbook.

The result? The business stabilized. The children stopped fighting. And Elaine—freed from the stress of managing family politics—told me, "I sleep better now."

Sometimes, the greatest superpower isn't fighting villains; it's removing well-meaning loved ones from roles they no longer fit, and doing it in a way that preserves their dignity, the family legacy, and the integrity of the plan.

A Trust Protector can do that when the structure is built right.

The Step-Up That Almost Got Stepped Over

Let's wrap up this superhero toolkit with one more example—this time, the Trust Protector shows up to rescue a missed opportunity that would've quietly cost the family millions.

In many well-drafted estate plans, when a beneficiary (say, a child or grandchild) receives their share in trust, they're often given a limited power of appointment. This allows the beneficiary to redirect how the trust passes when *they* die, usually to any of the grantor's descendants, spouses, or charities. But not to themselves, their estate, or their creditors.

Why?

Because a *limited power of appointment*, by design, doesn't pull the trust assets into the beneficiary's taxable estate. That means no estate tax on those assets at the beneficiary's death. Sounds great, right?

Well, it depends.

Because here's the trade-off: when trust assets aren't included in someone's estate, they also don't get a step-up in tax cost basis at death. If that trust holds appreciated stock, real estate, or other low-basis assets, the family could be paying massive capital gains taxes if they ever sell.

But what if the beneficiary has plenty of unused estate tax exemption left? What if they're in a position where they could include those trust assets in their estate *without* triggering any federal estate tax? In this case, they're throwing away a free basis step-up for no reason other than inertia. And that's where the Trust Protector steps in.

Consider a client's son who was the lifetime beneficiary of a continuing trust. The son was nearing the end of his life, and the trust held a sizable portfolio of blue-chip stocks, most of which had been in the family for decades. The capital gain on the sale would have been staggering. However, upon reviewing the trust provisions, we found that he only had a limited power of appointment. There was no estate inclusion, and therefore, no step-up.

Now, the son had a substantial estate tax exemption left—thanks to planning, frugality, and frankly, outliving his wealthier sibling. He could've absorbed the full value of the trust assets in his estate and still not paid a dime in estate tax.

But the trust didn't allow it.

Until we called in the Trust Protector.

The trust had a built-in safety valve: a provision allowing the Trust Protector to grant a general power of appointment under specific circumstances. In this case, the beneficiary could appoint assets to his own creditors—a technique known as an intentionally defective general power of appointment, or IDGPOA.

"To his creditors?" sounds scary, but it's a legal fiction. No one expected the creditors to collect. The point was to *intentionally* trigger *estate inclusion* to unlock the step-up in basis. The Trust Protector executed the amendment, narrowly tailored to apply only to the appreciated assets, and only up to the amount that wouldn't trigger estate tax under current law.

When the son passed away, those trust assets received a full step-up in basis, and millions of unrealized capital gains were eliminated. The family could now sell without triggering capital gains tax, and they preserved the trust structure for future generations.

That's the kind of move most attorneys don't think about—or if they do, it's often too late to act.

But when you've installed a Trust Protector with the proper authority, and more importantly, the right foresight, your trust can evolve to take advantage of these strategies when they matter most.

Because let's face it: no one knows what the estate tax exemption will be ten years from now. No one knows which beneficiary will end up with room to spare. But with a Trust Protector, we don't need to know today. We just need the *option* to act tomorrow.

And that's the real superpower.

Not brute strength. Not speed. But the ability to adapt. To pivot. To quietly preserve wealth in ways that no formulaic, one-size-fits-all plan ever could.

So, if your trust doesn't have a Trust Protector, it's like Batman without a utility belt. Still brave. Still noble. But woefully under-equipped for the chaos ahead.

Mindset Shift: Structural Agility Is the New Control

Entrepreneurs like you are wired to lead. You've built, grown, and steered your enterprise with vision and grit. However, when it comes to your estate, that instinct to *control every-thing* can quietly become a weakness because **you can't micromanage from the grave, yet you can still lead.**

The trust continues to act in your absence. Consequently, you need to design a system to think and act on your behalf long after you've gone.

The Trust Protector is that system—a legal utility belt that doesn't simply defend your plan—it adapts it. It responds to tax changes, replaces underperformers, and shields against equity courts, creditor attacks, and family politics.

So, ask yourself:

- Is your estate plan flexible enough to outlive your original assumptions, or is it frozen in time the moment you sign it?

- Have you built a trust that can course-correct, or one that's stuck waiting for a court to intervene?

- If tax rates spike or laws shift, can your plan pivot automatically, or will your heirs be stuck paying for your rigidity?

- When your trustee falters—emotionally, legally, or strategically—do you have a system to replace them without conflict quietly and quickly?

- Finally, does your plan have a guardian with the authority to act, or are you hoping nothing ever goes wrong?

Structurally Sound thinking isn't about cementing your wishes but engineering evolution. It's recognizing that a plan isn't finished when you sign it. It's just getting started.

Risk Vigilant entrepreneurs don't only defend against lawsuits; they build layers of contingency. They anticipate threats from outsiders and breakdowns from within: poor trustees, family rifts, tax surprises, or even aging matriarchs with too much heart and too little restraint.

And **Tax-Aware planning?** That's not about squeezing deductions. It's about knowing who pays the tax—and *when*—can destroy or supercharge a structure. The ability to flip PWBDOT on and off and execute an IDGPOA at just the right moment is tax awareness at its highest level.

Your fundamental shift is to

- Stop thinking about control as a grip you maintain.
- Start thinking of it as a system you install.

Because lasting wealth doesn't come from a powerful document; it comes from a structure built with intelligence and flexibility and includes a quiet sentinel ready to act when no one else can.

That's the mindset of a Perpetual Wealth architect. And it's why, after reading this chapter, you'll never again ask whether to include a Trust Protector.

Instead, you'll ask yourself: Why did I ever build a plan without one?

CHAPTER 9

Future-Proofing Without Handcuffing Your Heirs

> Even if you're on the right track,
> you'll get run over if you just sit there.

—*Will Rogers, American actor and social commentator*

In 2007, Steve Jobs stood on stage at the Macworld Conference and changed the world.

He introduced the iPhone as a phone, an iPod, and an internet communicator—an all-in-one device. It was sleek. It was shiny. It was disruptive. And it was surprisingly limited.

The first iPhone didn't have the App Store. No Instagram, no Uber, no mobile banking. You couldn't download third-party apps. Apple controlled everything inside that phone—every function, every button, every feature. For a while, that worked. Until it didn't.

Jobs knew something most business owners and trust creators forget: Even your best ideas need room to evolve. So, in 2008, he made a bold decision—he opened the App Store. He handed over creative control to others. Suddenly, the iPhone wasn't just a device. Now, it was a platform built to adapt to whatever came next.

And that's exactly what a power of appointment does in your estate plan.

Powers of appointment turn a rigid, irrevocable trust into something flexible without compromising the original purpose. It allows someone you trust—usually a child or spouse—to modify who receives the trust assets and how they're distributed, either during their lifetime or at their death. You permit them to evolve the plan inside the walls you've already built.

But just like Jobs didn't give developers full access to Apple's source code, not all powers of appointment hand over total control. There are two key types, and each comes with trade-offs.

General vs. Limited: Understanding the Levers of Flexibility

The two types of powers of appointment—general and limited—function like two versions of the App Store.

Limited power gives flexibility within guardrails. The beneficiary can redirect the trust assets to a defined list: their children, a spouse, or a charity. They can't use it for themselves or their creditors. It's like offering curated apps in a sandbox environment.

A general power, on the other hand, allows you to do whatever you want with it. You can appoint it to yourself, your estate, or your creditors—anyone. You're handing over the master password. Doing so, however, brings more risk and some tax opportunities, as you'll see.

Let's walk through how this works in families who use these tools wisely.

Margaret and the Hidden Battle

Margaret's father completed his planning decades ago. He left her a trust that paid income for life, then passed it to her children in equal shares. It was clean and predictable.

But life didn't unfold according to plan. Margaret's youngest son struggled with addiction. The idea of handing him a seven-figure inheritance outright, in one check, made her stomach turn.

Thankfully, her father had given her a limited power of appointment. She used that power to place her son's share into a continuing trust—managed by a professional trustee, with distributions tied to health and stability milestones.

She couldn't have changed the terms of the trust for herself. But for her children? She had the authority to shift course because her father had the foresight to build in that option.

Paul's Sister and the Second Act

Paul's sister had gone through a divorce years ago and recently remarried a man who had become a loving step-grandfather to her children and grandchildren.

The trust left to her by her mother had a default language that passed her share down to her kids, but did not mention her spouse. However, her mother had included a limited power of appointment.

With it, Paul's sister redirected a portion of her trust to a continuing trust for her husband to ensure he'd be cared for if she predeceased him. She also carved out separate trusts for each grandchild, tied to education milestones.

It was all possible because her mother didn't just leave a trust. She left options.

Powers of Appointment Comparison

Feature	General Power of Appointment	Limited Power of Appointment
Who Can Receive Assets?	Anyone—including the beneficiary themselves, their estate, or creditors	Only a defined class (e.g., descendants, spouses, or charities)
Included in the Beneficiary's Estate?	Yes—assets are included for estate tax purposes	No—assets stay outside of the estate for tax purposes
Asset Protection from Creditors?	Low—considered "owned," so exposed to lawsuits, divorce, etc.	High—assets remain protected inside the trust
Step-Up in Tax Cost Basis at Death?	Yes—included assets get a step-up in basis, reducing capital gains taxes	No—original basis carries forward unless advanced strategies used
Control Given to Beneficiary?	High—beneficiary has total discretion	Moderate— beneficiary can redirect within limits
Best Used For	Strategic tax planning, inclusion for basis step-up, charitable gifting	Multi-generational protection, asset shielding, flexible family planning

Figure 9-A

Barbara and the Tax Bill That Didn't Need to Happen

If you read Chapter 8, you saw how a Trust Protector swooped in to save the day, granting a surgically tailored general power of appointment just in time to avoid a massive capital gains tax. That was a reactive strategy. Innovative, legal, and practical, but also one that required quick thinking and a little luck.

Let's add a twist to the general power of appointment issue. What if the beneficiary has some exemption remaining to eliminate the potential capital gain, but not enough to cover the entire trust? Let's examine Barbara's situation.

Barbara was the lifetime beneficiary of a *testamentary Credit Shelter Trust* worth $1 million, funded when her father died years ago. The trust was drafted the traditional way—with strong protections and a limited power of appointment. That limited power allowed her to redirect the trust at her death, but only among her father's descendants, their spouses, or charities, not to herself, her estate, or her creditors.

Over time, the trust's assets appreciated significantly. What was once a $1 million portfolio of blue-chip stocks and real estate had ballooned to $9 million. But the cost basis? Still $1 million. Assume further that Barbara only has $4 million of exemption remaining at her death.

When Barbara died, her children inherited the trust. They could be saddled with $8 million of unrealized taxable gain if they were to sell the assets at a combined capital gains tax rate of 28 percent (23 percent federal + 5 percent state), resulting in a $2.24 million capital gains tax.

Why?

Because there was no general power of appointment. No estate inclusion. And no step-up in basis when doing so wouldn't have otherwise triggered estate taxes. Again, we needed a general power of appointment like we saw in Chapter 8.

Rigging the System—Intelligently

Of course, when I propose granting a general power of appointment to clients, I often get a raised eyebrow and a question like:

> "Wait—you want me to give my daughter a general power of appointment? Couldn't she leave the entire trust to her yoga instructor or some guy she meets on a cruise ship?"

Fair question. But no, you wouldn't give her an open-ended power like that.

Instead, we draft an intentionally defective general power of appointment, or IDGPOA.

The IDGPOA allows Barbara to appoint the trust assets to the creditors of her estate—a technical requirement for estate inclusion and, therefore, the step-up in basis. However, in practice, no one uses this power to leave amounts to Capital One. That'd be like writing your will to say, "Everything to Visa, MasterCard, and the guy who fixed my roof."

Instead, Barbara exercises the power in favor of her children, grandchildren, or surviving spouse, just like she would have under a limited power. The point is not to change her intent but to unlock *tax efficiency*.

And to be clear, this power isn't granted lightly. The Trust Protector only steps in near the end of her life, evaluates her available estate and GST exemptions, and confirms that no estate tax will be triggered. This is not roulette; it's *precision tax planning*.

Remember, Barbara only has $4 million of exemption remaining. A Trust Protector can't insert a general power of appointment over the entire amount without triggering another problem, an estate tax in Barbara's estate, because the value of this Trust elevates her estate to one that would be taxable.

Comparing a Re-Rigged System

Now, let's imagine Barbara's inherited Credit Shelter Trust had included two subtle but powerful provisions:

1. A **Trustee's** authority to subdivide the trust into subtrusts, one will be named "exempt" because it is exempt from Barbara's estate, and the other will be nonexempt. and

2. A **Trust Protector** empowered to grant a general power of appointment—specifically, one that allowed Barbara to appoint the assets to the creditors of her estate.

With those tools, the Trustee subdivides the Credit Shelter Trust into two $4 million subtrusts. The Trust Protector causes one of the $4 million subtrusts to be included in Barbara's estate using an IDGPOA—**not so Barbara could rewrite her estate plan over piña coladas with Chad,** giving her just enough power to unlock the step-up in basis without any real loss of control.

(Chad is fictional. Any resemblance to Barbara's yoga instructor or cruise companion is purely coincidental unless he's trying to inherit the trust assets—in which case, you included the right restrictive power.)

Let's see how the numbers change:

Barbara's Credit Shelter Trust	Non-Exempt Subtrust ($)	Exempt Subtrust ($)
Fair Market Value after division into subtrusts	4,000,000	4,000,000
Original Cost Basis (½ applied to each)	500,000	500,000

Unrealized Capital Gains	3,500,000	3,500,000
Potential Capital Gains Tax	1,120,000	1,120,000
Potential Capital Gains Tax After IDGPOA Applied	**1,120,000**	**$0**
Will Barbara have a Taxable Estate because of the IDGPOA?	**No**	**No**

Figure 9-B

That's a **$1.12 million difference**, all based on a single, well-timed power.

A Rigged System Isn't Reckless— It's Responsible

Barbara's situation—and the $1.12 million lost to capital gains taxes—isn't rare. It's just rarely *anticipated*.

Too many estate plans are built to freeze, not to function. They're designed to avoid mistakes, not create opportunities. But when the landscape shifts—whether it's tax law, family structure, or market conditions—frozen plans crack.

Most trusts lack the necessary mechanics to adapt. They lack subdivision powers, don't appoint Trust Protectors with meaningful authority, and don't include intentionally defective general powers of appointment as a planning lever.

Why?

Because designing a trust that adapts takes more than drafting—it takes engineering. The design requires technical depth and creative foresight. Many estate plans are written with templates that prioritize uniformity over evolution.

However, building a Perpetual Wealth system takes a different tack.

You won't be giving your heirs a blank check. Instead, you will be identifying pressure points—like basis management—and baking in smart, surgical tools to respond to them.

The two provisions that would've changed everything for Barbara—a trustee's power to subdivide and a Trust Protector's authority to grant a targeted GPOA—aren't gimmicks. They're intelligent features of a trust built to thrive across decades, tax regimes, and changing family dynamics.

That's the difference between protection and preservation—between a trust that parks itself on the right track and gets run over by tax consequences and one engineered to switch tracks, pick up speed, and arrive exactly where the family needs it to.

As we saw earlier, Donald Trump said it best when he quipped, "That makes me smart," after navigating the tax code to his advantage. Whether you admire or roll your eyes at the approach, the principle stands: those who understand the system—and are bold enough to rig it legally—win.

That's not exploitation; that's strategy.

And that's what powers of appointment, Trust Protectors, and intentionally flexible design make possible for families who don't just want to protect their wealth but position it to grow, adapt, and endure.

Mindset Shift: From Lockdown to Liftoff

Rigidity is a quiet danger hiding in even the best-laid estate plans.

Many plans are technically sound and legally precise, but they're built for a world that won't exist when your kids need them.

You've seen it in this chapter: a missed step-up in basis, an inflexible power of appointment, a trust without the tools to adapt to changing law or family dynamics. These aren't rare scenarios. They're *predictable patterns*. And how they're solved separates Perpetual Wealth architects from well-intentioned amateurs.

Pause for a moment and ask yourself:

- Have you designed your estate plan to respond to change or resist it?
- Are your powers of appointment forward-looking, with surgical precision, or locked down out of fear?
- Is your trust built to adapt across generations, or will it break the moment the rules change?
- Have you given your team—the trustee, Trust Protector, and beneficiaries—the tools to pivot when an opportunity appears? Or are they stuck executing a legacy plan written for yesterday's tax code?
- And perhaps most importantly: Are you structuring around today's exemptions and brackets, or are you building a legal platform that can be reprogrammed in real time?

Structurally Sound planning isn't static; it's system intelligence. It includes subdivision clauses, tax-switch valves, and strategic appointment powers that can be toggled when needed, not just imagined at the outset.

Tax-Aware entrepreneurs don't just aim to avoid estate taxes. They ask, "Who's paying the tax now? Who *should* be paying it?" They know that managing *basis* is as critical as managing *estate exposure* and that $1.12 million can vanish because of one unchecked box.

Risk Vigilant means you're not just shielding wealth—you're making sure the tools to preserve it don't expire when you're gone. Because when the IRS or a probate judge knocks, you don't want your heirs opening a sealed vault. You want them to open a control panel.

And **Growth-Oriented** means you're not building this alone. These tools only work if your advisors know how to use them. Are they talking to each other? Do they understand how to rig a system legally, without tripping it?

This isn't about handing over control. It's about programming the controls in advance.

Your trust should not be a frozen plan; it should be a launchpad. Your trust should preserve your vision while allowing your family and advisors to land where the opportunity lies, even if the map looks different today.

Ask yourself:

Is your plan a snapshot? Or is it a system?

Because only the latter will keep working after the world changes.

CHAPTER 10

Rigged for You! Perpetual Wealth™ Engineering Case Studies

> Numbers don't lie, but they sure do hide—
> until you put them in a spreadsheet.
>
> —*Charlie Munger, longtime business partner of*
> *Warren Buffett at Berkshire Hathaway*

By now, you've seen how powerful the Perpetual Wealth system can be when you build it with flexibility, foresight, and the right tools. We've talked about Trust Protectors, powers of appointment, subdivision clauses, income tax strategies, and more. If it's starting to feel like a lot, that's good. That means you're beginning to understand what goes into rigging a system that isn't just legal but also *adaptive*.

Now, it's time to see these ideas in action.

This chapter brings together five real-world case studies that show how entrepreneurial families have applied these concepts—sometimes proactively, at the eleventh hour—to solve problems, seize opportunities, and future-proof their plans. You'll see trusts used as launchpads, not just vaults. You'll learn about strategies that preserve family control, minimize tax exposure, and expand options instead of shrinking them.

These concepts aren't just hypotheticals. They're windows into the kinds of issues high-net-worth families face and the creative planning that separates reactive documents from a living system built to endure.

Let's get into the playbook.

Case Study Alpha

Coding the Future, Structuring the Wealth: Inside the AI Empire You Can't Sue or Tax

Client Background

Edward is a successful sixty-two-year-old entrepreneur with a net worth of $30 million. He's worked hard, invested wisely, and built up his wealth through real estate, private equity, and a few well-timed exits. His estate plan is tight, thoughtful, and conservative.

His son, Travis, twenty-eight, is driven like his father but has very different, modern capabilities.

Travis is a tech prodigy. He has built an AI engine that can transform manufacturers' operations—optimizing logistics, predicting maintenance failures, and reducing waste at a level unmatched by any current platform. Several manufacturing executives have already shown interest. The upside is staggering.

But to take it to market, Travis needs capital—around $1 million to hire engineers, developers, and marketers and build out the go-to-market infrastructure. He doesn't want to give up control, and Edward wants to support him strategically.

Our objective is to structure a Perpetual Wealth system to accomplish the following goals:

1. Keep this explosive growth asset outside both Edward's and Travis's estates while benefiting both.
2. Limit self-employment taxes.

3. Minimize ongoing income taxes.

4. Limit personal liability.

Let's break it down.

1. Keep the Growth Outside of Both Estates

Figure 10-A

We begin by structuring Travis's AI venture inside a new entity owned by a *specially drafted irrevocable trust*—one that benefits Travis, but one that he didn't establish, but that he can control.

Enter the Intentionally Defective Grantor Trust (IDGT).

Edward can "seed" this trust with the $1 million Travis needs, either as a completed gift (using some of his lifetime estate and gift exemption) or via a combination of a seed gift and an installment sale. Because the trust is defective for income tax purposes (but effective for estate tax exclusion), it lets Edward pay the taxes on the trust income *without further gift tax exposure.* That tax burn is an estate reduction strategy in disguise.

A Trust Protector will be built into the IDGT, who may grant various powers, including the ability to override defective grantor provisions, exercise general powers of appointment, and install and remove trustees. The IDGT is drafted to comply with Qualified Subchapter S Trust provisions so that the underlying entity can be an S Corporation.

Figure 10-B

Once funded, the trust can own a Subchapter S Corporation, Travis Manufacturing Solutions (TMS), that becomes the holding entity for Travis's AI venture, removing the appreciation from Edward's and Travis's estates. Travis also creates a single-member LLC that owns the trademarks and patents on his AI called "Travis AI Company (TAI)." The AI is leased to the Operating LLC that is taxed as an S Corporation.

2. Limit Self-Employment Taxes

TMS is a Subchapter S Corporation owned by the trust. Travis receives reasonable compensation for his services via W-2 income through a management company (or salary if he takes on a formal operating role). Still, any excess profits can be retained and distributed as passive K-1 income, not subject to self-employment tax.

The TMS agreement clearly distinguishes between Travis's earned income and the trust's equity ownership, further reinforcing the separation from his estate and reducing payroll tax exposure.

3. Minimize Ongoing Income Taxes

Jurisdictional strategy meets entity planning at this point.

The venture will likely lose money at its inception, flowing through to Edward's income tax return. As the venture makes money during Edward's lifetime, TMS's income is attributed to him. If he's in a high-income tax bracket, the benefit of the additional "gift" of paying the income tax may be mitigated entirely by the income taxes he owes.

Instead, he may want the Trust Protector to turn off the grantor trust provisions. If the IDGT is established in a state with no fiduciary income tax (like Florida, Nevada, or South Dakota), and if the trust is administered correctly there, income retained in the trust avoids state-level income taxation. At that point, it may instead be structured as a PWBDOT so that the income, even if retained, pays a lower income tax rate than the compressed federal income tax rate that the trust would otherwise be subject to.

As the company earns vast amounts of money, the trust can make *discretionary distributions* to Travis (or other beneficiaries, including his children one day) when the timing is optimal, for instance, in years when Travis's income is low. Further, Travis can siphon off income by having his TAI charge licensing fees for using Travis's intellectual property, which is passive income and not subject to self-employment taxes.

If the company sells down the road, the capital gains flow through the IDGT, which remains outside Edward's and Travis's estates. Thanks to the IDGT structure, Edward continues to pay income taxes, letting the trust grow tax-free.

Figure 10-C

4. Limit Personal Liability

The combination of a manager-managed LLC and trust ownership offers robust protection:

- Travis doesn't own the LLC directly; he manages it or works for it.
- The trust owns the LLC, and its structure includes spendthrift provisions and asset protection features.
- Edward has no legal ownership or control once the trust is funded—his involvement ends with the setup.

Even if the business hits legal bumps (which startups often do), neither Edward's nor Travis's personal assets are exposed.

Optional Enhancements

Installment Sale to the Trust: If Edward wants to limit gift tax use, he can sell the equity to the IDGT in exchange for a promissory note at a low valuation (due to lack of marketability and control).

Directed Trust Structure: Appoint an independent investment trustee to hold the LLC interest and separate administrative roles, reinforcing the estate exclusion.

Trust Protector Role: As mentioned earlier, there will be built-in authority to modify the trust, change situs, or even grant a narrow power of appointment if it's ever tax-advantageous to do so.

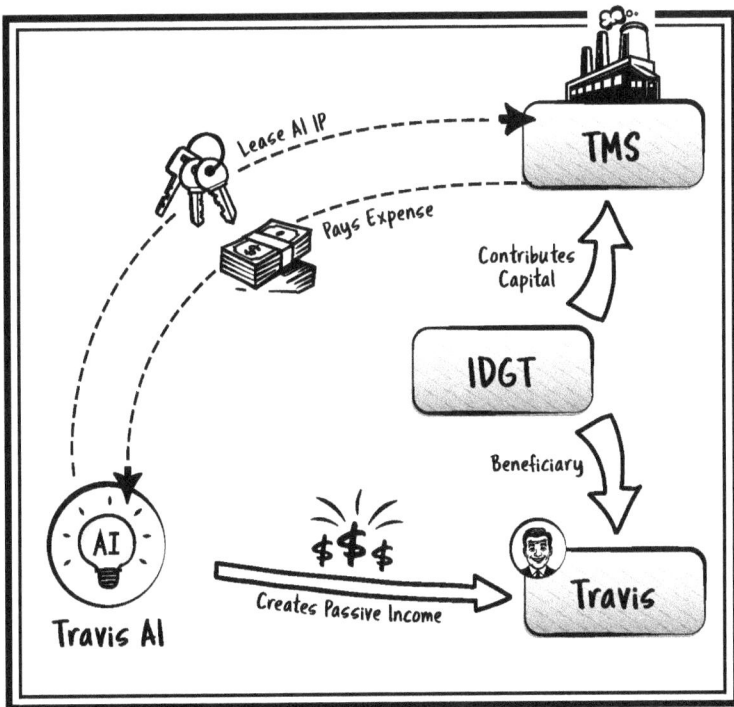

Figure 10-D

Mindset Shift for the Modern Entrepreneur

Most parents in Edward's position would write the check to Travis directly or invest through a family LLC. But doing so would expose them to tax, liability, and a lack of flexibility.

A Perpetual Wealth system doesn't just give. It *guides, shields, and scales.*

This system creates:

- a tax-efficient launchpad for Travis's innovation
- asset protection and liability mitigation for father *and* son
- a flexible trust structure that will endure, even as the company pivots, grows, and eventually exits

That's good planning—generational planning done right.

Case Study Beta

The Tax Strategy Hiding in Grandma's Pantry

Client Background

Samantha, sixty-three, is a seasoned entrepreneur with a net worth of $20 million. She and her husband, Gary, sixty-seven, have built significant wealth through years of real estate investing. Their crown jewel? A **$7 million portfolio of rental real estate**, all of which has been fully depreciated.

The income is solid, the properties are stable, and the cash flow is consistent. But there's a looming problem: the entire portfolio sits on a *zero tax basis*.

If Samantha sells, the capital gains tax and depreciation recapture would be punishing, likely exceeding $2 million in combined federal taxes. She wants to clean up the basis, eliminate future taxes, and remove future real estate appreciation from her estate without disrupting her family's lifestyle.

She and Gary have plenty of other assets and liquidity. Their two adult sons are financially stable. And Samantha's eighty-nine-year-old mother, Mollie, is still alive, healthy, and lives independently. Mollie's estate is modest and well below the federal estate tax exemption.

We want to structure a Perpetual Wealth system to accomplish the following goals:

- eliminate over $2 million of embedded capital gains and depreciation recapture tax;
- move the real estate appreciation outside of Samantha's estate;
- provide ongoing income to the family;
- limit the use of Samantha's gift and avoid using any of her GSTT exemptions; and

- establish long-term wealth protection for her sons and future generations.

Let's break it down.

1. Eliminate Capital Gains with an Upstream Transfer to Mollie

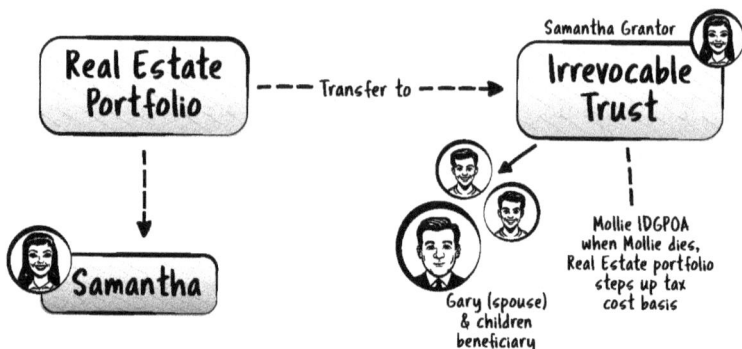

Figure 10-E

The first move is a carefully structured *upstream transfer*. Samantha places her entire $7 million real estate portfolio into a newly drafted *irrevocable trust* for the benefit of her husband, Gary, and their children.

But this isn't just a gift; it's a precision tax maneuver.

The trust is built around an Intentionally Defective General Power of Appointment (IDGPOA)—a strategy we explored in Chapter 9. Mollie holds a carefully tailored general power of appointment that ensures the portfolio is included in her estate for estate tax purposes at her death, triggering a full step-up in basis.

But here's the catch—Mollie's power is *intentionally* limited.

She can only appoint the assets to her creditors or to a narrow class of individuals. That way, even if Mollie were to become vulnerable due to dementia or undue influence later in life, the trust would be protected. She cannot be persuaded—or manipulated—into giving the assets to a neighbor, caregiver, or a well-meaning but completely unrelated charity.

The family preserves tax advantage without giving up control of disposition.

What does that buy the family?

A **full step-up in tax basis** to $7 million at the moment of Mollie's death.

After Mollie's death, Samantha or her family can sell the real estate, liquidating the properties free of capital gains and depreciation recapture tax, saving over $2 million in immediate taxes.

Even better? Mollie's estate is well below the federal estate tax exemption. Her inclusion of these assets triggers no estate tax; we're simply recycling unused exemption that would have otherwise gone to waste.

Instead of transferring assets *downstream* and incurring tax, Samantha looks *upstream*—turning Mollie's mortality into a tax benefit without giving up the keys to the castle.

Samantha Grantor

Irrevocable Trust

Real Estate Portfolio

If Gary dies, Mollie exercises POA to Samantha

Gary and /or children

Figure 10-F

2. Income Remains in the Family via Spousal Design

Giving away the portfolio doesn't mean giving away the income.

The trust is drafted so that while Mollie holds the power of appointment, the income beneficiary is Gary, Samantha's husband. This allows the full income stream from the real estate portfolio to continue flowing into the family's household.

Even though the trust owns the portfolio, Samantha and Gary continue to enjoy the same cash flow as before the transfer.

What if Gary dies before Mollie?

No problem.

The trust includes successor provisions allowing income to shift to

- Samantha directly (at the trustee's discretion);
- their two adult sons, if Samantha doesn't need the income; or
- remain in trust, protected and compounding.

This ensures *continuity of benefit* no matter what happens.

3. Exclusion from Samantha's Estate

Because the $7 million portfolio is transferred to a completed gift trust, and because Samantha retains no power of appointment, no control, and no benefit, the assets are excluded from her taxable estate.

This means:

- The real estate won't be taxed again at Samantha's death.
- She preserves her own estate exemption for her remaining assets.
- The $7 million in real estate, once stepped-up, can now be positioned dynastically for her sons.

This strategy is a *leveraged estate freeze:* Samantha swaps $7 million of taxable real estate with $7 million of *clean, tax-free value* that's entirely off her balance sheet.

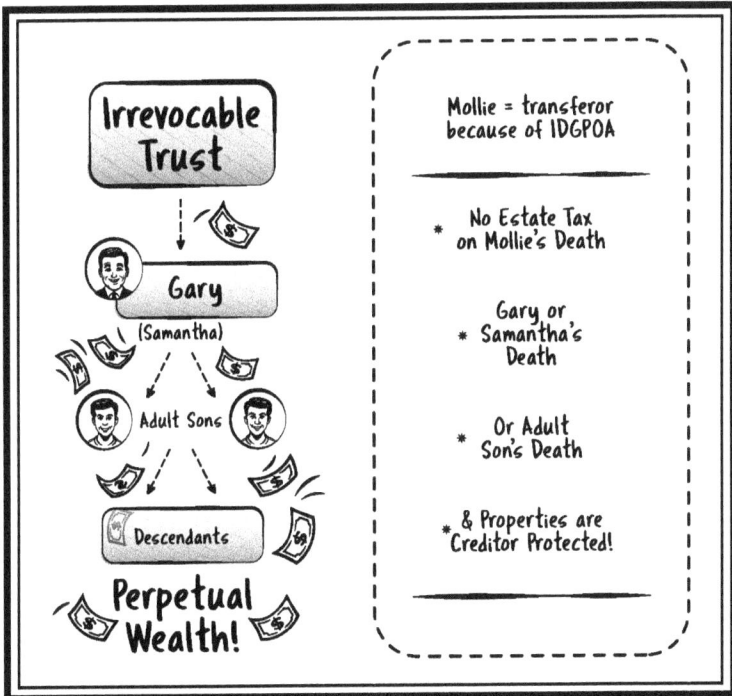

Figure 10-G

4. GSTT Allocation at Mollie's Death

Because the trust is drafted properly, Mollie is considered the *transferor* for GSTT purposes.

At Mollie's passing, her GSTT exemption can be allocated to the trust, effectively converting it into a *dynasty trust* that will

- benefit Samantha and Gary during their lifetimes;
- pass down to their sons **free of estate and GST tax;**
- remain **protected** from creditors, divorcing spouses, and other threats; and
- enable multigenerational **tax-free compounding** on future growth.

Instead of letting Mollie's exemption lapse, we use it to create a fortress for future generations.

Side-by-Side Comparison: Upstream vs. Do-Nothing Strategy

Issue	No Planning (Status Quo) ($)	Samantha's Upstream Strategy ($)
Capital Gains Tax	2.1 million due at liquidation	**0 post step-up**
Estate Tax Exposure	7,000,000 in Samantha's estate	**Excluded from Samantha's estate**
Use of Samantha's exemption	Yes	**No (all but 10%)**
Use of Mollie's exemption	Wasted	**Efficiently used to offset 7,000,000**

Ongoing Income	Samantha collects	Gary collects—seamless income continuity
Gary's mortality contingency	N/A	Income can shift back to Samantha or sons
GSTT Planning	Not Utilized	**Dynasty Trust created with Mollie's exemption**
Legal Control & Liability	Samantha	**Trust owned, protected, and structured**
Tax Savings	Capital gains + estate tax due	**2.1 million saved plus appreciation and multi-generational shield**

Figure 10-H

Optional Enhancements

Directed Trust Structure: Add independent investment trustees to oversee real estate management and help shift future assets into diversified holdings.

Trust Protector Role: Empower a trust protector to grant powers of appointment, change situs to a tax-friendly jurisdiction (e.g., Nevada or Florida), or convert trust structure as needed over time.

Dynasty Trust Provision: Build out the next generation's sub-trusts to provide asset protection for Samantha's sons and eventual grandchildren.

Mindset Shift for the Real Estate Entrepreneur

Most real estate owners nearing retirement would do what their CPA recommends: hold the properties until death, then hope for a step-up. However, that strategy exposes the assets to their own estate tax and offers *no multigenerational leverage*.

Samantha flipped that logic.

She turned an elderly mother's unused exemption into a *multimillion-dollar tax wipe*, kept the income in the family, and secured long-term protection for her sons—all while retaining her liquidity and preserving flexibility.

A Perpetual Wealth system doesn't just preserve— it *amplifies*.

Results of the strategy:

- a $7 million portfolio receives a full step-up in basis
- $2.1 million plus in tax savings realized
- limited use of Samantha's gift exemption and no use of her GST exemption
- Gary receives income, and successors are protected
- a tax-free, asset-protected, and multigenerational dynasty trust is created for her sons

That's generational tax arbitrage done right.

Case Study Gamma

Cooling the Estate Tax, Heating the Legacy

Client Background

Frank didn't start with much more than a work truck, a few tools, and an ironclad work ethic. He figured out early that in the sweltering heat of Southwest Florida, folks didn't just want air conditioning—they *needed* it. Over the next four decades, he and his wife, Maria, built CoolMaster, Inc., from a tiny one-man shop into one of the most trusted HVAC providers in the region.

At sixty-eight, Frank's still sharp, still up early, managing fifty employees, walking the warehouse with a coffee in hand and a ballcap with the company logo stitched on the front. But he's also realistic. "I can't be doing this forever," he jokes. "And the boys are ready."

Those "boys"—Ryan and Chris—aren't boys anymore. They've been running field teams, building the maintenance subscription business, and driving the company's digital transformation through scheduling and remote diagnostics. They respect the foundation Frank laid, but are ready to scale it further. There's no question about their competence. The question is how to transfer the value without killing the golden goose—or getting clobbered by taxes.

Here's what we're working with:

Business Snapshot

- S Corporation, 100 percent owned by Frank
- Gross Revenue: $20 million annually
- Net Profit: $7 million

- 60 percent recurring revenue from maintenance contracts
- 40 percent from HVAC equipment sales and installations

The company operates out of a commercial building valued at $5 million, which is fully paid off and owned by Frank and Maria through a separate entity, Coolmaster Building LLC. Rent is $30,000/month. The building's tax basis? Only $250,000. Ouch.

Personal Estate Snapshot

- Primary residence in Florida: $2.2 million
- Summer home on a Wisconsin lake: $700,000
- Total estimated estate: $40 million plus

Frank and Maria are staring down the barrel of looming estate tax changes. They've got a thriving business, valuable real estate, and two sons ready to lead. But they're worried that if they don't do this right, a third of what they built could disappear to taxes. "I don't mind paying my share," Frank says. "I just don't want to tip extra."

Let's build a Perpetual Wealth strategy to

- avoid triggering capital gains on transition
- create passive income streams for Frank and Maria
- move appreciation outside their estate
- protect the real estate's embedded gain
- empower Ryan and Chris to grow what their parents built

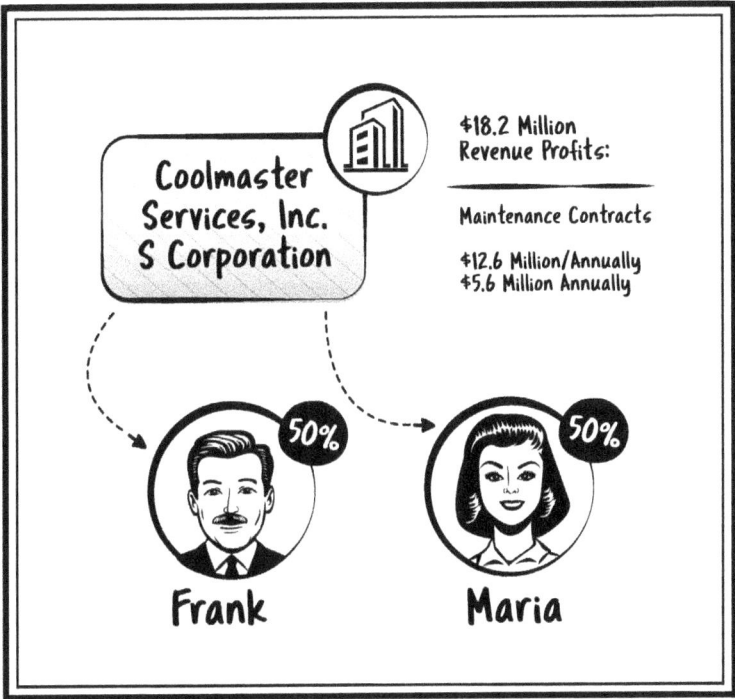

Figure 10-I

1. Carve the Business into Strategic Components

Most folks think of a business as a single block. But a company like CoolMaster is really multiple businesses in one.

CoolMaster Services, Inc. is the operating company (OpCo)—the boots-on-the-ground HVAC services company that dispatches trucks, sells new units, and maintains customer relationships. For purposes of valuing OpCo, we separate the revenue streams, using a 3x multiple of maintenance contracts and a 2x multiple of equipment sales:

- Maintenance (60% of profits = $4.2) × 3x multiple = $12.6 million

- Equipment sales (40% of profits = $2.8M) × 2.0x multiple = $5.6 million
- Total valuation: ~$18.2 million

Maria and Frank aren't interested in transferring the business to a competitor or other purchaser. They'd rather give it to Ryan and Chris, whom they trust and who have already invested their sweat equity in the company's growth. Maria and Frank, however, do want to ensure they have sufficient funds for their retirement years.

2. Extract and Monetize the Intellectual Capital

Frank didn't just build a business. He developed a method—how to sell maintenance packages, how to price ductwork replacements, and how to train junior technicians without compromising quality. This is intellectual property. And it's too valuable to sit unnoticed on Frank's hard drive or in a dusty binder.

To monetize Frank's intellectual property, we create **CoolMaster IP, LLC**:

- It owns service manuals, training systems, workflow SOPs, pricing models, and even the customer intake and CRM flow.
- The operating company licenses the IP from CoolMaster IP and pays a royalty fee—say 5–7 percent of revenue.
- That's $1.5 million flowing to Frank and Maria via a passive, non-W2 income stream.

But here's the best part: CoolMaster IP is owned by Spousal Lifetime Access Trusts. A Spousal Lifetime Access Trust (SLAT) is a smart estate planning tool that lets you remove assets from your taxable estate while maintaining indirect access to them through your spouse.

A SLAT sounds complicated, but think of it like this: you gift assets out of your estate, but your spouse can still benefit from them. It's like stepping out of the room—but leaving the door cracked open. This is what we do to the IP company shares. When Frank and Maria die, Ryan and Chris inherit the shares.

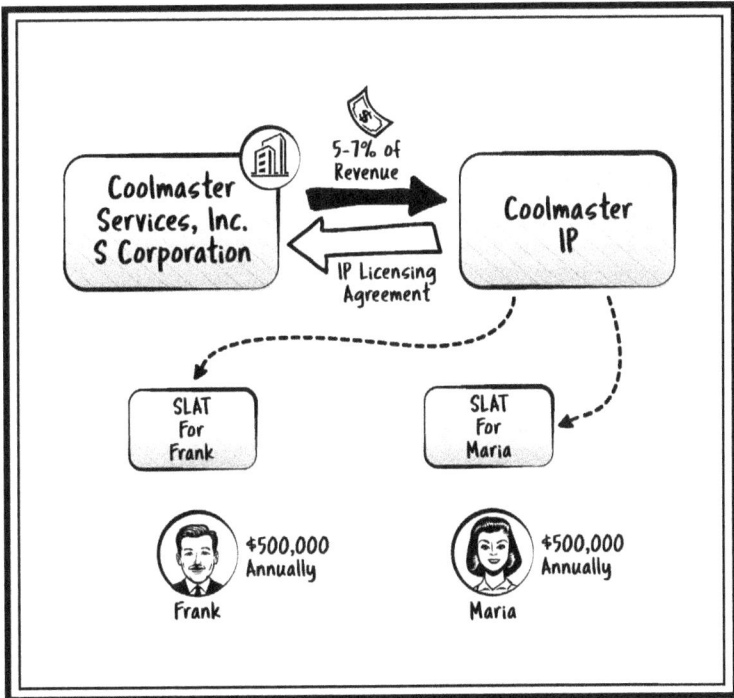

Figure 10-J

To make the SLAT work, create an irrevocable trust and gift assets into it. The trust benefits your spouse during their lifetime—and potentially your kids or grandkids too. Because the assets are no longer in your name, they're excluded from your estate, which helps reduce or even eliminate estate taxes down the road.

But here's the clever part—your spouse can receive distributions, and since you're married, that money benefits both of you. You've moved the assets out of your estate, but you haven't cut the cord completely.

Which means:

- the trust is **outside Frank and Maria's estate**
- income flows to them (we need to be careful of something called the reciprocal trust doctrine, but we can manage that)
- but the appreciation of the IP's value stays in the trust for Ryan and Chris.

Frank and Maria own the *how* of the business without being taxed on the *what*.

3. Establish a Management Company to Provide Central Oversight

Behind every successful contractor business is a pile of administrative work nobody wants to do—HR, payroll, compliance, accounting, scheduling. Instead of keeping that inside the operating business, we pull it into **CoolMaster Management, LLC,** which

- charges OpCo a management fee;
- employs the admin team;
- creates another source of income that can either go to Frank and Maria or be gradually transitioned to the sons; and

- can one day manage multiple OpCos if Ryan and Chris expand into new territories.

This creates a repeatable, franchise-ready structure that scales.

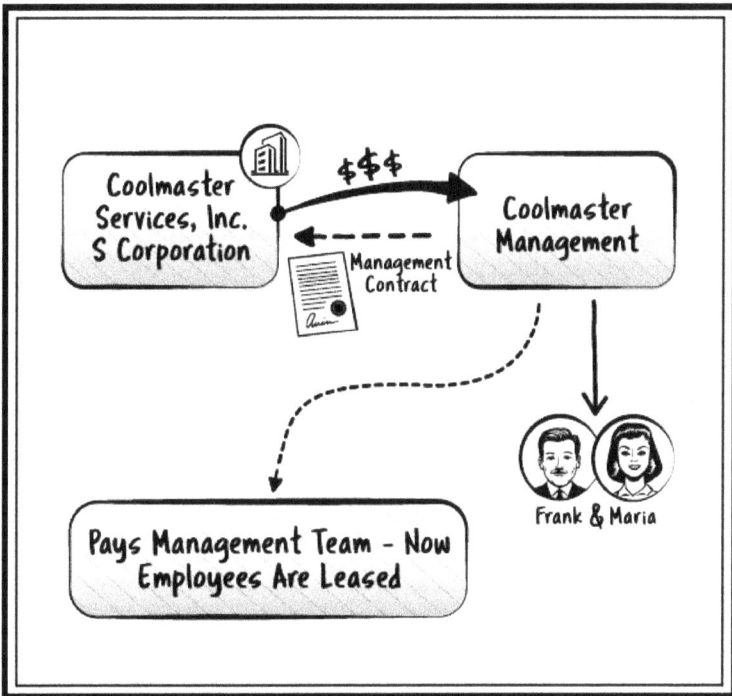

Figure 10-K

4. Sell the Business (At a Discount) to two IDGTs

Now, we address the estate tax elephant in the room.

Instead of gifting or selling the business outright, Frank and Maria sell their respective interests in the operating and management companies to two different IDGTs.

Instead of gifting the business (using up their gift and estate tax exemptions) or selling it outright to an outside buyer (incurring capital gains), Frank and Maria take a more elegant approach—they sell ownership interests in the operating company and management company to a grantor trust, specifically an Intentionally Defective Grantor Trust (IDGT).

The IDGT breaks down like this:

- The total business valuation approximates $20 million.
- Apply a 30 percent discount for lack of control and marketability, which means $14 million fair market value for transfer, or $7 million for each of their respective interests.
- Frank and Maria each make a small seed gift to the trust—usually 10 percent of the value, or around $700,000 each—which consumes a small part of their gift tax exemptions.
- Then, each sells their remaining $6.3 million interest to the IDGT in exchange for a promissory note. The IDGT's beneficiaries are Ryan and Chris.
- The IDGTs are timed and drafted to minimize a potential "reciprocal trust doctrine" IRS challenge. In other words, the timing of the sales and the provisions of the trusts cannot be identical, or the IRS would have a good argument that the entire transaction is a disguised gift or sale and tax the transactions accordingly.

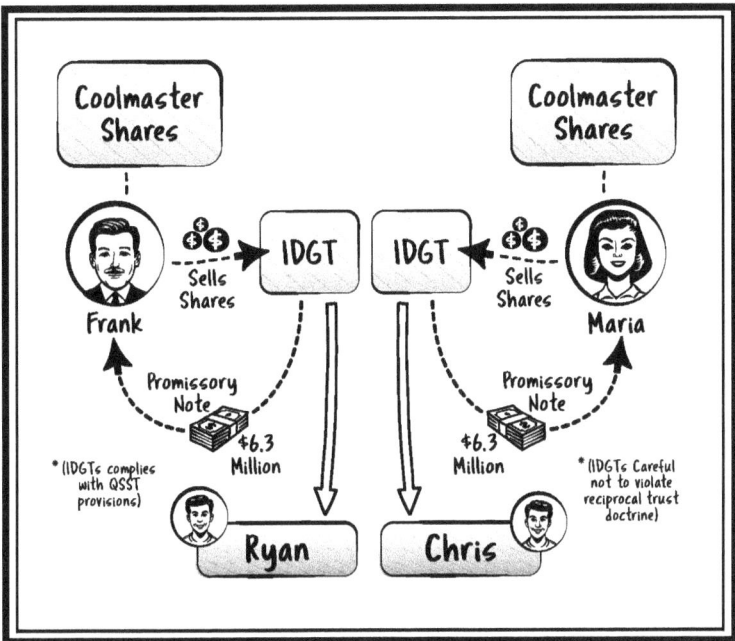

Figure 10-L

Key Benefits

- *No capital gains tax* on the sale because the IDGT is a *grantor trust*—Frank and the trust are treated as the same taxpayer for income tax purposes.

- Only a *small portion of the gift exemption* is used for the seed gift.

- *Future appreciation* grows inside the trust—outside Frank and Maria's estates and Chris and Ryan's estates.

- Income from the promissory note flows back to Frank and Maria, providing retirement cash.

- The estate is frozen at the discounted value, and everything above that escapes estate tax.

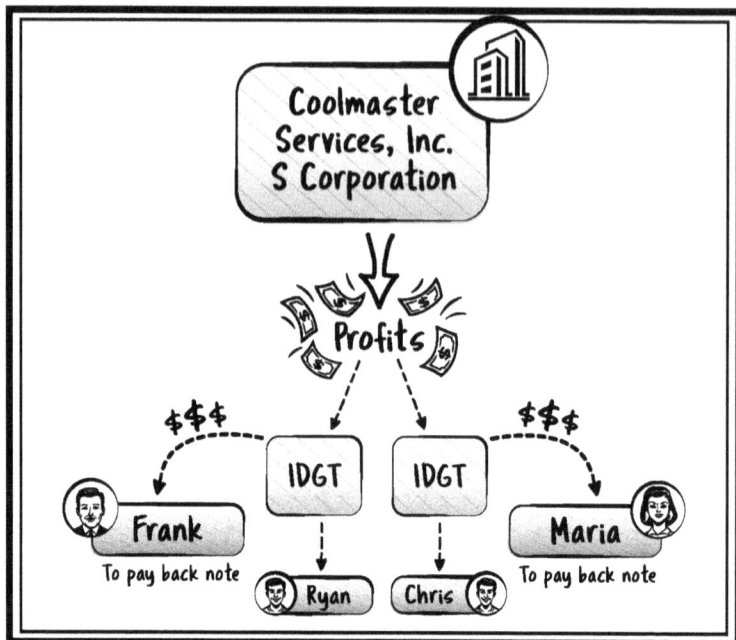

Figure 10-M

Liability Protection: An Overlooked Advantage of the Structure

Frank and Maria have always kept solid insurance—general liability, commercial auto, workers' comp—but even Frank knew lawsuits don't always stop at policy limits. And the more successful he became, the more he felt like a target.

He needed to eliminate the target on his back, and the Perpetual Wealth structure has the solution. The system does more than save taxes; it fortifies the walls around Frank's personal balance sheet.

How?

- OpCo is separated from the IP and Management companies, so those assets aren't exposed if there's a lawsuit from a botched install or a truck accident.

- The real estate is held in a separate LLC, and ultimately inside a *trust*, so plaintiffs can't attach it in a business suit.

- The IP company has no employees or trucks; it licenses know-how, making it a low-risk, high-yield entity.

- Income-producing assets (like IP royalties and note payments from the IDGT) flow into trusts, with spendthrift provisions that prevent creditors from reaching them.

- Frank and Maria don't "own" the company anymore on paper; they just hold a secured note, which is much harder to attack than equity.

- Similarly, Chris and Ryan don't "own" the company. Instead, they have beneficial interests in trusts that own the company.

There could always be a lawsuit against the company, but extracting wealth from one of the principals is now increasingly complex.

And the Real Estate? Let's Step It Up

The $5 million building—with its $250,000 basis—is a capital gains problem waiting to happen. If Frank sells or dies owning it, the tax bill could bite hard.

To minimize that tax bill, he should implement *upstream planning using an IDGPOA trust.*

Just like Samantha did in Case Study Beta, Frank transfers the building into a trust for Maria's elderly mother, Ynes, that

- gives the parent a *general power of appointment*, but only over Frank and Maria's descendants;
- ensures the property is included in Ynes' (parents') estate; and
- guarantees that Ynes's death triggers a *step-up in basis* at death to the full $5M.

Frank and Maria still receive rent. The family still controls the building. But the tax bomb? *Defused.*

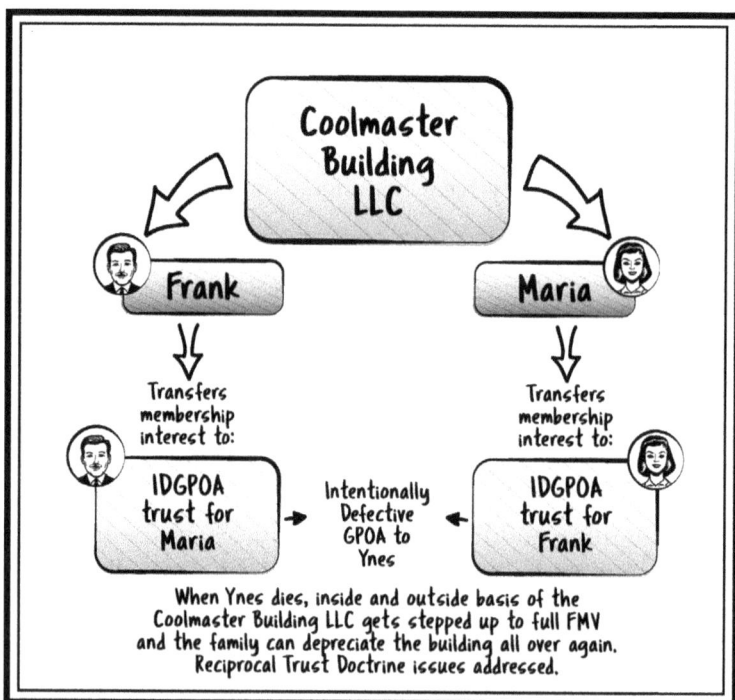

Figure 10-N

Strategy	Do Nothing (Status Quo) ($)	Perpetual Wealth Strategy
Business Transfer	Gifting or Selling Triggers Tax	**Installment sale to IDGT—no gain**
Estate Tax Exposure	12M included in 25M estate	**Excluded via IDGT/SLAT trust structure**
Real Estate Capital Gain	~400K tax at sale or death	**Step-up via upstream trust planning**
Owner Income	W-2 salary, SE tax owed	**Royalties, rent, and note income = passive**
Intellectual Property Control	Unprotected, tied to Operating Company	**Held in low-risk IP entity + trust-owned**
Business Appreciation	Included in estate creating estate tax liability	**Escapes estate tax— held in trust**

Real Estate Liability Protection	Owned personally, high liability	LLC ownership + trust-layered firewall
General Liability	Everything reachable in lawsuit	Only OpCo exposed; other assets insulated
Total Tax Savings Over Time	Taxed at every stage	$3M+ in tax savings + long-term protection

Figure 10-O

Mindset Shift for the Family Business Owner

Most business transitions are rushed, reactive, and riddled with emotion—a handshake and hope. But hope isn't a strategy.

Frank didn't build CoolMaster that way. From the very beginning, he thought in terms of *structure*—how systems created scalability. Now, when it comes time to transition the business, he's leaning into that same mindset.

He isn't handing over a business with fingers crossed. He's transferring it with *intention, framework,* and *vision*.

Structurally Sound

Frank didn't just give Ryan and Chris a business. He gave them a strategic separation of assets, clear operating roles, and built-in legal protections. By breaking the company into operational, IP, and management entities, he created a platform that could scale, attract future investors, and replicate itself, while protecting each piece from the risks of the others.

Tax-Aware

He also knew the traps: depreciation recapture on the building, capital gains on the business, and estate tax on future growth. Frank didn't just know about them; he planned for them. He legally eliminated millions in avoidable taxes by utilizing an IDGT, an upstream trust for the real estate, and royalty structures to create passive income. Doing so saved money and compounded future freedom.

Risk Vigilant

Frank has spent enough time in people's homes—and courtrooms—to know lawsuits are just part of doing business. But they don't have to reach your core. By separating legal entities, holding IP and real estate in trusts, and pushing income through protected channels, Frank made sure that one problem could not bring down the whole operation. His personal wealth—and his family's peace of mind—remain insulated.

Legacy Spirit

This wasn't just about money. Frank could have sold to a third party and cashed out. But his real legacy isn't the company—it's the *family* who will carry it forward. By giving Ryan and Chris something structured, protected, and scalable, he gave them more than a job. He gave them a mission. A foundation they can build on. A future he helped shape—but doesn't need to control.

Frank isn't just passing down a business. He's passing down a *Perpetual Wealth system*.

What Happens When These Mindsets Are Ignored

Now, contrast that with Tom, another HVAC owner in the same town.

Tom was proud of what he built. His sons worked in the business and were capable. So, when he turned seventy, he handed over the S corporation in one shot. No trusts. No structure. No plan. "You boys figure it out," he said.

As a result:

- The business and the real estate were in the same legal entity.

- A customer injury turned into a personal lawsuit that reached Tom's bank accounts.

- The company's trade secrets were shared across multiple software platforms and ultimately lost when one son exited the business.

- There was no voting agreement. The brothers fought. One quit. The other tried to buy him out, incurring additional debt.

- When Tom died, the IRS valued the business at $10 million, but it was all still in his estate.

- The estate tax bill was over $4 million.

- The boys had to liquidate real estate to pay the estate tax.

Do you see the difference?

Tom ignored *structure.*
Tom ignored *tax risk.*
Tom left his family *vulnerable.*
And in the end, Tom's business was sold—not scaled.
Frank planned. Tom reacted. The first created a platform. The second left a problem.

The Perpetual Wealth Question:

Are you transitioning a business—or designing a legacy system?

Because the next generation isn't just inheriting your company. They're inheriting the consequences of your planning, or your lack of it.

Case Study Delta

The Blended Balancing Act

Client Background

Richard had built everything himself from the ground up. Precision Industrial Services, Inc. started with a dusty desk in a shared warehouse and a few reliable clients. Forty years later, Richard was fielding a $12 million offer from a private equity group. He didn't need the money, but he wanted to ensure the transition didn't unravel the family he'd worked just as hard to protect.

Richard, now sixty-one, was remarried to Monica, fifty-two. Monica had no children of her own, but she was a devoted partner through years of late nights, trade shows, and emergencies that only family-run businesses understand.

From his first marriage, Richard had three adult children:

- Taylor, who managed sales for the business
- Ben, who handled day-to-day operations
- Lila, a middle school art teacher, who preferred kilns and canvas to spreadsheets and staff meetings

The business was his largest asset. But Richard also had $5 million in brokerage investments, a primary home in Florida, a lake house in Wisconsin, and a strong desire to avoid the fate of friends whose blended families blew apart in probate court.

"Monica gave me support. My kids gave me purpose. I want us all to live harmoniously, and I'd like to transition the business to the boys. However, I want to have enough to live off of for Monica and Monica, and I want to treat Lila fairly."

Richard's family situation, as well as the fact that he didn't want to sell the company out from under his sons, was a perfect Perpetual Wealth situation. The balance sheet and plan follow:

Client Balance Sheet

Asset	Value ($)	Ownership
Precision Industrial Services	12,000,000	S Corporation
Brokerage & Investment Accounts	5,000,000	Joint w/ Monica
Florida Primary Residence	1,000,000	Richard
Wisconsin Lake House	750,000	Richard
Miscellaneous Assets	250,000	Richard
Life Insurance	2,000,000	Richard
Total Net Worth	21,000,000	Strategically placed across entities and trusts

Figure 10-P

Let's Break It Down

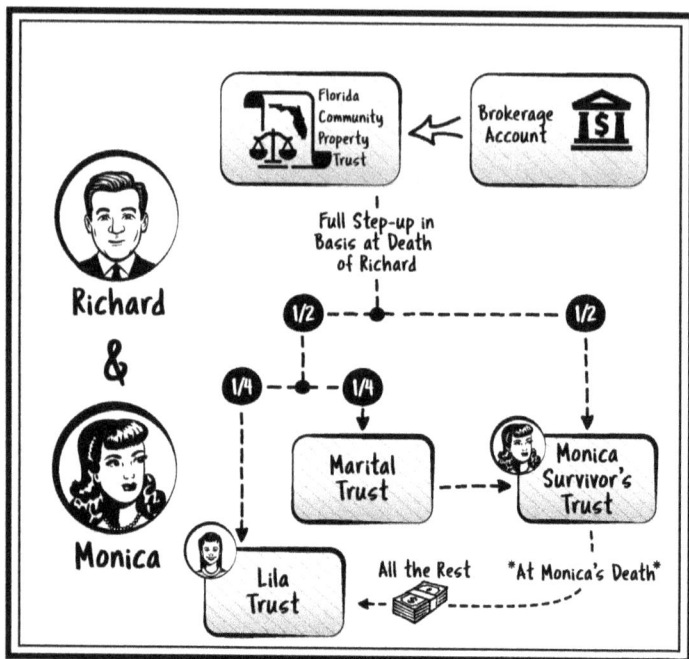

Figure 10-Q

Florida Community Property Trust (FCPT) for Brokerage Assets

Richard and Monica contributed their $5 million joint brokerage account to a *Florida Community Property Trust (FCPT)*. Why?

- To secure a 100 percent basis step-up at Richard's death
- To allow his $2.5 million share to pass into a QTIP trust for Monica
- To give the remainder of Richard's half share to Lila, after Monica's death

Monica retains her half and continues to receive income, and Lila gains a secure, liquid asset that doesn't involve her brothers or their business.

The FCPT was Richard's quiet solution to a loud problem: how to care for his wife and daughter without pitting them against each other. Monica's dignity is protected. She doesn't have to rely on goodwill or wait on distributions.

2. QTIP Trust for Monica—Funded from FCPT and Devise Planning

At Richard's death, his $2.5 million share of the FCPT flows into a QTIP trust for Monica's benefit. Monica retains the other half and owns it outright. Her estate plan bequeaths it to Lila, but she can change it anytime. Should she remarry without a nuptial agreement, a new spouse would also have rights to her half. Richard understands this and is fine with it.

- Monica receives a lifetime income, with access to principal as needed.
- Upon her death, the assets pass to Lila.
- Monica remains supported.
- Lila receives liquidity and security with no entanglement in the business.

This QTIP structure avoids gift and estate tax while protecting both family branches.

3. Postnuptial Agreement: Essential for Florida Homestead Planning

Richard knew that Florida's laws treat homestead differently and dangerously.

You can't leave your Florida primary residence to anyone other than your spouse unless that spouse signs a valid waiver of the specific homestead rights under Florida law. Otherwise, the devise fails, and Florida's default rules take over, which would create an unsatisfactory result.

So, Richard and Monica signed a *postnuptial agreement* stating that

- Monica waived homestead rights under Florida law;
- The agreement allows the home to pass *by devise;* and
- Richard's estate plan now puts the home into a *Marital Trust*, assuming that Monica survives Richard, then splits the Florida home with one-third to each child at Monica's death.

No ambiguity. No conflict. And most importantly, no invalid devise. It wasn't about trust, but rather about law. Monica understood that, and so did Richard.

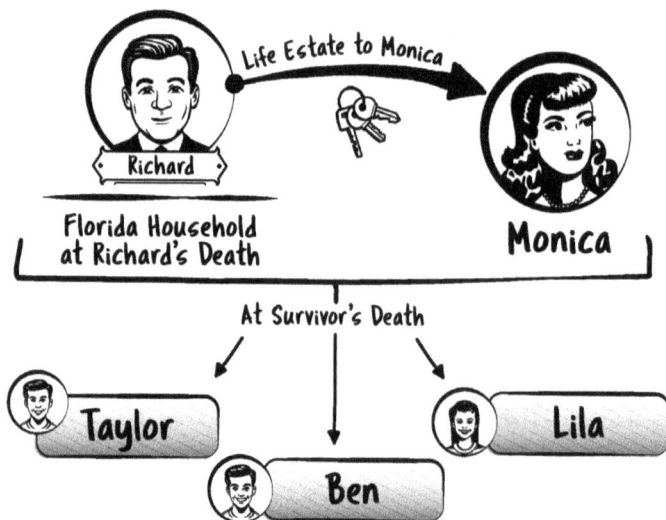

Figure 10-R

4. Lake House to Lila—Direct Ownership, Total Clarity

Some assets are more than just value; they're emotional landmarks.

The Wisconsin lake house had always been Lila's favorite place. Richard's trust will transfer it outright to her without a trust, partnership, or co-ownership with her brothers. Another estate tax savings strategy would include transferring the Wisconsin residence into a Qualified Personal Residence Trust (QPRT).

She could live in it, rent it, or sell it. But it would be hers, unconditionally.

"Giving her something of her own—without complications—that mattered to me," Richard said.

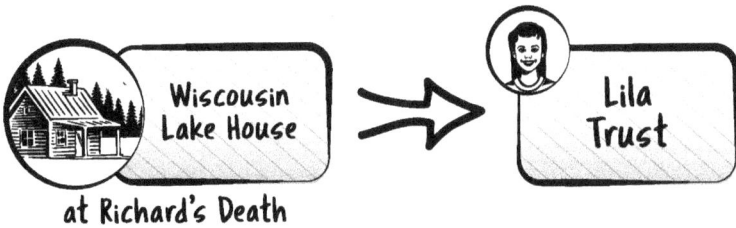

at Richard's Death

Figure 10-S

5. Business Transition to IDGT—For the Boys, Not for Lila

The business isn't just an asset; it is a career for Taylor and Ben. But for Lila, it was a spreadsheet with a last name she'd never put on her résumé. Further, it's generally a bad idea to give closely held business interests to children who aren't part of that business when others depend on it for their livelihood. Passive ownership by a non-participating sibling often leads to conflict over distributions, decision-making, and especially over compensation. If Lila had remained a co-owner, she might one day resent the salaries Taylor and Ben draw as operators, especially if dividends were thin. At the same time, Taylor and Ben might feel she was getting paid dividends from their labor and risk-taking.

By keeping the business in the hands of those who run it, Richard prevented the trust from becoming a battle-field—and preserved the relationships behind the balance sheet. Richard didn't name her a beneficiary of the company; instead:

- he gifted 10 percent of the company to an *Intentionally Defective Grantor Trust (IDGT)*;
- he sold 90 percent at a discount to that same trust in exchange for a note;
- Taylor and Ben received *sub-trusts* based on their operational roles; and
- Lila was intentionally and respectfully *excluded*.

By using this design, Richard avoided the common trap where a non-operating child becomes a beneficiary who expects distributions, while the working siblings resent the pressure to perform and pay out. This gave Taylor and Ben clarity and control.

"It's not fair to make her an owner of something she didn't want. And it's not fair to make the boys send checks to someone who's not in the fight."

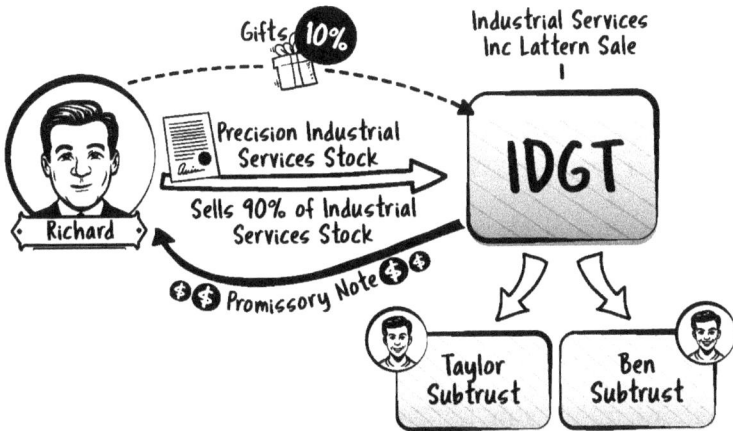

Figure 10-T

6. ILIT with $2 Million Life Insurance for Liquidity

Richard used part of the business sale proceeds to fund a $2 million permanent life insurance policy, held inside an *Irrevocable Life Insurance Trust (ILIT)*.

The ILIT provides

- liquidity for taxes and expenses
- no estate tax impact
- optional use for equalization or buyouts

This was Richard's way of ensuring that nobody had to sell something they wanted to keep, or keep something they couldn't afford.

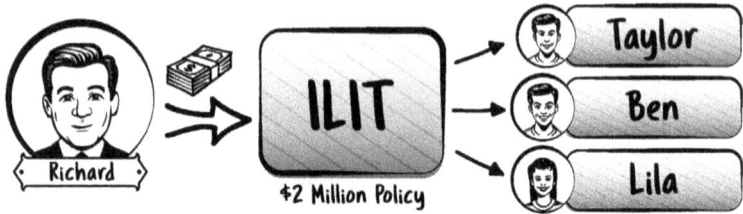

Figure 10-U

The Fairness Conversation

Richard didn't aim for equal slices. He aimed for equal satisfaction.

- Lila got real estate she loved and liquidity she could rely on.
- Taylor and Ben got the business they helped build.
- Monica got the income she deserved and the security she needed.

No one had to justify their share. No one had to resent the others. And no one had to guess what Richard meant.

A *Legacy Intent Letter* accompanied the plan, offering instructions as well as insight.

Strategy Comparison: Hope vs. Structure

Strategy Element	Typical "Hopeful" Approach	Perpetual Wealth Strategy
Business Transfer	No structure = risk of estate tax and confusion	10% gift + 90% sale to IDGT; avoids estate inclusion, honors work-based succession
Beneficiary Fairness	Equal shares of everything	Lila receives FCPT/QTIP assets and lake house; boys receive business + homestead share
FCPT Usage	Not used— misses basis step-up	Entire $5M brokerage moved into FCPT; 100% step-up and clean split at Richard's death
Spousal Protection	All proceeds taxable	IDGT strategy freezes value, shifts growth to heirs
Florida Homestead	Invalid devise to QTIP	Postnup waives homestead so QTIP can legally hold it
Real Estate Usage	New spouse may inherit everything	QTIP lock in Richard's family as remainder beneficiaries
Internal Business Conflict	Forced asset sales or borrowing	ILIT provides tax-free liquidity

Tax Efficiency	Equal shares, unequal outcomes	Equal value, unequal access: Customized to each life path
Liquidity Planning	Pays taxes out of estate or forced sales	$2 Million ILIT provides tax-free liquidity
Family Harmony	No one knows what's coming	Clarity, intent letter, separate trusts reduce resentment and confusion

Figure 10-V

Mindset Shift: Fairness Doesn't Mean Equal. It Means Right.

Richard knew this wasn't just about estate tax or probate avoidance. It was about relationships—fragile ones. A spreadsheet can't feel tension at Thanksgiving dinner. Trust documents can't sense unspoken resentment between siblings. But Richard could. And he'd seen too many families torn apart by a plan that was "technically sound" but emotionally tone-deaf.

He respected that Lila lived in a different world than Taylor and Ben—one where fulfillment came from creativity and autonomy, not payroll reports. He valued Monica's presence and loyalty, but he didn't want to saddle her with the burden of managing assets she never built. And most importantly, he understood that structure isn't about restriction; it's about release. The right plan frees people from ambiguity, tension, and future battles they never asked to fight.

Richard embraced the Perpetual Wealth mindset to guide his plan.

Structurally Sound

Everyone had what they needed, wrapped in the correct legal container. No shared bank accounts between stepmom and stepchildren. No overlapping ownership of businesses or homes. Each piece of the plan was precisely allocated and easy to administer.

Contrarian Curious

The plan spoke long after Richard was gone. It didn't leave Monica guessing. It didn't leave Lila waiting. And it didn't leave the boys fighting. It created clarity, so his family could focus on what they meant to each other and not on what they expected to receive.

Tax-Aware

By using IDGT, FCPT, and QTIP trusts, Richard sidestepped unnecessary capital gains, captured full basis step-ups, and trimmed the estate tax bill without trimming his family's future.

Liquidity Conscious

With life insurance held in an ILIT, no one had to sell something they loved to pay taxes on something they inherited. Cash would be available without emotion, without argument, and without delay.

Growth-Oriented

Richard had questions. He asked them. He took advice. He listened—not just to his advisors but to his family. Then he built a plan that reflected what he had and who they were.

This plan wasn't just a balance sheet. It was a love letter in legal form that said, "I saw each of you. I planned for your future. And I did it with care."

Case Study Epsilon

The Legacy Builder Without Heirs

Client Background

Evelyn is fifty-two and lives in Monterey, California, in a redwood-and-glass house perched above the sea. The walls are lined with original art. A grand piano sits near the window—not for show, but for late-night improvisations after a good bottle of wine. Her prized 1790 German violin rests nearby, always perfectly tuned.

She's built and sold two software companies, mentors young founders, and volunteers at the Monterey Symphony. She has no children and has never married. Her only sibling, Jeff, is a soft-spoken artist who lives simply. Evelyn calls him "brilliant with oil paint, hopeless with money."

But Jeff's daughters (Evelyn's nieces)—Maya and Tess— are her greatest joy. She calls them her "heart family." And she's committed to lifting them up, giving them every opportunity to rise without the weights she carried.

Evelyn lost her mother to pancreatic cancer—a quiet, brutal goodbye that left a mark. Since then, her legacy planning has been focused, almost mission-driven. She said, "This isn't about leaving things behind. It's about planting seeds that grow after I'm gone."

Evelyn's Financial Profile

Asset	Value ($)	Notes
Investment Accounts	8,000,000	Taxable, diversified, low basis
Traditional 401(k)	4,000,000	Growing at 10% annually
Monterey Home	4,500,000	Owned outright
Life Insurance (UL)	500,000	Individually owned
Artwork (Dali)	2,150,000	Donate to CRT
Net Worth	**19,150,000**	**Diversified, tax-sensitive, asset-rich**

Figure 10-W

Let's Break It Down

1. Launching Her Nieces with 529 Plans

Evelyn doesn't believe in dangling opportunity. She believes in handing it over, pre-wrapped and ready to be used. She contributes $90,000 each to *529 plans* for Maya and Tess—fully front-loading the five-year IRS gifting limit so that

- a total of $180,000 is removed from her estate;
- accounts grow tax-free;
- funds can cover tuition, grad school, study abroad, or eventually roll into *Roth IRAs*;
- a *fiduciary successor custodian*, not Jeff, will manage the accounts.

"This is their launchpad," Evelyn says. "And no one has to wait for a scholarship to make a dream real."

2. Art with a Second Life: A Charitable Remainder Trust (CRT)

Evelyn's Salvador Dalí sculpture and a contemporary paint-ing—valued at $2.25 million combined—were not just décor. They were her personal symbols of ambition and imagination.

"I lived with that art for decades. Now, someone else can love it—and a lot of people can benefit from it." Now, they will fund something more.

She places them into a **CRT**, which will

- sell the pieces at auction;
- pay her 6 percent annually for life (~$135,000/year), which she'll use to fund additional trusts for Maya and Tess;
- provide an immediate charitable deduction; and
- leave the remainder to the Monterey County Community Foundation for cancer research and music education.

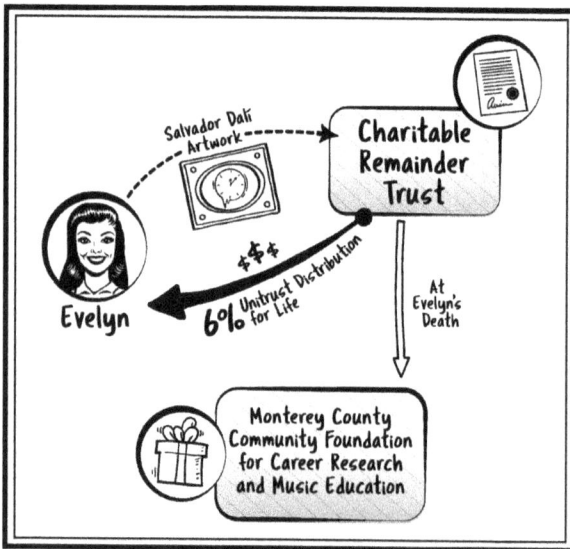

Figure 10-X

3. Monterey County Community Foundation (MCCF): A Legacy Partner

Instead of building a foundation from scratch, Evelyn designates **MCCF** as the primary beneficiary of her

- Roth IRA (partial)
- life insurance policy
- residual estate

She writes a *Legacy Intent Letter* outlining allocations for

- pancreatic cancer research and to assist families of patients with pancreatic cancer
- a music education endowment
- a women-in-STEM scholarship, named after Maya and Tess

She personally meets with MCCF leadership to ensure mission alignment.

"I don't need to manage another board," she said. "I just need to know the right people will carry the torch."

4. Her Monterey Home: Anchor and Asset

The $4.5 million home is more than a view; it's a legacy resource.

Evelyn outlined two future uses:

- If her health declines, her care team can sell the home to fund care, investments, or endowment gifts.
- If she doesn't need it, the home will transfer to MCCF, with sale proceeds divided among her scholarship and medical research designations.

About her home, Evelyn said, "It gave me peace. Now, it can give someone else a shot at life or a seat in an orchestra."

5. A Family Office That Walks Beside Her

Evelyn partners with a **boutique family office**, not for hand-holding, but for capacity building.
The office

- manages investments for her $8 million taxable portfolio;
- executes Roth IRA conversions and tracks tax offsets; and
- coordinates her CRT auction, grant-making, and DAF.
- provides personal support by sourcing medical professionals, coordinating care, managing property repairs, and even helping her buy her following EV.

They meet quarterly with her *Legacy Advisory Committee (LAC)* to align wealth, giving, and future care decisions.
"I don't want to guess who will help me later. I want to choose them now and build trust while I still run the show."

6. IRA Planning: Roth + QCD Strategy

With her IRA compounding at 10 percent annually, Evelyn faces a future RMD tsunami.
So, she balances two strategies:

- Converts $2 million to Roth over six to eight years

    o Offsets taxes with *CRT and DAF deductions*
    o Leaves Roth to the nieces' trusts—income-tax free and fully deployable

- Holds the remaining $2 million for *Qualified Charitable Distributions (QCDs)*

  o Beginning at age 70½, she'll make *$100,000 annual gifts* to MCCF
  o Satisfies RMDs, *lowers taxable income*, and keeps Medicare premiums down

"I'm not trying to avoid taxes. I'm trying to ensure every dollar goes where I want it, not where Congress sends it."

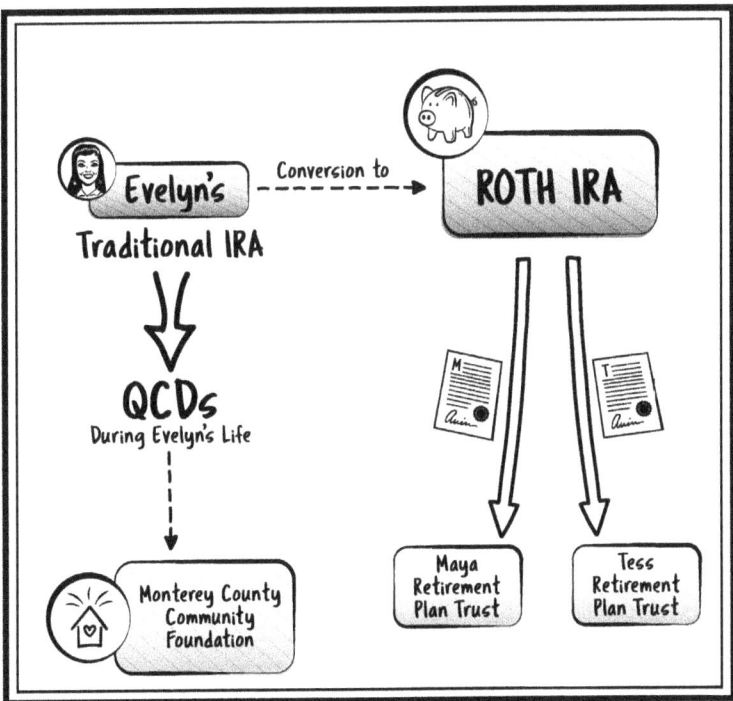

Figure 10-Y

7. A Trust That Protects Without Hovering

Evelyn's **revocable trust** is her command center that

- avoids probate;
- names a professional trustee; and
- gives her Legacy Advisory Committee (LAC) full review rights, including:

  ○ trustee oversight and replacement power
  ○ approval of discretionary distributions
  ○ alignment of endowment and charitable fund activity

She also appoints a *fiduciary care manager* to activate at age seventy-five (or earlier if needed) to coordinate:

- medical care
- in-home support
- financial oversight during incapacity

Depending on her needs, the home can be retained or sold as part of this care plan.

"This isn't paranoia. It's delegation. I'm the CEO of my life, and I just built a good team."

Strategy Element	Typical "Hopeful" Plan	Perpetual Wealth Strategy
Niece Support	College Checks or promises	**529s are front-loaded**, trustee-managed, and offer long-term flexibility

Art & Charitable Planning	Bequest at death	**CRT funds auction**, lifetime income, remainder to MCCF
IRA Strategy	Wait until RMDs are necessary	Half Roth Conversions and half QCDs at 75 (RBD) professionally executed
Monterey Home	Unused	**Held or sold** funds directed to cause-specific grants or LTC needs
Investment Oversight	Retail advisor or DIY problem if incapacity arises	**Family office manages investment, giving, and execution**
Elder Protection	Hopeful family or DPOA	**Care advocate + Legacy Committee + coordinated fiduciary plan**
Philanthropic Legacy	Bequest to national nonprofits	**MCCF-directed funds with an impact-specific intent letter**
Liquidity & Tax Efficiency	Piecemeal or reactive	CRT income + Roth flexibility + QCDs = precision + purpose

Figure 10-Z

Mindset Shift: Independence Isn't Isolation; It's Intelligent Design.

Evelyn didn't wait for someone else to define her legacy. She designed it herself while still having clarity, conviction, and the right people to build with. She wasn't trying to control everything from the grave. She was trying to **create freedom now, reduce the burden later, and leave a legacy without confusion**.

She embraced the *Perpetual Wealth* mindsets:

- **Structurally Sound**. Every account, asset, and role is placed with surgical care.

- **Legacy Spirit.** Whether or not you have biological heirs, you desire a life that echoes in every scholarship and symphony.

- **Tax-Aware**. CRT, Roth, QCDs, and offset strategies dialed in by an innovative team.

- **Liquidity Conscious.** She has options, income, and no fire-sale risk.

- **Coachable Attitude**. Evelyn built a strategy by listening first, then acting with bold precision.

Evelyn didn't have heirs, but she had vision. And *she planned like someone who knew her values were bigger than her lifetime.*

TRUTH #4

Tax-Free War Chest

Freedom Requires a Tax-Free War Chest: Liquidity isn't just about having cash; it's about having the right kind of cash—one Uncle Sam can't siphon off. Tax-free liquidity survives downturns—and seizes opportunities. Whether funding business growth, protecting your family, or ensuring you're never at the bank's or IRS's mercy, having a reservoir of tax-free capital provides freedom to navigate uncertainties.

By now, the rigged nature of the system is no longer just your suspicion; you understand that it's a fact. You've seen how taxes, lawsuits, and static planning sap the potential from even the most successful entrepreneurs. But recognizing the game is only part of the journey. To win, you need leverage—and not the kind that asks for permission. You need a war chest that is *accessible, tax-advantaged*, and *answerable to no one but you.*

Chapter 11 begins that transformation by asking the question most entrepreneurs don't think to ask until it's too late: what if the banks say no? What if the market tanks? What if your next big opportunity arrives... and your money is tied up or taxable? The chapter pulls back the curtain on liquidity—why it's more than a balance sheet line, and why true entrepreneurial freedom depends on *unrestricted, tax-free access to capital* when you need it most.

Chapter 12 builds on this by introducing the *Perpetual Wealth Bank™*, where you stop borrowing from institutions and start borrowing from yourself. Using overfunded life insurance as your personal liquidity engine, this chapter reveals how to create a vault of tax-free cash that you can access for investments, opportunities, or even tax-free retirement—all while it remains protected and compounding behind the scenes.

Chapter 13 takes it even further with *premium financing*, a strategy so powerful—and so misunderstood—that most advisors either ignore it or actively discourage it. But when you structure it properly, you can fund millions in life insurance without tying up your own capital. You'll see how this strategy becomes the cornerstone of your tax-free dynasty, generating liquidity without liquidation and empowering your trust structures to fund generations, not just preserve them.

Chapter 14 reveals what most CPAs and attorneys miss entirely—the quiet revolution of *Cash Balance Plans*, where the tax code allows business owners to shelter hundreds of thousands per year beyond 401(k)s. This isn't retirement planning. It's income tax surgery—sophisticated, compliant, and engineered—to let entrepreneurs catch up on retirement in the blink of a few high-contribution years.

Finally, Chapter 15 shows how the best structures don't just protect; they evolve. It pulls together liquidity, trusts, premium financing, and tax-sheltered retirement strategies into a living, breathing framework. You'll see how to fund your future, unlock growth capital, and retire from the grind without retiring from the game. Because Perpetual Wealth doesn't mean sitting still. It means building a system that moves with you—and beyond you.

In these five chapters, we don't just look at tools; we build the *Tax-Free War Chest*™, a liquidity system that doesn't ask for permission, isn't hostage to the IRS, and gives you the confidence to act when it matters most.

Because the real win isn't having capital; it's having capital that answers to *you*.

CHAPTER 11

Caffeinated Capital: What a Coffee Giant Can Teach You About Liquidity

In business, cash isn't just king—it's oxygen.
You don't notice it until you're gasping for it.

—*Howard Schultz, CEO of Starbucks*

Thousands of people preload their Starbucks cards or apps with money daily. Not because they have to, but because they're buying convenience. They don't realize, however, that they're also funding Starbucks's global expansion.

In an August 24, 2024, story, *Marketwatch* reported that Starbucks has nearly $1.8 billion in stored value from unspent gift cards and mobile app deposits. That money isn't revenue until you buy a cup of coffee. But in the meantime? Starbucks can use a zero-interest, tax-deferred cash reserve however it wants—open new stores, invest in tech, or buy beans in bulk.

It's a masterclass in *liquidity strategy*.

Starbucks didn't borrow from a bank. They didn't issue stock. They quietly built a cash war chest by turning coffee buyers into capital providers.

Now, imagine if you could build a private reservoir of capital that's unencumbered, tax-efficient, and under your control. That's what this chapter is about.

Whether you're running a billion-dollar public company or a family business, one thing doesn't change:

Liquidity is your edge. When others hesitate, you move.

Liquidity: The Most Underrated Asset in an Entrepreneur's Arsenal

Entrepreneurs talk about net worth like it's gospel. "I'm worth thirty million," they say, pointing to their real estate holdings, the value of their business, or what their stock options might fetch on a good day.

What goes unsaid: Nothing matters when the bank account is empty.

You can't buy time, opportunity, or payroll extensions with equity. You need cash. Not just cash, but accessible, unencumbered, tax-efficient cash.

That's liquidity.

However, liquidity is the one thing most business owners don't plan for. They're so busy maximizing growth, reinvesting in the business, and "letting the money ride " that they forget that one unforeseen event—a downturn, a lawsuit, a lost key employee—can leave them asset-rich and option-poor.

The truth is, profit doesn't protect you; liquidity does.

Cash Is for Cowards. Tell That to Your Payroll

Somewhere along the way, "cash is for cowards" became a badge of honor among entrepreneurs. Sure, it's a clever line at cocktail parties, but try telling that to your team when you can't meet payroll during a short-term cash crunch. Suddenly, liquidity sounds a lot more noble.

Liquidity is about staying in the game long enough to win.

During economic chaos, like the early days of COVID-19, those with cash weren't panicking; they were pouncing. Real estate investors scooped up distressed properties, business owners absorbed struggling competitors, and families locked in generational opportunities.

They could do this because they had access to capital, not a line of credit the bank could yank at any time, not a retirement account locked up behind early withdrawal penalties, not phantom equity.

But actual, usable liquidity.

False Liquidity: The Mirage Most Entrepreneurs Chase

Many business owners think they have liquidity because they can access a line of credit or "just sell something if I need to."

Try selling an industrial building during a down market. Try liquidating your partnership interest with 90 days' notice and a full partner vote. Try converting paper stock into real dollars in under a week, without taking a bath on taxes.

Liquidity isn't what looks good on paper. It's what shows up when you need it.

That's why we call it a lifeline; in moments of crisis or opportunity, it's the one thing that keeps you from going under or missing the boat.

Liquidity for the What-Ifs and the What-Nows

It's easy to think of liquidity only in terms of opportunity—buying a business, pouncing on a real estate deal, scooping up assets when the market is down. And yes, those are all critical reasons to access immediate capital.

But what about the less glamorous reasons?

What about life?

I've always taken pride in pushing my limits, especially in physical endurance. At age forty, I had a midlife crisis. Others might say I just rediscovered my competitive streak. I'd been a swimmer in high school and swam intramural races for my college fraternity. That foundation, and a love of long-distance bicycling, eventually led me to triathlons.

First sprints, then Olympic distances, then Half-Ironmans. At fifty, I crossed the finish line of my first full Ironman. For those unfamiliar, a full Ironman isn't a casual Sunday 5K. It's a 2.4-mile open water ocean swim—with 2,500 other competitors thrashing, which feels like a brutal water polo match rather than a race—followed by a 112-mile bike ride, and then, just for fun, a full 26.2-mile marathon. No breaks. No mercy. Just forward motion.

By the time I hit fifty-five, I'd completed nine half-Ironmans and three full-distance ones. Training was part of my identity.

Then, during a routine swim practice, something felt off. I had trouble breathing. I'd brushed off a few earlier warning signs, but this time, even my coach, Angie, could see something wasn't right. She offered to call an ambulance, but I declined. I drove home. In the meantime, Angie tattled, calling my wife, Patti.

Patti wanted to take me immediately to the ER. I stalled long enough to shower, put on sweats, and eat a chicken thigh off the rotisserie bird in the fridge. (Hey, I was hungry!)

At the hospital, when I told them I was experiencing some chest tightness and trouble breathing, they whisked me back. Tests ruled out a heart attack—thankfully—but the next morning, after spending the night on a bed in the middle of an ER hallway, Patti next to me on a folding chair, a cardiologist ordered a heart catheterization. Jeff Rosen, another cardiologist I know, performed the procedure. We were joking around in the OR, trading one-liners with the surgery techs and nurses before they put me under.

When I woke up, Jeff's tone had changed. He leaned over and said, "Craig, we need to talk."

I replied, "No good words follow that sentence, Jeff. What's up?"

"I couldn't fix them with stents."

"Them?! With what?" I asked, still groggy from the anesthesia.

"Buddy, you need a triple bypass."

That wasn't in my training plan.

They transferred me to another hospital for surgery. It was Labor Day weekend, and I was supposed to fly to Croatia with Patti for our thirtieth anniversary biking tour. Instead, I was being prepped for open-heart surgery.

As they wheeled me into the OR on the morning of the surgery, Patti—always quick with a zinger—leaned over and said, "You'll go through no amount of trouble to avoid buying me a nice anniversary gift!"

That moment of levity reminded me that this was a pit stop, not the end.

I came through just fine. And I'm back to swimming and biking. I gave up running, not because I can't, but I don't want to! But here's the thing—I never once worried about money. Not during those hospital days. Not during recovery. Not when the Croatia tour had to wait.

Why? Because I had maintained liquidity.

And that's the point. Liquidity isn't just about investing in new opportunities; I've also used it when I launched my trust company. It's about being able to handle life without panicking. Liquidity allows you to say "yes" when opportunity knocks and "I've got this" when the unexpected hits.

Liquidity is the buffer between stress and security, whether covering estate taxes without a fire sale, helping aging parents with care, supporting a child in crisis, or simply giving yourself breathing room to recover from surgery.

Mindset Shift: Liquidity Is the Set of Tires—Not Just the Spare

Liquidity isn't just a number. It's a strategy. A position. A mindset.

And yet, most entrepreneurs treat it like a just-in-case fund. They tuck it away and don't view it as serious or strategic. Until, of course, everything goes sideways, or an opportunity screams their name. Then they realize they can't move without selling, borrowing, or paying through the nose in taxes.

Here's the uncomfortable truth: You aren't ready if your money isn't readily available.

Liquidity doesn't mean cash in the bank. It means capital you can control, *without triggering taxes, penalties, delays, or drama.*

Ask yourself:

- Is your liquidity yours, or is it stuck in someone else's rules, timelines, or covenants?
- If an eight-figure opportunity hits your desk tomorrow, could you move on it, or would you need to call your banker first?
- Could you fund a new venture, help a child in crisis, cover estate taxes, or ride out a multi-year market dip without selling something, borrowing, or panicking?
- Do you have liquidity, or do you have paper wealth and optimistic assumptions?
- And when you're no longer here, will your heirs have liquidity to act, or a fire sale to clean up?

Being **Liquidity Conscious** doesn't mean hoarding cash. It means building liquidity into your structure—life insurance, irrevocable trusts, tax-advantaged accounts, business cash flow strategies—*on purpose*, not by accident.

Tax-Aware entrepreneurs don't simply access money. They access it efficiently. They know how to avoid turning liquidity into a tax trap. They engineer systems that let them move money without triggering unnecessary gains or exposure.

Structurally Sound planning means that liquidity isn't an afterthought. It's woven into the blueprint. It exists across multiple vehicles, is aligned with long-term goals, and is built for generational access, not just monthly bills.

And **Systems-Oriented** entrepreneurs don't build liquidity in a vacuum. They assemble a team of professionals—legal, financial, tax, and especially the best insurance experts—who design systems they can rely on in the middle of life's mess because access isn't just about assets. It's about *team alignment.*

The Perpetual Wealth mindset doesn't treat liquidity as a cushion. It treats liquidity as a command center, launchpad, life preserver, or even a buy button.

Because when your liquidity is designed correctly, you're not reacting to life.

You're leading.

So, ask yourself one more time:

Are you building a liquidity system that puts you in control, or one that keeps you dependent?

Because when the moment comes—and it always does—you won't rise to the level of your net worth. You'll fall to the level of your liquidity.

Up Next: Life Insurance—Your Family's Private Bank

In the next chapter, we'll unpack why cash-value life insurance is a misunderstood and underutilized asset for business owners. We'll talk about tax efficiency, strategic structuring, and how the smartest families use insurance not just as protection, but as a platform for liquidity, opportunity, and freedom.

If Starbucks can do it, why can't you?

CHAPTER 12

The Perpetual Wealth Bank: Borrow from Yourself— Never Ask Permission Again

Life insurance is one of the few assets that gives you tax-free money exactly when you need it most, without anyone's permission.

—*R. Nelson Nash, author of* Becoming Your Own Banker: Unlock the Infinite Banking Concept

If you've ever felt that the wealth game is tilted, you're right. But what most entrepreneurs never realize is that the tilt isn't always against you. If you know how to read the rules—and I mean *really* understand them—you can start playing a completely different game.

In this new game, one of the most misunderstood yet powerful tools is *indexed universal life insurance (IUL)*. Not the off-the-shelf kind or the product your cousin with a license tried to sell you in 2014. I'm talking about over-funded, engineered, max-cash-value life insurance built for entrepreneurs who understand leverage, liquidity, and legacy.

This chapter is about more than just life insurance. It's about building a *Perpetual Wealth Family Bank™*—a financial system that outlives you. However, before we delve into charts, trusts, and financing strategies, we must look at how this tool has become the quiet workhorse of generational wealth.

Public Policy, Not a Loophole: Why Life Insurance Is Tax-Free

If a single financial tool enjoys the kind of protection, tax advantage, and legislative privilege most other assets could only dream of, it's life insurance. And it didn't get that way by accident.

To understand why our tax code treats life insurance with velvet gloves, we must go back to the late nineteenth and early twentieth centuries, when industrialization was booming, but the social safety net didn't exist. No Social Security, no welfare, no disability income. If the family breadwinner died, the income disappeared, and the family was often left destitute.

Life insurance was the solution. Unlike today's insurance, it wasn't a product of financial engineers—it was a matter of survival. Life insurance was a contract that guaranteed a grieving family wouldn't be homeless or left to starve. Congress and most state legislatures recognized its societal benefit and deliberately enshrined protections into law.

So, when people today marvel at life insurance's tax benefits, they often assume it's some quirky loophole. Actually, it's **public policy**, plain and simple.

Even today, that policy guarantees that

- **Death benefits are income tax-free under IRC §101(a).** If you die with a $5 million policy, your beneficiary will receive the full $5 million. No 1099. No income tax. Just a check.
- **Cash value grows tax-deferred, like an IRA**. But unlike an IRA, it doesn't have required minimum distributions (RMDs) and doesn't show up on your tax return.

- **Policy loans are tax-free.** You can borrow against your policy's accumulated value with no tax penalty. Why? Because it's a loan backed by your own money. The IRS doesn't tax you for borrowing against your investments or home equity. Same principle.
- **Protected from Creditors.** Life insurance—especially its cash value—is shielded from lawsuits and bankruptcy in many states. Why? Because lawmakers didn't want widows and children to lose the only financial protection they had just because Dad got sued.
- **Paperwork is limited.** No 1099s. No annual reporting. No capital gains. You can hold a properly structured life insurance policy for thirty years and never have to tell the IRS a thing.

Why? Because the government *wants you to own it.*

The government would rather have private insurance protect families than create more public assistance programs. Life insurance is one of the few places where private planning aligns with public policy, and that's precisely why it's been given this tax-advantaged lane.

When Did Life Insurance Become an Investment Tool?

Life insurance was initially designed as a straightforward agreement: you pay premiums, the company pays a benefit if you die. It wasn't until the mid-twentieth century that insurance companies and policyholders began to explore how these contracts could do more.

As early as the 1930s and 1940s, participating *whole life policies* began to accumulate *dividends*, providing policyholders with a means to grow their death benefit or reduce premiums. The policies provided protection, but they became vehicles for accumulation.

By the time the 1980s rolled around, inflation had hit savers and investors alike, and interest rates were fluctuating wildly. **Insurance companies, never ones to miss a beat, rolled out a new breed of policy—Universal Life**. These weren't your grandfather's life contracts with fixed premiums and rigid guarantees. They were designed to be flexible, responsive, and interest-sensitive. Fast forward a few more decades, and Indexed Universal Life entered the scene. It still offered life insurance protection, but now with cash values linked to stock market indexes, such as the S&P 500.

Important caveat: You don't *own* stocks inside an IUL. Your returns are *based* on the market's performance, and are not subject to its direct losses. That's not just clever—it's engineered safety.

Yet despite all that, critics still circle like vultures squawking a tired refrain: "Too expensive! Just invest the difference!" They point to the early costs—commissions, fees, policy charges—and declare the whole thing a racket. However, those critics overlook that they're judging a tax-free asset against tax-deferred accumulation—*tax-free access and tax-free death benefit against a fully taxable investment*. That's apples to oranges; as if one of the apples came with a built-in IRS delay, and the orange didn't even report to the IRS at all.

They also miss the *why* behind those early costs. Insurance has public policy advantages precisely *because* it delivers a death benefit first and foremost. Those up-front charges fund the guarantees and safety net that make it possible for entrepreneurs, business owners, and high-income earners to grow a tax-advantaged pool of capital that isn't tethered to Wall Street's whims or the government's shifting tax code.

In the following pages, you'll see charts that put this argument to bed. Over time, the efficiency of properly structured insurance, especially when it's designed with the same rigor as trusts, asset protection, and tax mitigation, can outperform taxable investments in both liquidity and legacy.

To be truthful, this is a matter of structure, not cost. Remember, insurance is a strategy, not just a product.

This surge in investment-like policy design caught Congress's attention and led to *Modified Endowment Contract (MEC)* rules in 1988. More on that later in the chapter.

What's the Difference Between Term, Whole Life, and Indexed Universal Life?

Building a *Perpetual Wealth Family Bank* starts with understanding your financial ingredients. Not all insurance is created equal; more importantly, not all insurance is designed for entrepreneurs. Let's unpack the key types.

Term Insurance

What it is: Temporary coverage with no frills. You pay premiums for a set term—say, ten, twenty, or thirty years. If you pass away during that term, your beneficiaries get the death benefit. If you're still breathing at the end, the insurance company keeps the premiums, and the policy evaporates.

Why it's sold: It's cheap and easy. For the price of a pizza night, you can buy coverage that will at least cover the mortgage and college tuition should the worst happen.

What it lacks: Everything that matters for long-term wealth strategy. No cash value. No liquidity. No leverage. It's like renting an apartment; it's functional, but you're not building anything that lasts.

Use case: Good for income replacement when premiums are low in your early earning years. Unfavorable for entrepreneurs seeking to establish long-term liquidity or fund multi-generational structures.

Whole Life Insurance (Participating, Overfunded)

What it is: The old faithful of insurance. Fixed premiums, a guaranteed death benefit, and cash value grow yearly, whether the stock market is flying or falling.

Why it's sold: Stability. Predictability. This is the workhorse of many estate plans, especially when overfunded for high early cash value.

What it offers: Tax-deferred growth, tax-free access, guaranteed accumulation, and potential dividends from mutual companies (not guaranteed, but reliably paid for decades). Think of it as the rock-solid foundation of the *Perpetual Wealth Family Bank*—slow, steady, and almost impossible to mess up.

Use case: This is ideal when your goal is stability. It is best suited for entrepreneurs who want early liquidity with minimal risk and are willing to aggressively fund policies.

Indexed Universal Life (IUL)

What it is: A modern twist on traditional insurance, IUL offers permanent death benefit protection and a cash value component that earns interest based on a market index, typically the S&P 500. But here's the catch: you're not *invested* in the index. Instead, your cash value *tracks* it with a cap on gains and a floor (often 0 percent) that protects against losses.

Why it's sold: Flexibility and opportunity. Premiums can be adjusted up or down. Returns are market-sensitive without the full downside risk. And because of its unique structure, IUL allows for the potential for *higher growth*, especially when designed with a focus on cash value over death benefit.

What it offers: Strategic liquidity. Tax-free access through policy loans. Downside protection. And the opportunity to grow your personal banking system faster than guaranteed products, without crossing into taxable or high-risk territory.

Use case: IUL is perfect for entrepreneurs who want control, growth potential, and tax-favored access to capital without tying their fate to Wall Street or Washington. It is ideal when used properly, with disciplined funding and a clear intent to build a *Perpetual Wealth Family Bank* that lives and breathes with your business.

Bottom Line: A System That Rewards the Builders

Congress didn't just "allow" insurance to grow tax-free. They *designed* it that way. It's public policy. The US government wants you to protect your family. They want you to build your safety net. And if you do it using life insurance, they'll reward you with tax-free growth, access, and a tax-free death benefit.

No sideways hedge fund schemes. No offshore LLCs. No heroic tax gymnastics. Just a system that's been quietly available for over a century to those willing to use it.

Most people ignore this. They chase market highs, trade too often, and lose liquidity to taxes, fees, and volatility. Meanwhile, those who understand the blueprint are stacking cash in a system designed to multiply—not erode—their efforts.

This is not a loophole. It's the law. The only question is: are you funding your Family Bank or someone else's?

Income Tax-Free ≠ Estate Tax-Free

Here's where most people get blindsided.

You've just finished reading that life insurance proceeds are tax-free. And that's true—*from income tax.*

But when you own the policy, the entire death benefit is included in your estate. If your estate exceeds the federal exemption ($13.99 million in 2025), everything above that threshold is exposed to a *40 percent federal estate tax*, not to mention potential state estate taxes.

So your tax-free policy could quietly become a *multi-million-dollar tax bill*.

The solution? Use an Irrevocable Life Insurance Trust (ILIT) to own the policy. That keeps the death benefit outside your estate. Put another way, your death benefit doesn't get counted when the IRS tallies your estate. That's millions that pass to your family with zero estate tax. However, it also introduces a new wrinkle: you must *gift the premiums* into the trust, which starts burning through your gift and estate tax exemption.

This becomes especially important when discussing large policies—$10 million, $20 million, and above.

Before we examine numbers, let's talk about how pigs get fat, but hogs get slaughtered.

When word got out that life insurance wasn't only a death benefit but a tax-favored, liquid asset class, some folks got greedy. They didn't just nibble at the trough. They dove in headfirst, stuffing policies with so much cash that the IRS couldn't help but notice. That's when the rules changed—and the slaughter began.

The Rise of MEC Rules
(And the Genius of Walking the Edge)

Once word spread that life insurance was tax-deferred, liquid, and creditor-protected, the strategy started to evolve. Wealthy families weren't just using insurance to protect against premature death. They used it to build *tax-favored personal banks*—policies stuffed with cash, earning competitive returns, and accessible by loan at any time.

One of these was referred to as a "single-premium life insurance" contract. You'd deposit a large sum—say, $1 million—and have immediate access to a growing pool of cash, free from tax reporting, 1099s, and early withdrawal penalties.

The IRS, as you can imagine, took notice.

What Is an MEC?

In response, Congress passed a 1988 tax law that gave us the *Modified Endowment Contract (MEC)* rules. These rules stipulated:

> If a life insurance policy is funded too aggressively—too much premium, too fast—it crosses a threshold and becomes an MEC.

More importantly, *once a policy becomes an MEC, it stays an MEC forever.*

This matters because when a policy is classified as an MEC:

- *Loans and withdrawals become taxable to the extent of internal gain* (i.e., any earnings).
- They're treated under *LIFO* rules (Last In, First Out)—meaning you're taxed first as ordinary income on the gain (not the lower capital gains tax rates) before you can access the tax-free principal.
- *Distributions before age fifty-nine-and-a-half* are also subject to a *10 percent penalty*, just like an IRA.

In one stroke, your "tax-free loan machine" becomes a *taxable annuity with penalties.*

Where's the Line?

The MEC line is defined by a technical IRS formula called the *7-Pay Test.*

Simply put, the 7-Pay Test calculates the *maximum premium* that can be paid into a life insurance policy *over the first seven years,* based on the size of the death benefit and certain assumptions about mortality and interest.

If you pay more than this allowable amount in any of those first seven years, the policy becomes an MEC.

Here's how it works:

1. Suppose a $2 million policy has a 7-pay MEC limit of $95,000 annually.
2. You've exceeded the line if you pay $100,000 in Year 1.
3. It's too late even if you only pay $50,000 in Year 2.
4. The policy has become and will remain a MEC—forever.

MEC in Action: An Example

Let's say John funds a whole life policy with the following inputs:

- Death Benefit: $2,000,000
- MEC 7-Pay Premium Limit: $95,000/year
- John wants to build cash value aggressively, so he pays $125,000 in year 1

What happens?

- The policy immediately becomes a Modified Endowment Contract.
- The cash value still grows tax-deferred, but

- If John borrows $50,000 from the policy in year 5 and the policy has a $100,000 gain, the loan is treated as a *taxable distribution.*

- He pays ordinary income tax on the $50,000—and possibly a 10 percent early withdrawal penalty if he's under fifty-nine-and-a-half.

- Now, just to be clear: even if your policy becomes an MEC, *the death benefit still passes to your beneficiaries' income tax–free.* The IRS isn't that cruel—they only penalize you while you're alive and trying to enjoy it.

That's a steep price to pay for aggressive funding.

Why MECs Didn't Kill the Strategy

You might think this ended the overfunded policy strategy, but it didn't. It just forced entrepreneurs and planners to become smarter.

Today, skilled advisors design policies to fund up to the MEC line, without crossing it. The best fiduciary advisors use blended term riders, paid-up additions (PUAs), and funding schedules that allow maximum early cash value while maintaining the tax advantages.

Think of the MEC line like a speed limit. You can drive sixty-five. You can't drive sixty-six. But if you know the limit, you can get where you're going as fast as legally possible.

And that's what to do.

Don't break the rules. Bend them into shape.

Indexed Universal Life vs. Qualified Retirement Accounts (IRA and 401(k))

You've probably heard the standard line from traditional advisors: "Just invest in an IRA and let the market do the work," or "Permanent insurance can't compete with equity returns." So, let's settle it without hype and sizzle. These are just numbers backed by 2025 illustrations and decades of tax law.

First, let's look at your traditional retirement vehicles. As of 2025, you can only contribute:

- $7,000 to an IRA if under age fifty
- $8,000 if age fifty or older
- $23,500 to a 401(k), plus $7,500 if you're fifty to fifty-nine, and an extra $11,250 if you're sixty to sixty-three

While those contributions are tax-deductible and grow tax-deferred, you'll pay ordinary income tax when you withdraw the money, often in your highest tax bracket. That's hardly a recipe for long-term freedom.

Is Indexed Universal Life (IUL) Ever Taxed?

Technically, yes, but only under specific conditions. Here's how it works when structured properly:

Action on IUL Policy	Consequence
Withdraw more than your basis (premium contributions)	**Taxed as ordinary income** on gain
Take policy loans against the cash value - Perpetual Wealth Family Bank strategy during life	**Not taxable** (loan against your asset)
Surrender the policy for cash	**Portion exceeding the basis is taxable** as ordinary income

Policy is **held to death**	**Death benefit is 100% income tax-free,** including all growth, to beneficiaries
Policy becomes a **MEC, and you take loans/withdrawals before 59½**	**Ordinary tax on gain, plus 10% excise tax penalty**

Figure 12-A

Used properly, the result is often zero taxation.

The Illusion of Control: Comparing 401(k) to IUL

I recall attending a retirement planning seminar when I was still more of a CPA than a lawyer. A gray-haired accountant leaned over and whispered, "The 401(k) is great—if you want to retire poor in the highest tax bracket." I laughed then, and I nod now.

Let's do the math and put the strategies to the test.

Designing a Policy for Control, Cash Flow, and Confidence

Ivan is a sharp and energetic forty-year-old. He's the kind of entrepreneur who doesn't wait around for things to happen; he builds opportunities. After successfully exiting a logistics business in his thirties, Ivan finds himself in a new role: capital allocator. He's got liquidity, vision, and ambition. What doesn't he have? Patience for traditional financial planning.

Ivan doesn't want to "max out a 401(k)" just to handcuff his money until some arbitrary government age. He doesn't like the idea of building wealth that he can't access without suffering taxes, penalties, and permission slips. And he certainly doesn't believe in parking capital in vehicles where volatility is passed off as "strategy."

Instead, Ivan wants to build something lasting—a Perpetual Wealth Family Bank—that supports his ventures, funds opportunities, and transfers wealth on his terms. He wants:

- *Liquidity now*, so he can pounce on investments or cover unexpected downturns
- *Tax-free income later*, not some RMD-defined drip schedule
- A *death benefit* that takes care of his family, bypasses probate, and transfers efficiently through his trust
- *Continual control*—because he didn't get where he is by outsourcing his decisions to Wall Street or Washington

The strategy that checks all those boxes includes a maximum-funded Indexed Universal Life policy. Here's what that strategy looks like:

- Face Amount: $5 million starting death benefit.
- Premiums: $290,000 annually for 15 years only—paid in full by age 55.
- Design: Using an option to increase the death benefit for years 1–15, switching to another option that will increase the death benefit in year 16 to maximize cash value growth.
- Loan Strategy: Beginning at age 60, Ivan starts withdrawing $720,000 annually through policy loans, tax-free.
- Purpose: Build an income stream without triggering income taxes, RMDs, or market losses—all while preserving a multi-million-dollar death benefit for his heirs.

This is not "buying life insurance." This is about building a *self-fueled wealth system*—a source of tax-free capital during life and a tax-free inheritance at death—utilizing a chassis designed by the IRS to be exempt.

Below is an illustration of Ivan's Indexed Universal Life policy as outlined in a May 2025 schedule:

Year	Age	Cumulative Premiums ($)	Cash Value ($)	Tax-Free Income (Annual Withdrawal in $)	Death Benefit ($)
5	45	1,450,000	1,075,794	0	6,075,794
10	50	2,900,000	3,087,602	0	8,087,6021
15	55	4,350,000	5,829,669	0	10,829,669
20	60	no additional premium payments after year 15	8,009,764	720,000 begins next year	10,733,084
25	65		6,789,747	$720,000 annually	8,283,491
30	70		5,267,854	$720,000 annually	6,587,858
40	80		1,437,708	Final 30,000 loan taken at age 76	2,099,446
50	90		10,045,102		5,368,934

Figure 12-B

The highlights include

- total tax-free income withdrawn from the policy: $10,410,000
- cash value remaining at age 90: $4.4 million
- death benefit at age 90: $5.4 million

But Wait—Why Is the Death Benefit So Low at Age 80?

This surprises a lot of people—and it should. At first glance, a drop from over $10 million to just over $2 million looks like something went wrong.

But it didn't. That drop is by design.

Behind the scenes, we see that

- in the early years, Ivan's policy used an increasing death benefit option, which means the death benefit includes both the face amount and the cash value. This structure maximizes accumulation and growth;

- after year fifteen (Ivan is fifty-five), the policy switches to another option, locking in a *level death benefit* and allowing the cash value to grow more efficiently;

- starting at age sixty, Ivan begins withdrawing *$720,000 per year* through *tax-free loans,* which accumulate over time and act as liens on the policy's death benefit; so

- by age seventy-nine, the insurer is subtracting nearly $10 million in outstanding loans from what would otherwise be a large death benefit.

This isn't a flaw—it's how the strategy works. Ivan gets the best of both worlds: tax-free retirement income while alive, and a respectable death benefit at death. And as the income tapers off, the policy begins to rebuild. By age ninety, the death benefit rebounds to over $5.3 million, all tax-free to his heirs.

Now, Let's Look at the 401(k)

Let's assume Ivan maxes out his 401(k) annually, adjusts for inflation, and earns a hypothetical 7 percent return (pre-tax). Here's how it compares:

Year	Age	Total Contributions ($)	Account Value (Pre-Tax) ($)	After Tax Value (@ 40%) ($)
10	50	332,120	519,888	*Penalty–can't access*
20	60	750,027	1,839,757	1,103,854
30	70	1,413,006	4,912,346	2,947,407
40	80	2,213,440	6,661,884	3,997,130
50	90	2,830,219	7,013,301	4,207,981

Figure 12-C

By age sixty, Ivan had contributed just over $750,000, and his account balance had reached $1.89 million.

Not bad, right?

But here's the kicker: Ivan's in the highest federal tax bracket—plus state taxes, let's assume a combined 40 percent effective tax rate. So, every dollar he withdraws in retirement is taxed as ordinary income. That $1.83 million is only worth about $1.1 million in after-tax cash.

Fast forward to age seventy, and the account might grow to $4.9 million. But again, 40 percent of that goes to the government. That's a tax hit of almost $2 million—money Ivan will never see.

Under current law, he also has to start taking Required Minimum Distributions (RMDs) at age seventy-five. It doesn't matter if he needs the money; the IRS wants its cut.

So, while the 401(k) is growing, it's also losing.

Even if the account grows well, Ivan's withdrawals are fully taxable. And he has no control over when he *must* take them—RMDs start at age seventy-five, like it or not.

And all of this assumes Ivan doesn't die early, doesn't have a market crash right before retirement, and doesn't need to tap the funds for emergencies (which, by the way, comes with a 10 percent penalty before age fifty-nine-and-a-half).

The Side-by-Side Comparison

Year	Age	IUL Cash Value ($)	IUL Tax-Free Income ($)	IUL Death Benefit ($)	401(k) Value ($)	401(k) Value After Tax (@ 40%) ($)
10	50	3,087,062	____	8,087,062	519,888	Penalty can't access
20	60	8,009,764	Begins 720,000/year	10,733,084	1,839,757	1,103,854
30	70	4,927,556	Still 720,000/year	6,233,396	4,912,346	2,947,407
40	80	1,437,708	Still 720,000/year	2,099,446	6,661,884	3,997,130
50	90	10,045,102	Distributions complete	5,368,934	7,013,301	4,207,981

Figure 12-D

These Figures Tell a Simple Truth

The real advantage of liquidity isn't just in the numbers—it's in the timing, control, and tax treatment of those numbers.

401(k)s grow tax-deferred, but you pay dearly on the back end. And heaven forbid you need that money early; it'll cost you a 10 percent penalty before age fifty-nine-and-a-half, and forced distributions begin whether or not you want them.

The IUL, by contrast, builds momentum early and com-pounds inside a *tax-favored structure*. By age sixty, Ivan had accumulated over *$8 million* in available capital, and unlike the 401(k), he could access it without a tax hit, penalty, or waiting for government approval.

That's what the IRS quietly allows through life insur-ance: a vehicle for self-controlled liquidity that can fuel your life, business, and family while delivering a tax-free wealth transfer at death.

For entrepreneurs, access to capital is often more valuable than the capital itself. That's why the UIL tells a different story—one of freedom, flexibility, and financial readiness.

In the real world of business ownership, the ability to use your money when you need it isn't a luxury; it's the edge.

Why Entrepreneurs Choose Liquidity Over Lock-Up

Entrepreneurs like Ivan didn't build wealth by playing the waiting game. They didn't climb by locking up their capital and hoping the IRS would cut them a break in the decades to come.

Yet that's the contract most people sign when they stuff money into a 401(k): Park your cash. Obey the rules. Hope they don't change. And give up a giant chunk to taxes when you finally access it.

The 401(k) system is designed for employees, not owners. It limits contributions, punishes early access, and eventually forces distributions—even when you don't want them. And always, always, the IRS is lurking with a claim on your future.

That's not freedom. That's *deferred dependency.*

Ivan recognized this early, which is why he built a Perpetual Wealth Family Bank—an overfunded IUL policy built for access, not restriction. His Family Bank is a reservoir of opportunity capital he can use anytime, without age limits, tax penalties, or permission slips.

Even when Ivan borrows from his policy, the cash value continues to compound, as if he had never touched it. That's by design.

He's not playing the tax-deferral game. He's playing the access game.

And in the long arc of entrepreneurship, *access beats accumulation.*

The Perpetual Wealth Takeaway

Ivan's strategy preserves wealth *and* puts it in motion.

- He's using after-tax dollars to build tax-free, on-demand capital.
- He's accessing liquidity without disrupting growth.
- He has created a creditor-shielded structure, estate-tax-minimized, and immediately usable.

The 401(k) is still growing quietly, while stacking an IOU to Uncle Sam.

The question isn't "Which account earns more?"

The question is:

When opportunity strikes, will you be ready—or restricted?

Mindset Shift: The Liquidity-Conscious Entrepreneur

Every entrepreneur believes they're financially savvy until an opportunity arises and their money is buried under red tape.

That's when the real mindset gets revealed.

The *Reactive Saver*

- follows traditional advice
- maxes out retirement accounts
- waits until fifty-nine-and-a-half and pays taxes to touch their own money
- thinks "saving on taxes today" is worth surrendering control tomorrow
- ignores liquidity until it's too late

- treats life insurance like a luxury, not a lever
- watches an opportunity pass by

The *Liquidity-Conscious Entrepreneur*

- builds systems to control capital, not chase it
- understands that liquidity is a weapon, not a safety net
- uses life insurance as a *living financial engine*, not just a payout at death
- moves when others freeze
- sees tax-free access as fuel, not fluff

This is the Perpetual Wealth *liquidity mindset*, which is about positioning yourself to act anytime, every time.

It's not about playing defense. Because liquidity isn't what you build *after* wealth.

It's what lets you build it.

Ask yourself:

Are you building a retirement account that waits on someone else's timeline or a system that lets you act on *your own*?

Remember, it's not about how much you've saved but how quickly you can access it.

"But it requires more cash outlay…"

Let's hit pause and talk about the elephant in the room. You saw how a properly structured UIL policy could build a powerful family bank with tax-deferred growth, tax-free access, and creditor protection—all good things.

However, you also saw the catch. That policy required *more after-tax money* than a 401(k). For entrepreneurs who are used to reinvesting every spare dollar back into the business, staring at slow-building value can feel like watching paint dry on a rainy day.

You're probably thinking, "I spent this much, and that's all the liquidity I've got?"

Fair reaction. It's also why traditional insurance strategies leave a lot of entrepreneurs cold.

And let's not forget the hidden toll: each dollar stuffed into that policy may have consumed some of your lifetime estate and gift tax exemption. That exemption is your stealth shield that keeps the IRS from lunging at your family's future. Waste it early, and the IRS isn't just knocking—they'll be walking right through the front door after you die.

Now, imagine reaching the same destination—more quickly, with less personal capital, and without torching your exemption. In Chapter 13, I'll show you how high-level entrepreneurs *borrow* to fund policies without draining their reserves. The same tax-free growth, same protection—just turbocharged.

You've seen what patience can do.

It's time to talk about power *without endangering your assets.*

CHAPTER 13

Leveraging Your Family Bank

*Leverage is the reason some people
become rich and others do not.*

—*Robert T. Kiyosaki, author of* Rich Dad Poor Dad

Doris Christopher didn't just create a kitchen empire. She built a wealth strategy that outlasted the brand.

Before she sold Pampered Chef to Warren Buffett's Berkshire Hathaway, Doris had already taken steps to protect what mattered—her family's future. While most people focused on her impressive buyout, she was quietly executing a premium-financed life insurance strategy designed to

- lock in a significant death benefit to protect her estate;
- use bank financing—*not* her capital—to fund the plan;
- leverage favorable interest rates and growing policy values; and
- transfer wealth tax-efficiently and privately.

When Berkshire came knocking, Doris didn't scramble to find liquidity. She'd already structured it. She didn't write checks from her portfolio to fund insurance premiums—she used other people's money, elegantly and securely.

This wasn't theory. It wasn't something dreamed up in a seminar to sound impressive. It was real, personal, purposeful, and tailored to her values: preserve wealth, maintain control, and avoid last-minute chaos.

Moreover, insiders say the premium finance deal she used didn't require blanket liens or pledging her business as collateral. A modest brokerage account as collateral kept at her investment custodian satisfied the bank's requirements. And even that was temporary. As the policy grew in value, the collateral vanished.

The result? The policy's death benefit was passed to her heirs tax-efficiently. Her liquidity stayed intact, and her business interests remained untouched.

Doris didn't just build a successful company. She built a Perpetual Wealth system that served her family long after she sold her final cookware set.

From After-Tax to Outsmarting Tax

In the last chapter, you saw Ivan structure a UIL policy with after-tax dollars. It became his private reserve—liquidity that grows tax-free, protects from lawsuits, and transfers wealth without triggering estate tax.

But if you're like most entrepreneurs, one line might still be echoing in your head:

"Wait a second… That $290,000 a year? That's all after tax. My 401(k) contributions, at least, are pre-tax."

And you're right. A 401(k) gives you a tax deduction now. Life insurance premiums? They come out of pocket.

So what if I told you there's a way to keep your cash, still build that Perpetual Wealth Family Bank, and have the bank fund the whole thing?

That's what Doris did, and it's called premium financing.

Using Other People's Money—
The Entrepreneur's Favorite Strategy

Thank goodness, entrepreneurs don't think like the 401(k) crowd.

You didn't save your way to success. You got here by leveraging teams, capital, and talent—not all of it your own.

Premium financing fits that mindset perfectly.

Instead of funding your life insurance policy yourself, a bank does it for you. You might post a relatively small amount of collateral—and the bank funds the rest.

What this means for you: the bank fronts the money, the policy builds value, and your family gets a multi-million dollar asset without you coming out of pocket!

You end up with a fully built policy—millions in death benefit and growing tax-free cash value—without locking up your own liquidity. Your money stays in play where you need it most: in your business, portfolio, or acquisition pipeline.

That's not just smart; that's leverage *done right.*

What Premium Financing Means

Let's make it real.

Premium financing is exactly what it sounds like: a *bank loans money to pay the premiums on a life insurance policy.*

Here's the basic framework:

- You want a significant death benefit, say $20 million.
- You could write annual checks for $1.1 million yourself, but you don't.
- Instead, the *lender* funds the premiums yearly, and depending on the insured's age, it might be for a short or longer period.

- You may post *a relatively small collateral account,* typically from a segregated brokerage account that remains at the financial institution you normally use.
- Over time, the *policy's cash value* becomes the collateral, replacing your own funds.
- The *loan is paid back* using distributions from the policy and is tax-free.
- Whatever is left—death benefit minus loan—goes to your beneficiaries, tax-free.

The key? *Structure it correctly*.

Ivan's $20 Million Strategy—Built with Bank Capital

Let's revisit Ivan. He's forty, healthy, and experienced in wealth strategies. In his case, the professional designed a *premium-financed IUL policy* with a *$20 million death benefit*.

- Annual Premium: $1,136,811
- Duration: Fifteen years
- Total Premium Financed: $17,052,165
- Loan Type: Alternate Loans
- Loan Interest Rate (Illustrated): Averages 5.33 percent, ranging from 4.90 percent to 5.83 percent over thirty years
- Growth Rate of Cash Value (Illustrated): Averages 2.00 percent spread over bank loan rate
- Collateral: Policy cash value + brokerage account early on
- Loan Repaid: Premium financing repaid by internal returns at age 69. Ivan does not come out of pocket
- Exit Strategy: Tax-free distributions repay the loan over time, and the excess death benefit goes to heirs

The policy is owned by a special type of *Perpetual Wealth Family Bank Trust.* This trust keeps it outside of Ivan's estate and avoids estate tax altogether. The Bank Trust can distribute cash to Ivan's spouse (achieving an indirect transfer to Ivan) and children, and can loan money to family entities and other irrevocable trusts.

Loan Interest is capitalized (not paid by Ivan out-of-pocket) into the policy loan, which may be repaid when the death benefit is received. In some cases, the design includes using cash values to pay interest to cap the loan or pay the loan off early, as I demonstrate below.

Most advisors miss this secret that Ivan can start paying back the loan early using the policy's tax-free distributions. That one decision shrinks interest costs, lowers the collateral requirement, and improves the long-term death benefit.

Projections With Early Loan Repayment

Age	Loan Balance ($)	Cash Value ($)	Collateral Required ($)	Death Benefit ($)
40	1,136,811	790,937	614,881	19,818,403
45	6,736,791	7,177,694	1,481,193	19,073,781
50	14,793,653	15,860,249	1,085,720	19,239,996
53	20,514,153	22,667,997	0	20,079,546
55	24,752,566	25,692,090	0	19,367,852
60	24,752,566	28,594,804	0	14,724,437
65	24,752,566	32,721,599	0	17,794,509
70	0	13,737,744	0	23,709,065
75	0	19,972,384	0	24,471,546
80	0	28,846,523	0	34,935,921

85	0	40,869,905	0	49,082,417
90	0	56,278,652	0	67,282,272
95	0	78,686,996	0	81,648,276

Figure 13-A

By age seventy, Ivan's more focused on accessing the policy for tax-free retirement income, and leaving amounts to his children and grandchildren to pursue their entrepreneurial ventures. This chart illustrates what that looks like. Through the trust, the family controls income, but Ivan's also managing the bank's exposure on his terms.

At age fifty-three, the trust loan balance stands at about $20.5 million. However, the cash value inside his life insurance policy, which the bank uses as its primary collateral, has already grown to $22.7 million. That means the policy itself fully secures the loan. No additional collateral is required. Ivan doesn't have to pledge a brokerage account or move liquidity from his business. His capital remains free and deployable for real estate investments, acquisitions, or sleeping better at night.

I should note that the cash value projections by law must be conservative. The actual cash value will likely exceed the projections in this table.

Now, jump to age seventy-five. There's $20 million of cash available for the family to tap tax-free. That's how you create a Perpetual Wealth Family Bank.

Fast-forward to age eighty. With early repayment, there's almost $29 million of cash value. The death benefit is nearly $35 million. By age eighty-five, the policy's cash value is an astounding $41 million, and Ivan has not put in one dime into the policy or the trust!

This illustrates the most underappreciated advantage of premium finance: you're not locked into a fixed, inflexible path. You can shape the outcome as you go. Want to increase income? You can. Want to reduce collateral exposure? Just redirect a portion of your tax-free income to pay down the loan. Need to pause distributions during a market cycle? You have that option too.

The traditional retirement vehicles don't offer this kind of dynamism. Once you're at your Required Beginning Date (age seventy-five for most readers), it's impossible to exit the RMD treadmill with your 401(k). But with premium finance, primarily when appropriately structured, *you're in control.*

The policy's cash value becomes your family's banker. The bank becomes your partner. And you orchestrate the timing, the risk, and the outcome on your terms.

And here's the kicker: all of this is unfolding within a contractually designed, tax-advantaged structure—approved and supported by IRS rules, established through public policy, and designed to deliver *a tax-free death benefit that still exceeds $82 million* by the time Ivan hits age 90.

This isn't "playing the insurance game."

It's designing a *liquidity strategy* that provides tax-free income, minimizes risk, protects estate value, and allows high-performing entrepreneurs like Ivan to stay nimble, even while building a financial fortress around their family.

Inside the *Perpetual Wealth Family Bank Trust*™

A Modern Structure for a 100-Year Vision

Imagine if your heirs didn't have to wait for a liquidity event, bank approval, or the next market cycle to fund their business, real estate, or philanthropic ideas. That's the power of the **Perpetual Wealth Family Bank Trust**™—a private banking system, inside your estate plan, built to last generations.

Here's how it works:

At the top sits a **grantor**—likely you—who creates the bank trust that acquires a large overfunded Indexed Universal Life (IUL) policy. When you pass, the massive **death benefit pours into the trust**, tax-free and estate-tax-exempt. But instead of distributing that capital outright, the trustee **lends it forward**—strategically.

Each beneficiary's share of the trust becomes a launchpad. The trust **purchases a new IUL policy for each beneficiary**, even while they're still young, using premium financing. The **cash from the your original policy** provides the temporary collateral. As those younger policies mature, they begin to self-fund, repay loans, and extend the cycle again—like a flywheel that never stops.

Beneficiaries don't receive lump sums. They receive **access to capital**—for vetted entrepreneurial ventures, real estate deals, or charitable initiatives—**backed by the trust, not a bank.** And unlike most financial aid or inheritance models, this one is structured. Disciplined. Regenerative.

It's modeled after what the Rockefeller family has done and continues to do. Here we update their strategy for today's entrepreneur facing liquidity, tax, and credit environments.

> No taxes on gains
> No estate tax inclusion
> No waiting for inheritance
> No handouts—only structured access

What you've created isn't just wealth.

It's an engine that builds leadership, responsibility, and opportunity across generations—with a built-in plan to pay it forward.

Well, Wait a Minute...

You're a savvy entrepreneur. You've read the Perpetual Wealth Plan and understand the mechanics of overfunded life insurance, premium financing, and trust structures. But part of you still wonders: why not just take that $290,000 per year (the amount earmarked to fund the premiums on the $5 million indexed universal life insurance policy in Chapter 12) and park that money in a taxable brokerage account? A good ol' diversified portfolio. You're in it for the long haul. After all, history shows the S&P 500 has averaged 8 percent annually over time, right? No financing. No insurance. Just good ol' equities.

It sounds reasonable. Rational, even.

You wouldn't be alone. Wall Street makes its money convincing high-income earners that tax-deferred or taxable growth is enough. "Invest the difference," they say, "and let compounding do its thing." But let's run the numbers and see how that plays out in the real world, with volatility, taxes, and timing risk.

The Illusion of Simplicity

That investment decision may look like a wise move. You're betting on long-term growth as your investment compounds. However, paper returns are one thing; real life is another.

What if the market drops 20 percent the year after you've borrowed against it? What if it crashes 30 percent, and your collateral suddenly isn't enough to support the loan you took? You might face a margin call. The lender doesn't care that the market "always bounces back";—they care about their risk today.

In such a case, you must liquidate at a loss (locking in your paper losses) or inject more collateral to cover the loan. Either way, the consequences can be devastating. You could lose access to your liquidity exactly when you need it most or, worse, trigger capital gains taxes while cashing out from a depressed portfolio.

That's not just poor timing; it's a financial hazard.

Now, contrast that with a properly structured, overfunded indexed universal life (IUL) policy, like the one used in our Perpetual Wealth Plan. It's linked to an equity index like the S&P 500, but not invested in it. That's a crucial distinction. When the market surges, you share in the upside—but only up to a cap. And when the market tanks? You don't go backwards. Why? Because your policy has a floor that is often set at 0 percent.

That means your policy credits zero for the year when the S&P drops 30 percent. You don't lose cash value. You don't trigger a margin call. And you certainly don't have to scramble to post more collateral or liquidate assets under duress.

The ceiling may limit the explosive years, sure. But that trade-off buys you peace of mind and, more importantly, predictability. It means you can confidently borrow against your policy, knowing the cash value won't evaporate overnight because of geopolitical unrest, a pandemic, or a few tech stocks tanking after earnings calls.

The truth is, the IUL was engineered to weather storms, which is why banks and family offices use them. Entrepreneurs who understand real-world risk, not just spreadsheet simulations, leverage these tools inside trusts as their liquidity engines.

In a world where capital needs to be ready when you are, not when the market cooperates, resilience beats raw return every time.

Wall Street's Got a Seat at the Table; Just Don't Hand Them the Gavel

Traditional investing—traditional stocks, bonds, mutual funds, and ETFs—has a role in a well-rounded portfolio.

Entrepreneurs are builders by nature, and builders like tools. Taxable investments, when used correctly, are excellent tools. They offer liquidity, exposure to innovation, and potentially outsized returns. Yet, having a seat at the table doesn't mean they should be sitting at the head, especially when it comes to building Perpetual Wealth.

These investments perform; the challenge is that they don't compound uninterrupted, and they don't offer the strategic leverage that comes with more sophisticated planning. Every time you sell an asset—even to generate income— you're handing Uncle Sam a piece of your growth. Every gain is split, taxed, and often stripped of the flexibility you actually need. You want performance but also control, predictability, and the legal structures to keep your wealth working across generations.

That's where the Family Bank concept shines. With overfunded IULs inside irrevocable trusts, you're not just investing; you're designing. You're converting capital into tax-free liquidity, protected from lawsuits and estate taxes, while giving yourself the ability to access funds during life without triggering a taxable event. Try getting that from your brokerage account during a market correction. Equities aren't bad, but they don't integrate into a cohesive, multi-generational wealth strategy as insurance-based planning does.

So, yes, keep your investments. Use them. Grow them. But recognize their limits. Just as a hammer isn't a saw, your brokerage account isn't a bank. It's not built to fund your liquidity needs while also protecting your family and shielding your estate. When you build a plan around Wall Street, you're at the mercy of its rules. However, when you build a Family Bank around your entrepreneurial ecosystem, you're setting the rules and collecting interest on the outcome.

Comparing Two Realities

Let's compare the stock market investments to the premium-financed plan. Assume you invested $290,000 per year for fifteen years, the same number of years we funded the $5 million policy in Chapter 12. Let's also assume you received a consistent 8 percent annual return—a respectable, even generous, return, given market history and the drag of taxes and fees. You don't pay taxes on the gains along the way (let's say you defer them), but if you liquidate, you'll pay capital gains tax—28.3 percent in 2025, not including state taxes.

Alternatively, you could borrow against your investments, just like you'd borrow against a life insurance policy. But even then, you're on the hook for loan interest annually, and the value of your portfolio becomes your collateral.

Let's Chart This Out—Borrowing Against Investment Account

Now, we will compare the value of your investment account, assuming that you withdraw the same amount you borrowed against the $20 million premium financed plan. Here are the assumptions made:

- $290,000 invested annually for fifteen years
- 8 percent growth
- 5.8 percent loan interest paid annually from the portfolio
- 60 percent loan-to-value cap enforced
- Net to family reflects portfolio value minus outstanding loan balance
- No estate tax applied

Stock Market Investments:
Borrowing to Obtain Tax-Free Income
Leads to Plan Collapse (in $)

Year	Cumulative Stock Market Contributions	Account Market Value	Cumulative Withdrawals (Loans)	Cumulative Interest Paid	If Death @ Year End Net to Family After Loan Payoff
10	2,900,000	4,247,480	0	0	4,247,480
15	4,350,000	7,942,256	0	0	7,942,256
20	4,350,000	11,669,780	720,000	0	10,866.260
24	4,350,000	9,133,940	3,600,000	876,960	8,205,140
25	4,350,000	8,205,140	Not enough equity to borrow	1,127,520	2,914,580
30	4,350,000	5,981,780	Not enough equity to borrow	2,129,760	1,661,780
35	4,350,000	4,728,980	Not enough equity to borrow	3,382,560	158,420
40	4,350,000	3,476,180	Not enough equity to borrow	**4,635,360**	Deficit

Figure 13-B

Observations

Despite no estate tax, the portfolio collapses if Ivan attempts to take out the same $720,000 that he withdraws from the $5 million IUL. After only five distributions totalling $3.6 million, the bank would likely require more collateral or call the loan.

In this scenario, you've come out of pocket $4,350,000, the same amount you would have paid to overfund a $5 million policy for tax-free income. Still, you've paid interest expense and haven't received nearly the tax-free income the $5 million policy generated. The $20 million premium financed, you'll recall, required no contributions or interest payments and provided significant distributions to the family.

> The same $4.3 million out-of-pocket either lost liquidity and collapsed—or created a tax-free estate worth over $35 million. *Design, not luck, made the difference.*

Let's Compare the Three Strategies

If we assume that Ivan lives to age eighty and dies, let's examine the total cash inflows and outflows, given our work in the previous chapter and this one.

Comparing Investments: $5 Million IUL and $20 Million Premium Financed ULI Cash Flows

Year 40	Investments ($)	$5 Million IUL ($)	$20 Million IUL Premium Financed ($)
Total Tax Free Withdrawals/ Available Cash in excess of loan	4,350,000	14,450,000	26,835,346
Total Amount to Family At Death	0	2,100,000	34,935,921

Total Contributions	(4,350,000)	(4,350,000)	0
Total Interest Expense Paid Out of Pocket	(4,635,360)	0	0
Net Benefit After Tax	**Deficit**	**12,200,000**	**35,000,000+**

Figure 13-C

> Ivan had $4.3 million out-of-pocket in a market strategy. After taxes, loan interest, and volatility, his projected estate value fell under $2 million. His $20 million premium-financed policy? It required no out-of-pocket, returned over $35 million to the family, and didn't collapse when the market sneezed. Same contribution window—completely different result.

Which Strategy Truly Builds a Tax-Free Bank?

There are moments in an entrepreneur's life when clarity arrives not from a spreadsheet or pitch but from lived reality. You've taken risks. You've bootstrapped and scaled. You've signed the front of the paycheck. However, at some point, you start asking different questions.

Not, "What should I invest in?" But, "What am I actually building here?"

That's what this chapter—and this book—is about. You're not looking for another product. You're building a *tax-free Perpetual Wealth Family Bank* that multiplies wealth and liquidity long after you've stepped away from the whiteboard.

Let's walk through the four roads entrepreneurs most often travel, and see which one leads where.

1. Invest in the Market

This is the classic "wealth accumulation" strategy. It's what the talking heads on Fox Business and CNBC tout and what your neighbor means when he brags about "just letting it compound."

It does work until it doesn't.

While the market is great for wealth accumulation, it isn't the best for building a tax-free bank.

Markets rise, but they also crash, stall, panic, and reprice when you least expect them to. Volatility isn't a bug in the system; it is the system. And when you layer on capital gains tax, interest cost when you borrow against it, and the risk of needing liquidity during a down year, the strategy starts to wobble.

Even when it performs, it leaves you exposed. The value is taxable, fully includable in your estate, and highly correlated to things you don't control. You're building wealth in a structure that evaporates when you touch it.

And if you die holding that portfolio? Your family inherits an asset deeply entangled with tax codes, probate rules, and a market that may or may not cooperate.

This is a bet, not a bank.

2. Fund Your 401(k)

This is the default for most high earners because it feels responsible and safe. "Tax-deferred" sounds like a win until you realize it's a *tax postponement plan*.

Your contributions are capped. Your access is restricted. And your partner in the plan—the IRS—has veto power over your entire exit strategy. They tell you when to take it, how much to take, and how much they get.

By the time you hit your seventies, your Required Minimum Distributions force you to cash out whether or not you need the money. And every dollar withdrawn is taxed at ordinary income rates. No step-up in basis. No capital gains treatment. Just ordinary income exposure on your life's work.

This is not a Family Bank; it's a toll booth.

3. The $5 Million Self-Funded IUL

The picture changes. This is no longer about chasing yield or beating benchmarks. This is about engineering outcomes. An overfunded Indexed Universal Life policy done right gives you tax-free growth, downside protection, and a *non-reportable cash access tool* for life.

When structured correctly, you control the inputs, the timing of withdrawals, and the death benefit. Your estate gets a tax-free payout, and your business succession plan is fully capitalized. And your liquidity? It's accessible when *you*, not the market, say so.

The limitation? You fund it yourself. That means tying up your capital; for entrepreneurs, as Howard Schultz says, liquidity is oxygen. You're creating the proper structure but carrying the weight alone.

Still, it's a powerful move. And for many, it's a solid middle ground between passive investing and full system design.

4. The $20 Million IUL Premium-Financed Policy

Now, we're thinking like a strategist.

This isn't a product; it's a capital deployment system that lets you build a $20 million tax-free death benefit using *other people's money*. You retain your liquidity. Your capital stays in motion. The bank funds the policy, and you only need to put up a relatively minor amount of legacy capital as temporary collateral.

Each year, the loan pays the premium. You may access tax-free income along the way. The policy grows, the structure matures, and one day, quietly, efficiently, the policy becomes self-sustaining. The outside collateral falls off, the death benefit stands on its own, and your family receives an unencumbered tax-free legacy.

You never sold assets, paid tax on withdrawals, or pulled cash out of your operating business to make it happen.

That's tax efficiency and *system-level thinking*.

Which Path Holds the Most Promise?

Any of these strategies could work if you want to build a retirement fund. But if your goal is to build a Family Bank that throws off tax-free liquidity, funds future investments, supports your estate plan, and exits cleanly, there's only one strategy that checks every box.

It's not the one that forces you to give up control.

It's not the one that ties up your capital in Wall Street's casino.

And it's not the one that defers your tax burden until the bill is bigger.

It's the strategy that uses leverage smartly, thoughtfully collateralizes risk, and gives you multiples on every dollar of effort without triggering tax, probate, or regret.

But before you go chasing the promise of premium financing, let me say something critical because what comes next is where it either unlocks your future or becomes a ticking time bomb.

Not All Premium Financing Is Created Equal

Before you get too excited, call the insurance professional who can set you up for one of these strategies. Let's hit the brakes for a moment.

Premium financing comes in many flavors—some excellent, others downright reckless.

In the more aggressive or poorly structured versions, your entire financial life becomes entangled in the loan. As the lending bank funds more premiums each year, it requires more than just the policy as collateral. Some lenders demand a *blanket lien* on everything: brokerage accounts, real estate, even your business.

The more the loan grows, the tighter its grip on your freedom.

That kind of leverage comes with shackles. But that's not how a knowledgeable professional does it.

The most sophisticated premium finance strategies flip the power dynamic. Instead of putting your empire on the line or shelling out significant out-of-pocket premiums, you use a small, controlled collateral account held at your own bank or investment custodian. It's pledged to the lender, but you maintain control, visibility, and flexibility throughout.

In the best-engineered structures, the loan itself is non-recourse. That might not sound like a big deal until you understand what that means. Let me explain.

Most loans—whether it's a business line of credit, a mortgage, or even traditional premium-financed arrangements—come with recourse. That's banker-speak for: "If this deal goes sideways, we're coming for everything else you've got." Not just what you pledged—everything. Imagine financing a car, and when its value drops, the lender doesn't just repossess the vehicle—they come after your boat, your kids' 529 plans, and your weekend condo too. That's a recourse loan. It may start with one asset, but it sure doesn't end there.

Now, picture a non-recourse loan where you lease a car, and the agreement says, "If something goes wrong, you give back the car; that's it." The lender can't crack open the rest of your garage. They can't raid your portfolio, call your CPA, or peek into your estate plan. Their rights stop where your boundaries begin.

That's how the best Perpetual Wealth strategies are designed. The only assets pledged to the lender are the policy's cash value and the temporary collateral account. Your home? Off-limits. Your operating business? Protected. Your investment properties, brokerage accounts, and retirement plans? Untouchable. For you, this means the life insurance policy becomes your business partner in creating capital, and the trust makes sure it stays protected from taxes, lawsuits, and your in-laws.

- No personal guarantees
- No cross-collateralization
- No open doors into the rest of your estate

Most premium-financed insurance programs require full recourse. Banks like to have as many hooks into your world as they can get because it minimizes their risk, not yours. However, the most innovative strategies take the opposite approach. They keep your financial house fortified, giving you access to leverage while locking the doors behind you. You decide what's at risk and what isn't.

That's real control.

What you're left with is a fully funded, tax-advantaged, high-performing life insurance contract that you didn't pay for. This policy throws off millions in tax-free liquidity, preserves your estate's value, and finishes with a death benefit that exits your estate untouched by taxes, probate, or drama.

Why Premium Financing Works for the Entrepreneurial Mind

Entrepreneurs think differently. They don't ask, "How much do I have?" They ask, "Where is my capital doing the most good?"

Premium financing is designed for that kind of mind.

- It lets you retain your liquidity, keeping your money in motion rather than locked in a policy.
- It creates a significant, tax-advantaged asset that works for income, estate planning, and long-term liquidity.
- It allows you to build a powerful Family Bank funded with *other people's money*, not your own.

And when it's done correctly?

- The collateral is limited and temporary.
- There are no personal guarantees.
- There's no interference with your estate or your business.
- You retain control.

Premium financing isn't right for everyone. However, if you're a qualified entrepreneur with a net worth over $25 million, with high income, strong credit, and managed assets, it may be the most efficient way to fund your legacy *without tying up your assets and capital*.

Because if you're going to build a system that creates liquidity, leverage, and legacy. Why not do it without cutting the check yourself?

Mindset Shift: From Funded to Engineered

Now, that you've seen what's possible—really seen it—ask yourself:

Has your thinking shifted?

Are you still comparing financial strategies like products on a shelf?

Or are you beginning to see them as components of a larger system—*your system*—where liquidity, leverage, and tax efficiency all flow in the direction you've designed?

Before this chapter, you may have looked at a 401(k) and thought, "Well, at least I'm saving."

Do you now see it for what it really is—a tax-postponement plan with rules, penalties, and a finish line the IRS controls?

Before reading this chapter, you may have felt that investing in the market was safe, straightforward, and smart.

But now you've seen how market-dependent liquidity collapses under pressure, especially when you try to replicate the income from a policy without triggering taxes or margin calls.

Before this chapter, life insurance felt like protection. A contingency. Something that kicks in after you're gone. Now, can you see it as a living, breathing liquidity strategy—a bank you build, not just a benefit your family gets?

And leverage, how has your thinking changed there?

Did you used to associate leverage with risk? With over-reach? With danger?

Now do you see how innovative, tax-efficient, non-recourse notes, collateralized-by-design leverage can amplify your control, protect your capital, and increase what your heirs receive without exposing your portfolio or business to claims of creditors or court judgments?

That's the shift. Not just a new tactic—but a new frame.

You're not accumulating assets anymore. You're building systems. You're not asking "What's the return?" You're asking, "What's the role of this asset in the bigger machine?"

You're no longer just thinking like a builder. You're thinking like a designer. You're Contrarian Curious!

That's the Perpetual Wealth mindset.

And if your perspective has shifted even a little, this chapter did its job.

Reducing Taxable Income NOW!

Premium-financed life insurance isn't just for your heirs—it's your personal source of tax-free income and an opportunity engine you control. For many entrepreneurs, another question looms large: How do I reduce the taxes I'm paying this year on a seven-figure income? Most CPAs and financial advisors either overlook or misunderstand the one strategy built precisely for that purpose. But after the next chapter, you won't. You'll understand how to use a *Cash Balance Plan* to legally deduct hundreds of thousands in income, protect those dollars from creditors, and build a future benefit that's entirely under your control.

Most entrepreneurs have never even heard of it. You're about to master it.

CHAPTER 14

The Workhorse No One Talks About—Custom Designed Pension (IRC §415 Retirement Plans)

Walk into a room full of high-income entrepreneurs and ask what their 401(k)-contribution limit is, and you'll get many confident answers. Now, ask them what other Retirement Plans are available to them, and you'll likely face blank stares or vague references to pensions from a bygone era.

This is a wild reaction because for the right entrepreneur, a *custom-designed retirement plan* strategy isn't just a retirement account; it gives you the keys to the kingdom. It's a tax shelter, compensation adjusting tool, business retention strategy, and liquidity accelerator all wrapped into one. Plus, these plans typically favor the entrepreneur so that most of the contribution goes to the company's top executives, which in most cases includes you. If you understand how to structure these plans correctly, they will work hand-in-hand with your Perpetual Wealth planning to turn tax dollars you were already designated to the IRS into permanent assets invested inside your estate that can enhance your retirement savings.

First, the Setup: What Are These Plans?

Let's get this straight: there are a few versions of these plans, and they are not a trick. These plans are not some bleeding-edge loopholes that will be shut down next year. They are fully IRS-sanctioned and have been part of the tax code for many decades. But because they are a little more complex than a standard 401(k), they don't get the airtime they deserve.

At the core, these plans are covered under IRC §415, which sets the guidelines for the different types of defined benefit plans. Under the defined contribution plans—a 401(k) and a Profit-Sharing plan—you are limited to how much you can contribute annually, and your final plan balance at retirement will be determined by the market returns you received over the life of the plan.

The custom-designed retirement plan models are designed backward. Instead, you should begin with the benefit you want at retirement, and then the actuary calculates how much you can contribute annually to get there. The plans provide you with a range of contributions so you can put more money in during great years and contribute less to tough years. Flexibility!

Here's where it gets interesting: the IRS allows significantly larger contributions for the older, higher-paid participants because they're designed to allow the participants to catch up; that is, to fund their retirement accounts faster to make up for years that they did not fund the plan, so the balances catch up to the plan limits. This is especially attractive for older entrepreneurs. We're talking $100,000 to almost $450,000+ per year in deductible contributions, depending on your age and income. That's in addition to having a 401(k) and profit-sharing plan as well.

So, with one custom-designed coordinated strategy, you could be deferring taxes on over $400,000 per year and building a large nest egg for your retirement.

What Happens Inside the Plan?

The plan contributions—made by your company—are invested by a plan trustee or investment advisor, usually into a conservative portfolio of assets. You're not investing in meme stocks here. Most actuaries structure these plans and build their assumptions to mimic a 5 percent annual return profile, using a blend of:

- Treasury and government bonds
- Institutional-grade fixed income

- Stable-value funds
- Conservative equity exposure (think large-cap ETFs or index funds)
- Sometimes insurance-based general accounts for guaranteed minimums

In these plans, the company (i.e., the employer) makes a promise to the participants. Specifically, the plan promises:

- A certain percentage of their annual pay at retirement for each participant's account (for example, 5% of salary), and
- It is funded with a fixed interest credit (say, 4 percent per year), which mimics a safe, bond-like return.

Those aren't just goals—they're guarantees under the plan's formula. Another thing to keep in mind is that, in many cases, the tax code permits the plan to carve out a specific group of employees to participate in this plan while covering the balance of the rank-and-file employees through a companion profit-sharing plan.

This option was introduced in the code because most employees tend to change jobs more frequently than in the past. This strategy is particularly beneficial for employees who do not intend to remain with their current employer for their entire career. The two-plan carve-out structure provides lower-paid employees with a larger cash distribution at termination. The benefit for the entrepreneur is that they receive larger contributions, which will make a huge difference in tax savings for the company, as well as a larger lump sum account at retirement.

Now, the money the company contributes to the plan is invested—typically in conservative assets as noted in the bullet point above—so that it earns enough to meet that promised interest credit.

However, if the investments underperform, let's say the market returns only 1 percent or even goes negative for one year. The employer is still required to fund the rank-and-file participant's profit-sharing account. However, the plan funding can be reduced for the year by using the range of contributions established by the actuary under the Pension Protection Act to give the employer financial flexibility in good and bad times.

If business remains challenging, the employer can also amend the plan to reduce the benefit formula for the plan, which gives the employer relief in the funding. This doesn't happen often because the plan is conservatively managed and reviewed by an actuary annually, which is what a TPA (defined below) helps coordinate. But it's technically and legally your obligation as the plan sponsor to manage the funding.

The goal isn't to hit home runs—it's to maximize contributions for you and manage the plan to create predictable, steady growth that aligns with the actuarial assumptions of the plan. You want consistency. If the investments outperform the assumptions, your required future contributions go down. If they underperform, the business makes up the difference.

Side-by-Side—401(k) vs. Custom Designed Pension		
Feature	401(k) / Profit Sharing	Custom-Designed Pension
Contribution Limit (Age 50+)	$76,500	$450,000+
Contribution Type	Voluntary, fixed annual max	Employer-funded, actuarially determined
Tax Treatment	Pre-tax contributions	Same—tax-deferred growth, deductible
Investment Risk	Employee bears risk	Employer bears risk of underperformance

Complexity	Low (requires a TPA)	Moderate (requires an Actuary)
Ideal Candidate	Any employee	High-income owners age 40+
Creditor Protection	Strong (ERISA)	Strong (ERISA + trustee protections)

Figure 14-A

But What About Employees?

Now the big question: do I have to cover my employees too?

Yes—but here's the good news. Unlike a 401(k), where employee deferrals are common, a custom-designed pension plan is employer-funded. That means you control all contributions, and you can design the plan in many ways using carve-out strategies to increase your contributions. However, in all cases, it is important to balance your generosity with smart economics.

Contribution Allocation at a Mid-Sized Firm ($)				
Participant	Salary	401(k)/ Profit Sharing	Custom Designed Pension	Total Annual Benefit
Owner— Age 55	300,000	66,000	207,000	273,000
Manager— Age 35	125,000	12,500	6,250	18,750
Admin— Age 28	55,000	2,750	2,750	5,500

Figure 14-B

Ironclad: Why a Custom-Designed Pension Plan Is a Fortress Against Creditors

You already understand that lawsuits and legal threats aren't abstract dangers; they're structural realities for entrepreneurs. When it comes to sheltering assets from legal predators, few tools are as underappreciated and as ironclad as the custom-designed pension plan.

Because it falls under ERISA, your pension plan is protected from:

- lawsuits
- creditors
- bankruptcy proceedings

Even in states with weak asset protection laws, ERISA stands tall. When your plan is trustee-managed, with a third-party fiduciary, the protections increase further.

But Here's the Catch—It's Still Taxable

Let's pause here. You've built an elegant, tax-deferring machine, but eventually, you'll face ordinary income taxes on every dollar you take out. And if you pass away before draining the account, your heirs get hit twice: income tax and estate tax. In other words, the IRS gets a second bite of the apple.

If that feels like a hollow victory, you're not wrong.

This is where most plans end. But in the Perpetual Wealth system, this is where things get interesting.

Making the Tax Bill Disappear—The Perpetual Wealth Way

The Pivot: Use the Tax Savings to Buy Life Insurance in a Trust

During your peak earning years, you might contribute $300,000 annually to your custom-designed pension plan. Doing so could save $120,000 in taxes.

Instead of spending those savings, use a portion to fund an overfunded *Indexed Universal Life (IUL) insurance policy*, owned by your *Perpetual Wealth Family Bank Trust*.

Redirecting Tax Savings into Life Insurance				
Scenario	Annual CDP Contribution ($)	Tax Rate	Tax Savings ($)	Portion Used for IUL Premium ($)
Owner A	275,000	40%	110,000	50,000
Owner B	375,000	37%	138,750	75,000

Figure 14-C

The IUL grows tax-free. It's not included in your estate because of the way we structure it with your Perpetual Wealth Family Bank Trust. More importantly, it creates liquidity exactly when your family needs it most—at your death.

Compare the two:

Taxed vs. Tax-Free Structures		
Feature	Custom Pension	IUL in Family Bank Trust
Subject to Income Tax	YES	NO
Subject to Estate Tax	YES	NO
RMDs Required	YES	NO
Lifetime Liquidity	Limited, Taxable	Flexible, Tax Free
Creditor Protection	YES (ERISA)	YES (IF IN TRUST)
Tax-Free Death Benefit	NO	YES

Figure 14-D

Later in Life: Using RMDs Strategically

At age seventy-five, you're required to begin RMDs. Why not use them to fund the policy?

Using RMDs to Fund a Trust-Owned Policy ($)			
Age	RMD (on 3.5M IRA)	Life Insurance Premium	Tax-Free Estate Protection
75	151,000	125,000	3.5M
76	157,000	125,000	3.5M

Figure 14-E

This is how you convert taxable income into tax-free wealth, even in retirement.

Disadvantages? Sure. But All Manageable	
Concern	**Solution**
Premium commitments	Tailor policy to peak earnings window
Complexity of trust coordination	One-time setup, long-term gain
Inflexible CDP access pre-retirement	Use IUL policy loans instead

Figure 14-F

Final Thoughts

The custom-designed pension plan isn't simply a retirement structure. The plan is a *tax-optimized launchpad* that, when paired with a Perpetual Wealth Family Bank Trust and strategically designed life insurance coverage, becomes a multi-generational wealth system.

- Deduct large sums now.
- Protect assets from lawsuits.
- Avoid the estate tax later.
- Pass on tax-free capital to your heirs.

You're not just postponing taxes. You're redirecting those taxes into a system that works for you now and for generations. That's the Perpetual Wealth way.

CHAPTER 15

Case Studies—Puzzle Complete

Capital isn't scarce; vision is.

—*Sam Walton, founder of Walmart and Sam's Club*

Bringing It All Together: Structure Meets Strategy

If you've ever pieced together a complicated jigsaw puzzle—five hundred pieces scattered across the dining room table, finally snapping into a vivid picture—you know the satisfaction of completion. That's what these case studies are all about. They take the concepts we've discussed throughout the book—tax minimization, asset protection, trusts, liquidity strategies—and demonstrate how they work together in real-world scenarios. If the rest of the book gave you the puzzle pieces, this chapter is the box cover. Now, we get to look at the picture on the front and say, "Ah, so *that's* how it all fits."

This is where many entrepreneurs get stuck. They hear one strategy here, read another over there, and before long, their estate and tax plans look more like a cobbled-together Rube Goldberg device than a well-engineered machine. That's not entirely their fault. Much of the estate planning, tax, and financial services world is siloed, reactive, and far too reliant on "let's address what's in front of us now" advice.

The entrepreneurs we highlight here chose differently. They didn't chase the next tax loophole or hot asset class. They built *systems*—cohesive legal, tax, and financial architectures designed to grow with them, adapt to change, and support both their lives and legacies.

These case studies are based on real-life entrepreneurs I've had the privilege to work with over the years. To protect confidentiality, we've changed names, professions, and facts. But the core lessons—the strategies, the challenges, and the transformations—are very real. You'll see how trusts, LLCs, liquidity planning, and coordinated tax strategies can create a living, breathing Perpetual Wealth system, which evolves as life does.

So, take a look under the hood. These aren't hypotheticals; they're actual experiences from clients who chose to play a different game. Not the game traditionally designed the way most lawyers and CPAs think, but creative strategies where we wrote new rules. And if you've been following along, you'll see how you can apply the same system-building mindset to your own situation. Swap out the names and numbers, and you're off to the races.

Case Study Zeta

From Blight to Blueprint: How Lou Transformed Risk into Reward

After decades of success in the construction industry, Lou retired with a solid net worth of $15 million. But Lou wasn't interested in golfing five days a week, unlike many retirees. Instead, he embarked on a highly strategic and uniquely personal journey that would blend real estate redevelopment with sophisticated tax and estate planning.

With an old F-150 pickup truck and a sharp eye for opportunity, Lou began crisscrossing the small towns of the American Southeast, not in search of leisure, but to identify overlooked strip shopping centers—the kind that most investors would write off. These tired plazas, often anchored by chains like Piggly Wiggly, Food Lion, or Dollar General, became the foundation of his next fortune.

An Investor's Playbook in Motion

Lou had a three-part formula: scout, analyze, acquire. His process was intentional and data-driven, yet personal and intuitive, born from decades of experience in construction. He targeted neglected strip centers in underserved rural or exurban communities, found by evaluating demographics to confirm trends. On those centers he identified as worthy, he contacted the owners, often aging landlords, and negotiated deals before they reached brokers or the Multiple Listing Service (MLS).

The Hidden Engine: Leveraged Liquidity Through Life Insurance

- Lou's financial strategy was as brilliant as his redevelopment vision. He held a $5 million premium-financed life insurance policy on his wife, Linda, in an Irrevocable Life Insurance Trust (ILIT). Linda was the insured; Lou served as trustee.

- Despite paying no out-of-pocket premiums, the policy had accumulated $2.5 million in cash value, exceeding the bank debt embedded in the plan to pay the premiums.

- The original ILIT collateral account was no longer necessary, making the funds easily accessible for investment purposes.
- This $2.5 million of built-up capital served as the down payment source for acquiring properties.
- Combined with third-party *bank loans*, Lou could swiftly act on deals, giving him a competitive edge in distressed markets.
- The structure elevated his effective purchasing power to the level of someone with an implied net worth of over $30 million.

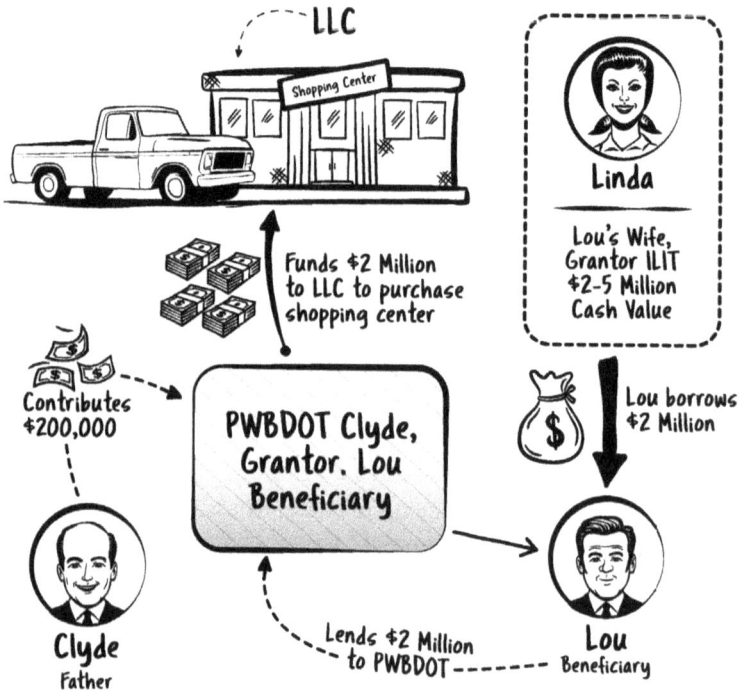

Figure 15-A

Ownership Through a PWBDOT: Smart Trust Architecture

Lou never purchased a property in his name. Instead, he created LLCs owned by a *Perpetual Wealth Beneficiary Deemed Owned Trust (PWBDOT)*—a structure initially seeded by his father, Clyde, with $200,000.

- Assets owned by the PWBDOT were outside of Lou's taxable estate.
- Lou had beneficiary-level access and full trustee authority, without formal ownership.
- Provided asset protection.
- Included powers of appointment to adapt to changing family circumstances, legal, tax, and financial conditions.
- The PWBDOT beneficiaries included his wife and adult children (and their descendants), so Lou could sprinkle the income to those he wanted.

All acquisition funds—whether borrowed or secured through third-party lenders—flowed into the PWBDOT, which, through the LLC, held title to each redeveloped property.

From Blight to Bright: The Value-Add Redevelopment Model

Lou approached each acquisition with the discipline of a seasoned developer and the strategic foresight of a financier. While the exterior of these neglected strip centers told a story of decline—crumbling pavement, dilapidated façades, and burned-out parking lot lights, Lou saw potential. He followed a consistent and highly effective formula: transform the property, lease to strong operators, maximize the income stream, and ultimately sell at a premium.

The rehabilitation process began immediately after acquisition. Drawing on his decades in construction, Lou assembled a network of reliable contractors. Their first order of business was to resurface the parking lots, restoring curb appeal and eliminating liabilities. Next came the installation of upgraded lighting systems, not only to improve safety and visibility but also to signal a fresh start to the community. Modernizing the storefront exteriors followed—fresh paint, uniform signage, and updated façades brought visual cohesion and commercial appeal.

Just as critical as the physical improvements was Lou's strategy for tenant turnover. He phased out underperforming or low-margin tenants, which typically included mom-and-pop beauty and nail salons, tattoo parlors, laundromats, and thrift shops that generated minimal foot traffic. In their place, he introduced a carefully curated mix of national franchise brands with proven performance in similar demographics.

Lou's access to these franchises wasn't incidental—it was a direct result of the relationships he cultivated by attending national franchise conventions held in Las Vegas. He became a known quantity among franchise development teams: a man who delivered quality locations in underserved markets. As a result, Lou had direct lines of communication with brands such as Starbucks, Dunkin', Verizon, Domino's, H&R Block, The UPS Store, Tropical Smoothie Café, and Subway.

These relationships enabled Lou to pre-lease units before construction was even complete, giving both tenants and lenders confidence in the project's viability. In many cases, his properties were fully leased before subcontractors applied the final coat of paint. It was a model built on consistency, reputation, and an eye for what small-town America needed—reliable services, familiar names, and safe, appealing retail centers.

Harvesting the Upside: Lou's Exit Strategy

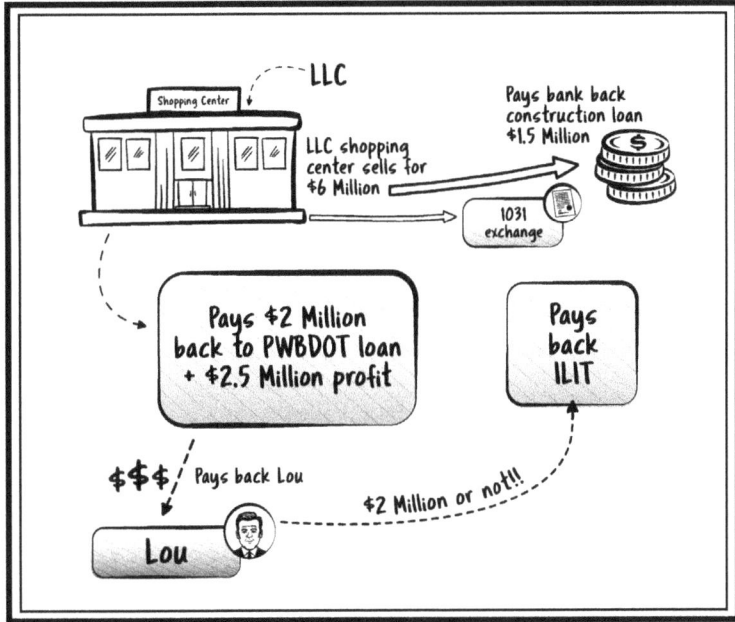

Figure 15-B

Lou understood that the key to sustainable success wasn't just in acquiring and renovating undervalued properties; it was knowing exactly when and how to exit. After each project's renovation, he held it for twenty-four to thirty-six months. This window wasn't arbitrary; it allowed enough time for the new tenant mix to settle in and for rental income to justify a premium sales price that would appeal to institutional buyers and real estate investment trusts (REITs).

Investors were drawn to the predictability of the rents and the proven appeal of the upgraded site, particularly in regions where new development was limited but demand remained strong. With timing and reputation on his side, Lou sold the properties at a substantial profit.

Rather than taking profits personally as distributions, adding to his estate, the sale proceeds accumulated directly back into the PWBDOT, albeit with income tax minimization based on the sophisticated powers contained in the document. This allowed him to repeat the process, growing his wealth outside of his taxable estate while preserving the benefits of asset protection, control, and multigenerational planning.

Strategic Layers: Income Allocation, Corporate Structuring, and Tax Minimization

Lou didn't just build wealth through real estate—he protected and amplified it through thoughtful tax planning and income structuring. While the strip centers were the visible face of his success, the real magic happened behind the scenes, within the layers of entities, trusts, and tax-savvy design.

Central to Lou's estate plan was the PWBDOT, which was a member of the LLC he formed to purchase a shopping center. The PWBDOT was no ordinary trust. It included a *trust protector*, a trusted individual who held the authority to make strategic adjustments to the trust's operation. Most notably, the trust protector could shift the income taxation from the trust to Lou to Lou's adult children, Benji and Gabi, who were also beneficiaries. By doing so, Lou could leverage their lower marginal tax brackets, retaining overall family wealth while keeping control firmly in place. And because the trust was domiciled in Florida, a state with no income tax, the structure shielded earnings from any unnecessary state-level erosion.

When selling and acquiring centers, Lou's entities and trusts took advantage of IRC Section 1031, strategically rolling gains into new properties to preserve capital and grow his portfolio tax-efficiently.

To further optimize his operations and earnings, Lou established two Florida *S corporations*, each playing a unique role in the ecosystem he built.

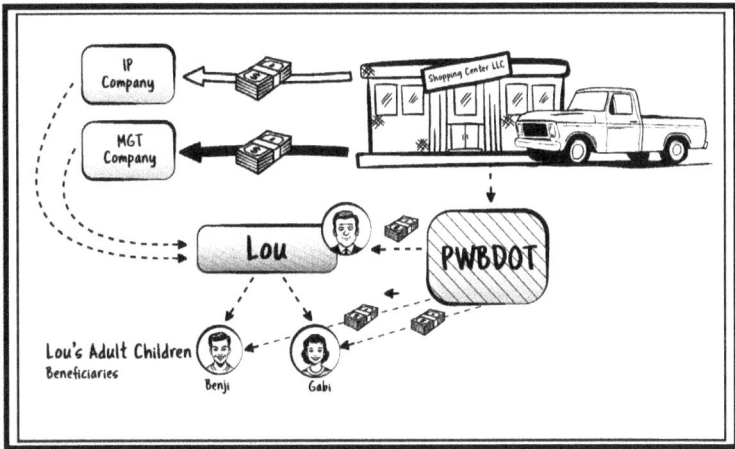

Figure 15-C

The first S corporation was a management company, through which Lou and his children were paid reasonable W-2 salaries for their active involvement. In addition to salary, the company issued dividends, which, under the S corp structure, flowed through to Lou without being subject to self-employment taxes—a crucial efficiency for high-income entrepreneurs.

The second was an intellectual property (IP) company, also taxed as an S corp. This entity held all of Lou's proprietary systems and know-how: his criteria for identifying undervalued shopping centers, his standardized methods for conducting due diligence and rehab, and his templates for lease negotiations and tenant onboarding.

The IP company licensed this intellectual property to the management company, which paid royalties in return. The IP was amortized, creating valuable non-cash deductions that lowered taxable income without reducing real cash flow.

Lou deliberately positioned the IP company outside the direct flow of rental and operational income, allowing him to significantly reduce state income tax liability in states that imposed such taxes on business activity.

Another strategy used was a *Cash Balance Plan* to siphon off taxable income from his management and IP entities.

Moreover, Lou strategically leveraged a range of real estate-specific tax advantages to minimize his annual tax burden. Through depreciation deductions on each strip center, including improvements to structures, roofing, and mechanical systems, he significantly reduced his taxable rental income.

In addition, his team targeted developments in qualifying communities to obtain property tax incentives and government-issued development credits. Where applicable, Lou also utilized Internal Revenue Code Section 179 to immediately expense capital investments such as HVAC systems, signage, and parking lot lighting. These accelerated deductions gave him added flexibility to optimize his tax position.

Together, this intricate framework of trusts and S corporations wasn't just clever—it was essential. It gave Lou the power to build, retain, and eventually transfer wealth, while staying agile in the face of shifting tax laws and economic cycles.

Conclusion: Engineered Legacy

Lou's story is not just one of wealth accumulation—it's a blueprint for how entrepreneurial drive, paired with disciplined planning, can create lasting impact during an entrepreneur's life and across generations. What began as a personal post-retirement venture evolved into a powerful model for building, protecting, and transferring wealth while remaining agile in the face of tax laws, market cycles, and life transitions.

At the heart of his success was a holistic estate planning framework, centered around using a Perpetual Wealth Beneficiary Owned Trust (PWBDOT). This structure enabled Lou to grow a substantial real estate portfolio while keeping those appreciating assets outside his taxable estate, ensuring his legacy would pass efficiently to his heirs.

His operations were designed with tax efficiency in mind. Lou could reduce his taxable footprint while maintaining operational control by layering S corporations and allocating income strategically, offset by robust *depreciation and expense deductions*.

Equally important was his attention to *asset protection*. Through the Perpetual Wealth Family Bank Trust holding a premium-financed life insurance policy and the PWBDOT owning real estate, Lou effectively insulated his personal and family wealth from potential creditors, estate taxes, and legal claims.

One of Lou's most powerful tools was the liquidity embedded in his life insurance structure. The policy's cash value provided flexible, tax-free capital, allowing him to seize investment opportunities without triggering income tax or liquidating appreciating assets. Better yet, that liquidity is also outside of his family's estate for tax purposes.

Perhaps most meaningfully, Lou integrated his family into the very fabric of the business. His children weren't just passive beneficiaries; they were active participants, learning from Lou, earning salaries, and gaining firsthand experience as future stewards of the enterprise. By splitting income across generations, Lou reduced tax burdens and instilled in his family the skills and values necessary to continue the legacy he built.

Lou didn't just retire from construction; he reconstructed his future. His case is a living example of how intentional design, rooted in legal tools and driven by an entrepreneurial spirit, can yield not just income but also impact. It's not just what Lou built, but how he built it that makes this story worth telling.

Case Study Theta

From Treatment Room to Enterprise: Courtney's Blueprint for Scalable Impact

Like many practitioners, Courtney began her professional journey in physical therapy, serving one patient at a time with focus, care, and a relentless drive for outcomes. What set her apart, however, was her clinical excellence and her ability to think like an architect, building not just a practice but a platform for scalable impact and intergenerational legacy.

From the outset, Courtney structured her business as an *S corporation,* allowing her to take a reasonable salary while enjoying distributions free from self-employment taxes. Her initial clinic opened in a modest, custom-built office space—paid for through a $100,000 capital contribution to a *Perpetual Wealth Spousal Lifetime Trust™ (PWSLT™)*, established by her husband, Philip, an irrevocable trust that offers income tax, estate tax, and asset protection benefits. That capital seeded the building's construction and gave the couple a foundational asset within a protected estate-planning vehicle.

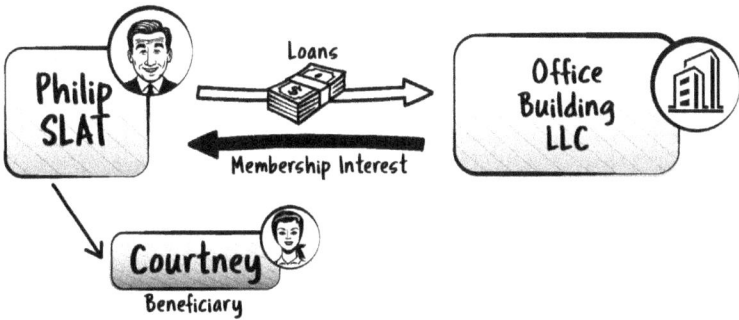

Figure 15-D

Scaling Through Systems and Segmentation

As her practice flourished, Courtney invested heavily in creating *repeatable systems*, including clinical protocols, staff training manuals, patient onboarding procedures, marketing funnels, and tools for measuring outcomes. Over time, these systems became their own asset class: *intellectual property with measurable economic value.*

Courtney segregated these systems into their own S corporation to shield that IP from operational risk and optimize income flow. This IP company would later license her systems to:

- Her own education company, which provided *continuing education and online certification programs* to physical therapists and clinic staff.
- A consulting company that helped other therapists establish and grow their practices in exchange for *minority equity stakes* or ongoing royalties.

This structure allowed Courtney to siphon off profits from those two companies, now surpassing her original clinic revenue, and direct them into the IP company. She took *dividends instead of a salary, avoiding self-employment taxes* on a significant portion of her income.

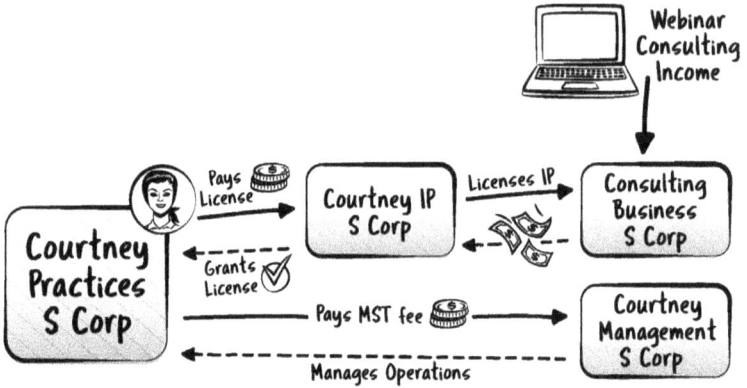

Figure 15-E

Layered Entities for Protection and Optionality

Courtney's brick-and-mortar clinics were no longer lumped under a single entity. As she expanded, she adopted a *hub-and-spoke legal model*:

- Each location operated as its own limited liability company (LLC), responsible for its own staff, lease, and liability.
- These LLCs were wholly owned by a parent holding company, which centralized management, tax reporting, HR, and capital decisions.

This entity segregation served multiple purposes:

- **Liability isolation**: If one clinic faced legal action or underperformed, it wouldn't drag down the others.

- **Strategic exits or partnerships**: Courtney could sell off or spin out a high-performing location as a standalone deal or offer phantom stock (a percentage of profits without ownership) to a promising therapist, retaining loyalty while freeing up capital.

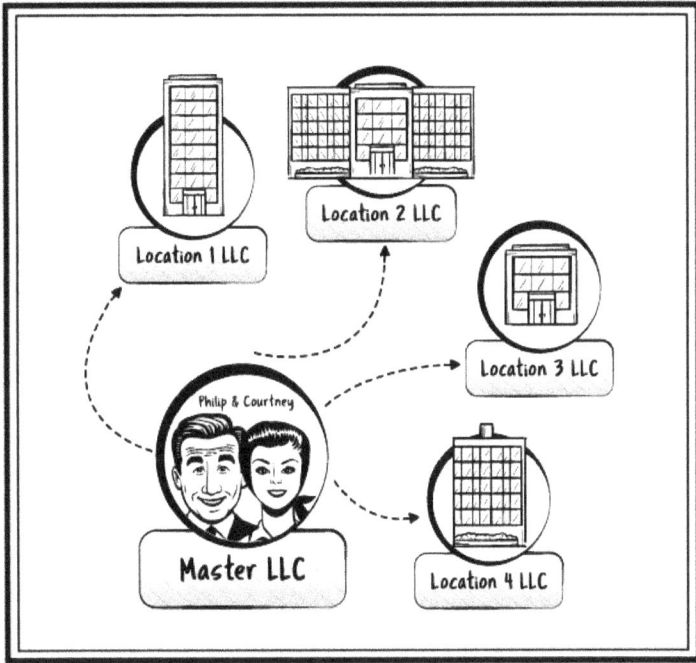

Figure 15-F

Trust Planning: Beyond the Business

Courtney employed the same critical thinking she brought to her business operations to her design for her estate and family wealth plan. In addition to the SLAT her husband created, she established two powerful trust vehicles to support their children and preserve the enterprise across generations.

True freedom comes from leading a team that manages the work for you.

Now, you're about to see how Perpetual Wealth becomes real.

Perpetual Wealth Family Bank Trust

Courtney formed a Perpetual Wealth Family Bank Trust (PWFBT), which became the owner of several multi-million-dollar whole life insurance policies insuring her children's lives. Even though her kids were teenagers with little income, the underwriting was based on Courtney's net worth and income. As a result, they could be insured for far more than their financial footprint justified, creating a massive store of tax-advantaged, creditor-protected capital.

These policies served as the family's internal financial management system. As her children matured and sought to start businesses, invest in real estate, or pursue philanthropic ventures, the *trust could lend funds against the policies' cash value* on favorable terms without needing to go to banks or tap into taxable capital.

As each generation passed, the life insurance death benefits flowed back into the PWFBT, replenishing its capital. New policies were then implemented for younger generations, ensuring a continuous, tax-free source of funding for the family, passed down from generation to generation.

The PWFBT was structured with key *trust protector* roles and carefully crafted powers of appointment, allowing each generation to adjust the trust to evolving legal, tax, financial, and family circumstances.

Teaching Financial Stewardship Early

Courtney didn't wait to teach her children about business until they graduated from college. As soon as they were old enough, she employed them in *age-appropriate roles*:

- One helped with video editing and social media content for her education platform.
- The other assisted with data entry and clinic inventory.

Because their income was legitimate and earned, Courtney *established Roth 401(k) accounts* for each of them— accounts that would grow tax-free for life, giving them a multi-decade head start on retirement and wealth building. This also allowed her to *shift income out of her own tax bracket,* creating an additional layer of savings.

A Personal Exit Strategy with Institutional Control

Rather than sell the operating companies or exit to private equity, Courtney chose *modular exits.*

- She retained full control of the IP and education companies.
- She sold off individual clinics when strategic buyers emerged or key team members wanted ownership stakes.
- She remained the content licensing source and landlord, ensuring recurring income even as she reduced her operational involvement.

This strategy gave her ultimate personal flexibility: she could travel, teach, mentor, or simply enjoy the fruits of her labor while still participating in the financial upside of what she had built.

Conclusion: A Practice, A Platform, A Private Enterprise

Courtney's case is a model of scaling a service-based business with strategic discipline and estate-planning foresight. She began with clinical expertise and transformed it into a multi-entity, multi-revenue enterprise designed to last generations.

Her story demonstrates several takeaways.

- When paired with a thoughtful business structure, trust planning enables control and protection without sacrificing opportunity while building value outside of a taxable estate.

- When extracted and appropriately licensed, intellectual property becomes one of the most tax-advantaged forms of recurring income.

- And how a service entrepreneur can evolve from a sole practitioner to a legacy architect, ensuring personal success and intergenerational empowerment.

Courtney didn't just build a business—she created a *wealth-building engine.*

The Final Shift

You've come a long way. You've seen how the system is rigged—and how entrepreneurs who know the real rules can turn the tables. You've seen how rigging legal and tax structures in your favor doesn't just save dollars; it reclaims power.

But if we stopped here, you'd still be missing something. Rigging the system is one thing. Scaling freedom is another.

Most entrepreneurs build success the way early settlers built houses: one board at a time, fixing leaks and cracks as they go. It works until growth outpaces the foundation. Then, what was once a strong shelter becomes a shaky liability.

If you want to truly rig the future—to expand revenue, protect liquidity, and create freedom that lasts longer than you do—the pieces can't simply be smart individually. They have to seamlessly and strategically work together.

That's what Entrepreneurial Truth #5 is about.

Your team should be your operating system, not your obstacle.

Too many entrepreneurs end up trapped by the people meant to free them. Not because they hired the wrong experts, but because no one ever taught those experts to think as a cohesive unit.

Let's finish strong.

TRUTH #5

From Doing to Designing: How a Unified External Team Unlocks Freedom

If you've reached Truth #5, you're not here by accident. You've already built something remarkable. You rigged the systems that tried to rig you. You turned unfair legal and tax frameworks into engines for your advantage. But now comes the final leap: turning personal hustle into enduring freedom.

Here's the trap most entrepreneurs fall into, and you might recognize it in your journey. You built your empire one brick at a time: A legal entity when you needed one. A tax strategy that made sense. Someone said an insurance policy was smart. Each move is in isolation, and each decision was designed to solve a momentary problem. And, against all odds, it worked.

Until it didn't.

Because no matter how successful you become, if your legal, tax, financial, and liquidity strategies were stitched together piecemeal, eventually you hit a ceiling. Growth stalls. Revenue leaks. Opportunities slip away. Worst of all, the freedom you fought to create starts eroding before your eyes.

It's not because you hired the wrong advisors. Most entrepreneurs I meet have a bench full of well-credentialed, well-meaning professionals. The problem isn't effort. It's architecture.

Freedom—real freedom—doesn't come from one-off advice. It comes from a team of experts operating under a single, coordinated system. When your attorney, CPA, financial advisor, and insurance strategist aren't working from a shared blueprint, you're not building Perpetual Wealth—you're patching potholes on a crumbling road.

This section is about fixing that permanently.

In Chapter 16, you'll learn about my epiphany that transformed me from a technician to an architect. That transformation led to the creation of the Perpetual Wealth system. I stopped solving problems in silos and started creating coordinated frameworks that unlocked freedom for my clients.

Chapter 17 zooms out from my personal experience and into yours. Wealth doesn't exist in a vacuum, and neither should your advisors. We'll explore true collaboration and why the standard "you talk to five experts separately" model is a recipe for missed opportunities and contradictory advice. You'll learn to spot fragmented systems before they cost you, restructure your team so they think *with* each other (not just for you), and build an external team that acts like a unified command center for your future.

In Chapter 18, the final chapter, we bring it all together in the Perpetual Wealth Program. This isn't about a stack of dusty documents. It's a living, breathing operating system — a team-based model that supports your freedom and expands it for generations.

You'll see how the right design transforms your advisors from separate vendors into a strategic force. When structured correctly, your external team doesn't just preserve wealth — they create a system that adapts to your life, scales your revenue, protects your liquidity, and ensures your family's freedom long after you're no longer steering the ship.

You weren't meant to do this alone. And with the proper structure, you never will again.

CHAPTER 16

From Technician to Architect

> If you want to go fast, go alone.
> If you want to go far, go together.
>
> —*African Proverb*

Fifteen years into my estate planning law career, I almost gave it up.

It wasn't because the firm was failing. On the contrary, business was exemplary. Clients referred friends and family. Revenue was healthy. From the outside, everything looked like success. But inside, I was drowning.

My phone rang off the hook every day. Clients weren't calling with emergencies but asking where their drafts were. "Did you finish the trust yet?" "When will I see a draft of the operating agreement?" "Can we fund the partnership interests before year-end?" It was a constant cycle of expectations, interruptions, and guilt. And the truth is, they had every right to ask. I couldn't keep up.

I worked long days and longer nights rewriting estate plans, redrafting structures, tweaking language, and trying to stay ahead of the next demand. Most nights and weekends, I was in the office. And most of that time, I was alone.

I told myself I was doing the real work, that clients paid me for the documents, and that if I just had more uninterrupted time, I could get everything done.

That's when my friend and fellow tax attorney, Alan Gassman, introduced me to Strategic Coach®. "It's not for lawyers," he told me. "It's for entrepreneurs who want to build a business that works *for* them instead of them constantly working *in* the business."

I was intrigued, and then I heard the price.

It was $8,000 a year, *back in 2005*. Plus, it meant flying to Chicago every quarter, covering airfare, hotel, and time away from the office. It felt indulgent, unrealistic.

I called Alan back, saying, "I can't justify spending the money or the time out of the office."

He replied, "Try it for one year. You'll see."

So, I did.

The Conversation That Changed Everything

In my first session, I walked in with what I thought was a legitimate complaint: "If my clients would just leave me alone, I could get their documents done."

Dan Sullivan, co-founder of Strategic Coach, asked me, "Why are you spending all your time on the commodity of your practice?"

I pushed back, hard. "The documents?!" I answered incredulously. "Because that's the value! That's what I'm being paid to do—get the trusts and provisions right. Drafting these matters!"

Dan nodded and then said something that would crack open the view of my entire career: "Do your clients know the difference between your documents and those from the lawyer down the street? Those less qualified and less expensive than your firm?"

I paused. And I had to admit they didn't.

That was in 2005, *before* LegalZoom and Rocket Lawyer offered do-it-yourself trusts and business entity templates online. Today, clients can whip up a trust in twenty minutes and never meet with a lawyer. Back then, those platforms didn't exist. But even without them, my clients couldn't tell whether my carefully crafted work product differed significantly from anyone else's.

And if they couldn't tell the difference, *what* were they paying for?

A Turning Point

Strategic Coach gave me space I didn't even know I needed to step out of the weeds and reevaluate how I was building my practice. The thinking tools and the environment helped me ask better questions. Not just "How do I do more?"—but "What do my clients want, and what's the best way to achieve it?"

That shift in perspective was invaluable.

At that point, my journey took a specific turn: I realized that for many entrepreneurs like myself, the next challenge wasn't *what* to think, but *how* to apply that thinking when structuring my clients' businesses and wealth.

Because in the legal, tax, and financial world, ideas aren't enough. You need infrastructure. You need vehicles that reflect those values and goals—entities, trusts, ownership models, intra-family transactions, and liquidity tools that function in harmony, not in silos.

That's what led me to build the *Perpetual Wealth™ Program.*

It wasn't a replacement for what I learned. The natural continuation was an implementation framework that turns big-picture thinking into real-world protection, opportunity, and freedom. It's where collaboration between advisors shifts from being theoretical to driving growth.

In other words, *mindset pointed the way. Structure made the journey possible.*

From Lone Technician to Collaborative Architect

That insight triggered a second breakthrough: I was trying to carry too much alone.

I realized the only way to scale my impact on my clients was to stop being the lone technician and start becoming the architect of a team. So, I began to build one.

First, I hired and trained lawyers who became board-certified, like I am, and built a support team within my office, including paralegals, client support staff, document drafters, and operations personnel. I empowered them with clear roles and held them accountable for their tasks. I stopped being the bottleneck.

Then, I expanded my team outward with seasoned CPAs, financial professionals, insurance advisors, and liquidity planners. I didn't just refer clients to these experts; I *collaborated* with them. Sometimes, a client already had a good professional or two, so I introduced those professionals into our systems.

That's when the fundamental transformation began.

When clients worked with us, they weren't just getting documents. They were getting a program—a structure—a set of coordinated, intentional decisions made by a team that could see the whole chessboard.

The client no longer had to be the go-between, asking each advisor what to do and hoping their answers didn't contradict each other. We handled the integration, and the client got to experience what they were really after all along: *confidence.*

You Can't Break the Ceiling Alone

Every entrepreneur hits a ceiling. I suspect you've hit a ceiling if you've read this far.

Maybe it's a time ceiling—you've got no more hours to give. Maybe it's a complexity ceiling—the business has outgrown your systems.

Maybe it's a capability ceiling—what got you here won't get you there.

But when that moment comes—and it *will*—trying to break through alone is a losing game.

You can't think your way out of a complexity you created by over-functioning. You need others, and specifically, *the right others*.

You need strategic collaborators. You need professionals who bring skills and expertise you don't have but who understand how those disciplines interact and are willing to work together toward your vision.

The Perpetual Wealth System: Where Thinking Becomes Execution

That's what the Perpetual Wealth system is designed to do. It brings together:

- **Liability and Asset protection:** minimizing exposure to lawsuits or liabilities.
- **Tax structure:** capital flows with minimal friction and maximum flexibility.
- **Ownership design:** controlling what you build, without having to be the one managing every detail.
- **Trust architecture:** taking care of you and your loved ones in a directed and purposeful way.
- **Liquidity planning:** Make sure opportunities don't slip by while you're waiting for a distribution or selling stock at the wrong time.

This isn't theoretical. It's a framework you can live in. A structure that grows with you, evolves as your business evolves, and supports your family long after you're no longer at the helm.

None of it happens in a vacuum.

It happens through collaboration with internal team members and external experts, with a network of "Whos" helping you get to your "How," and with a clear process that transforms complexity into clarity.

Collaboration Isn't Overhead; It's a Wealth Multiplier.

Some entrepreneurs still hesitate. They think, "I can't afford a team of advisors."

But here's the real cost:

- a lawsuit you could've avoided
- a tax bill you didn't expect
- a family dispute that splits your business in half
- a once-in-a-decade opportunity you missed because the cash wasn't there when you needed it

Collaboration isn't overhead; it's leverage.

The right team, working within the right structure, gives you something no spreadsheet can calculate:

- time
- confidence
- options
- peace of mind

Have You Hit the Ceiling?

You may not know you've hit the ceiling until you're already nose-to-glass. Here are a few signs it might be time to stop pushing harder and start building smarter.

1. You're the bottleneck.

Everything still flows through you—decisions, revisions, sign-offs, and client requests. If you take a day off, things slow down. A week? They stop entirely.

2. Your time doesn't belong to you anymore.

You used to have control of your calendar. Now, you're lucky to get through Monday without rescheduling Friday. Deep work? Forget it.

3. You've built success, but you're not free.

Revenue might be up, but so is stress. You don't trust that the system can run without you. And maybe… it can't.

4. Your professional team feels more like a patchwork.

Your CPA, attorney, insurance advisor, and financial planner are all good people, but they don't talk to each other. You're the middleman, hoping they don't contradict each other (or worse, overlook something big).

5. Your structures don't match your ambitions.

You're playing a bigger game, but still using legal and tax strategies built when your company was half the size. You've outgrown your foundation, and it's starting to show.

If any of these sound familiar, you're not broken. You've simply reached the next level.

And it's time to build the system that gets you through the ceiling—without crashing through it alone.

Mindset Shift: From Lone Operator to Visionary Architect

Take a breath.

Let's step back from the technicals for a moment. The trusts, the entities, the liquidity systems. Yes, they matter, but none of it sticks unless you ask the deeper question:

Do you believe you can scale this alone?

If reading this chapter stirred something—some low-level discomfort, some quiet recognition that you've been white-knuckling the controls for too long. Good. That's a signal. Your ceiling is talking.

What would change if you stopped treating collaboration like a cost and started viewing it as an accelerator? What if you looked at your current structure—your legal setup, your tax planning, your advisor relationships—and asked, "Is this correct?" but also, "Is this cohesive? Is this built to grow?"

More importantly, *is this built to grow without me growing?*

Too often, entrepreneurs end up building wealth that depends entirely on them—on their judgment, energy, inbox, and availability. But that's not Perpetual Wealth; that's a job wearing a fancier suit.

You can have the best ideas in the world, but if your structure can't carry them—if it isn't integrated, resilient, and driven by a team aligned with your values—then you've built something fragile. And fragility is freedom's worst enemy.

So, pause here, and ask yourself:

- Have you built a system or just a career with an LLC?
- Are your advisors truly aligned or just loosely affiliated?
- Is your wealth insulated by design or vulnerable by default?
- Most importantly, are you still trying to prove your value through effort when what you want is to lead with vision?

Mindset isn't just thinking bigger. It's choosing to stop being the hero and start being the architect.

Because Perpetual Wealth doesn't emerge from isolation. It's forged in collaboration. And it begins when you decide to stop managing complexity and start engineering freedom.

Most entrepreneurs don't realize that risk hides in plain sight without collaboration.

You won't spot the tax trap buried in a trust provision until your CPA and attorney finally meet at the audit.

You won't see the lawsuit exposure tied to an outdated entity until your insurance guy says, "I didn't know you had that property in your name."

Being *Tax-Aware* and *Risk Vigilant* isn't about hiring specialists. It's about orchestrating them, so no one assumes someone else is covering your blind spot.

That's the cost of going it alone. And it's a cost your next chapter can't afford.

From Mindset to Move

If this chapter resonated with you, take a moment before sketching out your current structure, not your organizational chart, but your *advisory ecosystem.*

Who are your legal, tax, financial, and liquidity "Whos"? Do they know each other? Do they talk? Do they work toward a shared vision, or just respond to your last email?

You don't need to solve everything today. But awareness is a decisive first step. Because every chapter from here forward builds on one central idea:

You weren't meant to do this alone.

And the next level of wealth and freedom can only be reached with others.

Collaborate intentionally. Build structurally. Live freely.

That's the mindset of Perpetual Wealth.

Coming Up Next: Building the System That Scales With You

In the next chapter, we'll start unpacking the actual elements of the Perpetual Wealth system from the only truly income- and transfer-tax-free asset to the overlooked liquidity strategies that create usable wealth. You'll see how these pieces come together not just to preserve wealth, but to create freedom for you, and for the generations that follow.

But it all starts here with the decision to stop going it alone and start building with others.

You may have built the business, but collaboration is how you scale the freedom.

CHAPTER 17

From Noise to Harmony: The Wealth Symphony Begins

Talent wins games, but teamwork and intelligence win championships.

—*Michael Jordan, six-time NBA champion*

Before Michael Jordan became an NBA champion for the first time, he was already the most talented basketball player on the planet. But he couldn't get past the Detroit Pistons in the Eastern Conference Finals. The Bulls would run head-first into Isiah Thomas, Bill Laimbeer, and something called the "Jordan Rules," a brutal defensive scheme to neutralize Jordan's brilliance.

And for a while, it worked because Jordan tried to do it all himself.

He averaged thirty-five points a game. He logged insane minutes. He left it all on the court. And the Bulls still lost.

The turning point didn't come when Jordan got better. It came when the Bulls got smarter. When Phil Jackson became head coach and implemented the triangle offense—a strategy that didn't rely on Jordan carrying the team, but on every player knowing their role, moving in sync, and reading the floor together—the whole game changed.

Jordan still got his points. But now, Scottie Pippen slashed through the lane. Paxson hit open threes. Horace

Grant owned the boards. And the Pistons? They never stood a chance again.

It wasn't just talent that got Jordan over the hump. What got them over was structure, harmony, and alignment.

Now, let's talk about your team.

Chances are, you've been running your wealth like 1989 Jordan—brilliant, relentless, and stuck in hero mode. Your CPA is playing isolation ball. Your attorney is guarding his half of the court, unaware of what the rest of the team is doing. And your financial advisor? He's running plays you didn't call.

And you? You're stuck in the middle, calling audibles, translating between playbooks, and hoping the whole thing holds together through another tax season.

Tangible wealth—the kind that protects your family, preserves your business, and creates generational opportunity—doesn't come from playing hero ball. Wealth comes from structure, rhythm, and collaboration.

From Talent to Flow: What Coordination Unlocks

Every entrepreneur starts with hustle, instinct, and raw execution. And it works until the game gets bigger.

You form an LLC. Add an S-Corp and then a trust when your first kid is born. Later, you sign a buy-sell agreement that your partner insisted on over lunch. Maybe you open a solo 401(k), and later, a family limited partnership because "someone said it gets stuff out of your estate."

None of this is wrong. But it's rarely built with orchestration in mind. You solve one problem at a time. The result is a noisy orchestra with everyone playing a different tune. And you are stuck trying to conduct it.

There's a reason it feels like everything flows through you. It's easier to jump in and fix something than to trust others to handle it. But when you solve problems in one area—tax, trust, liquidity—another advisor unknowingly undoes it.

That's a design flaw, not a coordination issue.

Your Life's Score Reads Like a Symphony But Plays Like a Jam Session

Most estate and tax planning for entrepreneurs is fragmented. It works in the moment but falls apart in the aggregate.

What looks fine on paper becomes chaos when you zoom out and ask:

- How do all these entities work together to minimize taxes, *not just this year*, but over a lifetime?
- Are my liquidity strategies aligned with my business exit, or pulling in opposite directions?
- Who's watching the whole board and adjusting as the game evolves?

Most entrepreneurs don't know—not because they're inattentive—but because no one has ever shown them how it could work differently.

That's why strategic collaboration is Entrepreneurial Truth #5.

Not because you need more advice, but because the *right team*, working from a shared plan, transforms potential into protection and possibility.

When Your Team Isn't a Team

You may have a CPA, lawyer, Certified Financial Planner, insurance advisor, or bookkeeper.

You may even have relationships with world-class professionals.

But unless they're talking to each other and operating from a coordinated framework, you don't have a team. You have a bunch of smart people with your cell number.

That's not collaboration; it's dependency dressed as delegation.

Collaboration Isn't a Buzzword; It's Infrastructure

When we talk about collaboration inside the Perpetual Wealth system, we're not referring to occasional Zoom calls or year-end tax reviews.

We're talking about structural integration.

- Your estate planner anticipates tax laws and liquidity needs.
- Your CPA shapes outcomes, not just reports on them.
- Your liquidity strategist isn't selling a product; they're solving a capital issue.
- Your investment advisor knows your business isn't just another asset; it's *the* asset.

And most importantly?
They all operate off the exact *blueprint*.
That's your orchestra, not just a team.

You're Not the Star. You're the Conductor.

You may not write the music, but you select the players. You set the tempo. You make sure the whole thing flows.

That's what Perpetual Wealth requires—not more effort, but more alignment.

And when the system plays in harmony? It's not just efficient; it's powerful and sustainable.

Collaboration by Design: A Model That Works

When working with entrepreneurial families across the country, we ask them to:

1. *Build their internal core.*

   A lean, trusted team that shares its values and helps manage the ecosystem.

2. *Identify their external collaborators.*

   Choose professionals who don't just deliver value, but also integrate across disciplines.

3. *Appoint a lead advisor.*

   Someone who owns the big picture and holds everyone accountable to the strategy.

4. *Align around a process.*

   The Perpetual Wealth framework gives every "who" a clear "how."

Collaboration Check-In

Is your team a team or just a list of vendors?

Ask yourself:

- Have your attorney, CPA, and investment advisor ever shared a call without you coordinating it?
- When one recommends something, do they verify it with others or assume it's fine?
- Is anyone quarterbacking your plan, or are you left connecting the dots?

If your answer is "me," then congratulations. You're the glue.

It's time for a better system.

When Collaboration Works

When collaboration works, you'll hear things like:

"We coordinated with your CPA to finalize that structure."

"Your liquidity plan just saved $200,000 in taxes."

"We prepped your trust for the next-gen transition; we're good until next review."

Consequently, you'll stop waking up at 3 a.m., you'll stop holding it all together, and you'll start casting vision.

A Word of Caution: Collaboration ≠ Abdication

You still lead. However, your job now is defining values, outcomes, and direction, not reacting to chaos.

The right collaboration *multiplies* your role.

Mindset Shift: From Holding It Together to Pulling It Together

You've built something extraordinary. But let's ask the tricky question:

Are you truly leading it or just holding it together?

There's a moment in every entrepreneur's journey where the tools that got you here stop working: the hustle, intuition, and solo problem-solving. They were necessary, but now they're your ceiling.

If you're still the glue holding advisors together, making calls between your CPA and attorney, juggling liquidity ideas from one advisor while the others are in the dark, you're not running a system; you're managing a mess.

It's not a people problem; it's a structural problem.

Ask yourself:

- Are your advisors connected by process or by your phone number?
- When one professional makes a move, does everyone else stay in sync or scramble to adjust?
- Is someone quarterbacking your entire strategy, or are you still the playbook and the waterboy?
- Does your family wealth plan run on trust and automation or reaction and memory?

- And when your team meets, do they even know they're a team?

Being **Coachable & Collaboration-Ready** doesn't mean abdicating leadership. It means defining your vision so clearly that others can execute it even when you're not in the room.

Structurally Sound at this level means systems talk to each other. Trusts, liquidity tools, and tax planning are not standalones; they're parts of a whole.

Being **System-Oriented** means your wealth grows not because you're in every meeting but because the system is designed to make decisions based on your principles on your behalf.

This is the transition from control to conduction, activity to alignment, and duct tape to design.

So, ask yourself one more time:

Are you still holding everything together?

Or are you finally ready to pull it together into a unified, Perpetual Wealth system that plays in harmony long after you've put down the baton?

Up Next: The Perpetual Wealth Process

The final chapter explains how all of this comes together, from discovery to design to ongoing stewardship. We'll also show you the framework we use to turn complexity into clarity, coordination into control, and chaos into freedom.

Collaboration may be the multiplier. However, structure is what makes the results stick.

CHAPTER 18

From Systems to Structure— Where Wealth Becomes Perpetual

> The skills that brought you out of Egypt are not the
> same skills that get you into the Promised Land.
>
> —*Rabbi Lord Jonathan Sacks,*
> *chief rabbi of the United Hebrew Congregations of the*
> *UK Commonwealth, author, philosopher, and theologian*

In the last chapter, we talked about Michael Jordan and how even the greatest of all time couldn't win it all alone.

For years, Jordan was a highlight reel with sneakers. However, the championships didn't come until Phil Jackson introduced the triangle offense—a system that distributed the load, synchronized the team, and turned one man's brilliance into collective dominance.

That's where you are right now.

You've built something real. You've pushed through resistance, scaled a business, and made money. You've done the hard things other people won't. But if you're honest with yourself, you still carry the weight of coordination. You're not just the owner or the CEO. You're also the de facto strategist, liaison between professionals, and executor of half a dozen financial plans never designed to work together.

It's exhausting and unnecessary.

Jordan didn't win by scoring more; he won by stepping into a system that matched his talent. And when you have a structure aligned with your vision, your wealth stops being a burden and starts becoming a platform.

That's the transition we're talking about—the shift from hustle to harmony, from rugged individualism to coordinated strength.

As Rabbi Sacks reminded us, the skillset that parts the Red Sea isn't the same one that builds a spiritual home in the land of milk and honey.

Getting your entrepreneurial venture off the ground—pushing through chaos, defying the odds—requires one set of muscles: grit, urgency, and scrappiness. However, those muscles won't carry you into sustained freedom.

Freedom isn't just about escape. Freedom is about arriving in a life designed around your terms, not someone else's defaults.

It's about arriving at a place where your business no longer owns you. Where your legal, tax, and financial structures aren't reacting to your success but fueling it. Where liquidity is a strategy, not a fire drill. Where your family isn't wondering what happens if something happens to you, because the plan's already in motion, aligned, and stress-tested.

Arrival means control, confidence, and clarity.

It means you're no longer running everything by memory and momentum. You've built a structure that holds the weight of your ambition—and frees you up to grow, mentor, invest, and lead from a higher place.

That's what the Perpetual Wealth Process is designed to deliver.

What We've Learned So Far and Why It Matters

This hasn't been a book about products. It's been a dismantling of default thinking. Over eighteen chapters, we've invited you to question almost everything you've been told by professionals who, though well-meaning, were operating inside narrow lanes.

We challenged the assumption that the traditional financial system was ever meant to serve someone like you. It wasn't. The tax code was designed to quietly extract as much wealth as possible from those who don't understand its loopholes, punishing those who conform. The legal system makes it difficult to protect assets, burdens intra-family wealth transfers with red tape, and often profits from the disharmony it claims to resolve. The banking industry was built to charge the highest interest on borrowed money while paying the lowest on the wealth you've parked there. These systems were not created with entrepreneurs in mind. And most advisors? Well, they've been trained to work within these traditionally built systems.

You, on the other hand, build. You take the risk. You're still in motion.

What the Five Truths Have Always Been About

By now, you've noticed this hasn't been a linear journey. It's been a deconstruction. Chapter by chapter, we've fractured the assumptions that keep entrepreneurs reactive, exposed, and out of control. And in their place, we've rebuilt a mindset anchored by the Five Entrepreneurial Truths.

These aren't just "things to know." They are *principles* to build with—truths to return to when a new opportunity lands in your lap, when you're making your next investment, or when the lawyer across the table says, "This is just how it's done."

Because *how it's done* has never applied to people like you.

Beneath it all—the new strategies, rethinking of trusts, taxes, liquidity, and control—was something more profound. A mindset shift. A new operating system. Everything in this book has pointed to five essential truths, not isolated lessons. Still, the framework behind how smart entrepreneurs rig the rules in their favor, protect what they've built, and multiply their freedoms. These truths aren't just worth remembering; they're worth using.

Truth #1: Man-Made Rules Are Just That

Don't play by default. Design your own rulebook.
The tax code, legal frameworks, and financial systems weren't handed down from on high—humans drafted them, many of whom never built a business. Your power lies in realizing these systems aren't fixed. They're *flexible*, but only if you know how to bend them.

Use this truth to challenge every advisor who says, "You can't do that." Ask: *Why not? And if not that way, what's a smarter way?*

Truth #2: Seven Entrepreneurial Mindsets Build Systemic Success

Linear thinking builds a business. Exponential thinking builds a system.
Entrepreneurs tend to carry their success on their backs. What starts as a hustle becomes an identity until the very thing that created momentum becomes the ceiling on future growth. That's not a character flaw. It's a mindset trap.

Growth is about thinking differently.

Real leverage doesn't come from being the smartest person in the room. It comes from building rooms where every seat is filled by someone whose capabilities complement yours. The greatest entrepreneurs aren't soloists. They're conductors.

Use this truth to escape the trap of *"I'll just do it myself."* That's the language of rugged individualism. Instead, adopt a growth-oriented, coachable mindset that seeks out aligned expertise, embraces better systems, and scales you out of the grind without losing control.

Truth #3: Flipping the Script: Turning the System in Your Favor

The rules are rigged, but they're riggable.

The system wasn't built to help you but to contain you. However, when you understand how it's wired, you can reverse-engineer it to serve your goals. The ultra-wealthy don't work harder. They work through structure. They build trust-based entities, strategically own assets, and shift from personal liability to protected leverage.

You don't beat the system by avoiding it. You flip it by deciding how your assets are held, how your income is characterized, and how your wealth moves across time and generations.

Use this truth to play offense, not defense, with the legal and financial tools quietly built for those who know how to use them.

Truth #4: Freedom Comes From a Tax-Free War Chest

Control doesn't come from having money. It comes from having access, on your terms.

You can have millions in equity and still be trapped. The real advantage isn't what you own; it's what you can use when you need it, without asking for permission or triggering unnecessary taxes.

Liquidity isn't just a safety net. It's a weapon. It lets you move when others freeze, buy when others panic, and lead when others hedge. The most successful entrepreneurs don't just plan for emergencies—they build liquidity into their system as a strategic advantage.

Use this truth to stop measuring wealth by net worth and start engineering freedom through access.

Truth #5: From Doing to Designing—Why a Unified External Team Unlocks Freedom

Solo brilliance fades. Coordinated strategy scales.

The heroic entrepreneur myth endures, but it eventually dies. Because true freedom doesn't come from being the most intelligent person in the room, it comes from building a room where every expert brings their best, and no one is duplicating or contradicting each other's work.

Perpetual Wealth is built on harmony. Your plan, your professionals, and your process must align—not just once, but repeatedly—as your life and business evolve.

Use this truth to evolve from piecemeal advice to synchronized execution, where every player moves in step with your vision.

From Truth to Action: Why the Process Is the Product

Knowing the five truths is one thing. Living them is another.

If you've ever looked at your estate plan, business structure, or tax strategy and thought, *I know this could be better; I just don't know how*—you're in the right place.

Because what you need isn't more effort. It's orchestration.

You may already have a team of professionals—CPAs, attorneys, advisors—doing their best to support your goals. That's not a problem. It's expected. But what most entrepreneurs don't realize is that even the best professionals often operate in silos. Even great advice can clash when it's not well-coordinated.

If you're curious about how I—and the team behind the Perpetual Wealth Program—approach these issues, we've created resources designed for that kind of curiosity. These include tools, masterclasses, podcast episodes, blogs, live coaching, and events that demonstrate how strategy, structure, and execution can work in tandem. And for entrepreneurs ready to move beyond curiosity and into coordinated action, we're here for that too.

What follows isn't theory. It's the actual process we use to build systems that turn complexity into clarity and wealth into freedom.

Let's walk through it—this time with real depth. What follows is the process my team takes an entrepreneur like you through to achieve their goals and desires.

The DEMERO™ Process: The Architecture Behind Perpetual Wealth

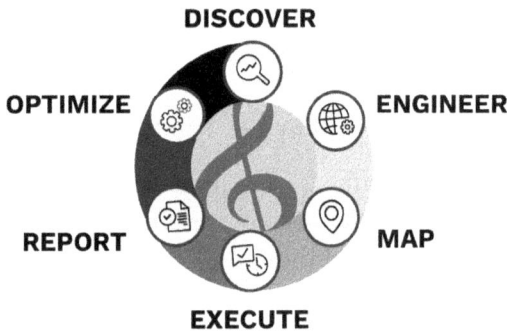

Figure 18-A

D – Discover

This is where the noise gets cleared and the real story begins.

The *Discover* phase is our diagnostic engine. Before recommending a single solution, we dig into what most professionals overlook: the full scope of your goals, constraints, exposures, and hidden opportunities.

We review your trusts, entities, tax returns, insurance policies, and partnership agreements. But that's just the start. We ask bigger questions:

- What are you building—*and why*?
- What keeps you up at night, and what do you want to protect most?
- What's working today that may not work three years from now?

We also identify:

- Gaps in legal protection (unfunded trusts, poorly drafted agreements, outdated titling)
- Tax inefficiencies tied to ownership structures, pass-through income, or embedded capital gains
- Risks related to business succession, liquidity constraints, or partnership dynamics
- Missing liquidity strategies that could create fragility in both opportunity and crisis

This isn't a surface-level questionnaire—it's a full forensic review, paired with an in-depth understanding of your aspirations.

Because a strategy built on assumptions is reckless. A strategy built on truth is where clarity begins.

You can't fix what you can't see.

E – Engineer

This is where vision becomes structure.

With clarity from Discover, we move into *Engineer*, the design phase where we architect the blueprint for your Perpetual Wealth system. This isn't just paperwork. It's a legal, tax, and liquidity strategy, structured in harmony and built around your outcomes.

Here, we design:

- Trusts that hold and protect assets, control distributions, and shift tax obligations while maintaining operational flexibility.
- Entity structures (holding companies, management companies, real estate partnerships) that isolate risk, optimize tax treatment, and preserve control.
- Intra-family sale or gifting strategies that shift value without triggering unnecessary taxes.
- Liquidity planning structures using lines of credit, private lending, or life insurance-backed access—so your wealth isn't locked away.
- Coordination across jurisdictions when offshore or out-of-state entities or trusts are appropriate.

Every recommendation is explained in plain language, backed by case-driven reasoning, and designed around your goals.

This phase isn't about plugging you into a templated "wealth plan." It's about reverse-engineering the desired results and designing a system to achieve them.

Your plan should be as original as your vision.

M – Map

This is where your potential paths come into focus.

The *Map* phase is about options, not mandates. In this phase, we present articulated strategies designed for your goals, risk profile, and operating reality. Each strategy is explained in plain language, and then visually modeled with flowcharts and spreadsheets so you can evaluate how it works in real life, not just on paper.

We show you:

- Multiple paths forward exist, each tailored to your specific needs, along with their tradeoffs, timing, and implementation complexity.
- How control, tax implications, asset protection, and liquidity behave under each scenario.
- What each strategy *looks like*—with flowcharts and spreadsheets that break down the numbers, timelines, and structures.

This phase isn't about deciding for you. It's about giving you the clarity to decide *intelligently*. When you can visualize the consequences and opportunities of each move, you don't just feel empowered—you become the architect of your wealth.

Clarity before commitment. Strategy before signatures.

E – Execute

Now, strategy becomes real.

Once the roadmap is clear and you've chosen your preferred structure, we move from theory to implementation. In the *Execute* phase, we build the actual architecture—drafting and establishing trusts, creating new entities, transferring ownership, and activating liquidity or tax strategies designed around your goals.

That includes:

- Establishing new trusts and funding them with the appropriate assets

- Executing intra-family transfers, recapitalizations, or gifting strategies
- Forming and structuring new entities as needed
- Repositioning asset ownership to align with the legal and tax plan
- Initiating liquidity strategies that support opportunity and protection

This isn't passive paperwork; it's precision restructuring. It requires foresight, sequencing, and alignment among multiple disciplines. Our team choreographs each step with your attorneys, CPAs, and financial partners so that everything integrates as intended.

This is where the real protection gets built—and where future freedom takes shape.

Vision without implementation is just a fantasy.

R – Report

Strategy without compliance is a liability.

Once your structures are created and funded, they must be properly reported across multiple jurisdictions and institutions. In the *Report* phase, we ensure that your strategy is legally sound and institutionally recognized, not just in concept, but also in the actual filings and records that matter.

That includes:

- Preparing and filing gift tax returns to document intra-family asset transfers
- Reporting intra-entity transactions properly on your income tax returns
- Filing annual reports with state agencies to keep your entities in good standing

- Maintaining corporate records, trust documentation, and capital account tracking
- Communicating with banks, title companies, and lenders to ensure correct titling
- Coordinating with business partners and advisors to align filings across entities

This is the operational backbone that preserves the strength of your strategy. Without it, even the most sophisticated plan may suffer an attack from tax and regulatory authorities for noncompliance. We handle the complexity, so your structure doesn't just work in theory; it works in the real world.

What the IRS doesn't know can still hurt you.

O – Optimize

Plans don't fail because they're flawed. They fail because they're frozen in time.

The final phase—*Optimize*—separates temporary structures from perpetual ones. Once your system is built and reported correctly, we shift into long-term maintenance mode. This is where we adapt and refine your strategy as life evolves: new businesses, new laws, new family dynamics, and new opportunities.

Optimize isn't reactive—it's proactive.

That includes:

- Monitoring changes in tax law, estate law, and regulatory frameworks that impact your plan.
- Adjusting structures when new entities are formed or business interests are restructured.
- Revisiting liquidity strategies to ensure they remain aligned with your financial needs.

- Updating trust provisions or trustee appointments as family circumstances change.
- Reassessing asset ownership, titling, or protection strategies based on market or personal shifts.
- Keeping your documents and strategies aligned—not just with your vision, but with reality.

Your system isn't static, and neither are you. That's why *Optimize* is ongoing. We don't "set it and forget it." We keep your structure functioning at a high level, year after year, generation after generation.

This is how Perpetual Wealth lives up to its name.

Perpetual Wealth isn't a noun; it's a verb.

EPILOGUE

The System Is Rigged— Now Re-Rig It For You

Take a moment.

Not because you're at the end of this book, but because you're standing at the beginning of something that most entrepreneurs will *never* fully understand. Most never even get close.

The truth is, a lot of smart business owners go their whole lives mastering operations, team leadership, and strategic execution only to unknowingly bleed out their wealth to taxes, creditors, courts, and disorganized heirs. They know how to build value, but they never learn how to *keep* it. Or how to transfer it. Or how to turn it into a flywheel that funds opportunity, tax-free, for generations.

But you're not like most entrepreneurs.

Because most entrepreneurs don't read this kind of book, and they certainly don't finish it.

You, on the other hand? You powered through each chapter like the entrepreneur you are—sharp, curious, and unwilling to settle for surface-level advice. You decoded the IUL mechanics, grasped the leverage in premium financing, confronted the lawsuit landmines, mapped out the role of trust structures, absorbed the realities of market risk, and maybe even cracked a smile once or twice along the way.

You didn't just learn how to *preserve wealth;* you learned how to *perpetuate it.*

And now? You're no longer walking into your financial future with your eyes closed. You're no longer hoping that your CPA "caught it," that your estate plan "covers it," or that your investment portfolio will "outpace it."

Hope is not a plan; structure is.

And what you've gained, page by page, is a lens through which you now see your entire legal, tax, and financial world differently. Your income streams, entities, distributions, trusts, and tax strategies are no longer disconnected. They're components of a *system*. A system you now understand. A system you can control.

That's power.

But it's more than that; it's a responsibility. Because now you know the truth: most legal, tax, and financial professionals are still playing checkers. You've started playing chess. And while that can feel invigorating, it can also feel a little lonely. You may already be realizing just how few people in your corner know how to have these conversations. Even fewer know how to execute them.

That's where we come in.

This book isn't a finish line. It's the on-ramp.

Because if something in these pages stirred something in you, whether it was the thought of your kids accessing capital without asking a bank or the realization that your life insurance isn't just about death—it's about *liquidity*—then now is the time to take action.

You're not building a business anymore. You're building a *Perpetual Wealth Enterprise*™—one that lives beyond you, funds opportunity for your bloodline, and pays dividends in confidence, clarity, and control.

And trust me, that enterprise won't run itself.

That's why we've created resources designed to meet you right where you are, in whatever stage of momentum or complexity your life presents:

- **Perpetual Wealth™ Podcast**: Bite-sized deep dives and expert conversations you can take with you on your drive, your jog, or your next flight. It's everything we couldn't fit into these pages delivered straight into your ears, minus the fluff.

- **Blog**: Real-time insights, legal updates, expanded case studies, and practical applications of the frameworks you've just mastered. You'll learn how others are applying these tools and what mistakes to avoid.

- **Masterclasses**: Not just theory. These are immersive, hands-on strategy sessions where we break down actual Perpetual Wealth blueprints for business owners like you. If this book opened your eyes, the masterclass will open the vault.

- **Live Events**: In-person intensives that bring together high-performing entrepreneurs, financial architects, and legal experts in a room full of possibility. No fluff. No upsell. Just real conversations, customized plans, and momentum you can feel in your bones.

The world isn't slowing down. Taxes aren't getting lower. Lawsuits aren't disappearing. Politicians aren't passing smarter wealth laws.

But you?

You're moving forward anyway. Armed. Alert. Aligned.

Now, you've seen behind the curtain, and you've learned how the game works. So, *you get to choose how to play it.*

Here's your final encouragement:

Don't go back to the default. Don't shrink back into the routine. You've come too far to let this just be an "interesting read."

Let this be the moment your entire financial life begins to *operate differently.*

Your future isn't just bright; it's designed.

Your income doesn't just pay bills; it funds capital systems.

Your wealth doesn't just accumulate; it *circulates*.

And your family won't just inherit dollars; they'll inherit *direction*.

You've earned this. Let's make your wealth as resilient as your ambition.

PERPETUAL WEALTH
MINDSET EXERCISE

Here are seven mindsets that entrepreneurs often don't realize can mean the difference between success and mediocrity. An entrepreneur who possesses the best mindset and works with their internal team and external advisors in each is much more likely to create exponentially growing businesses that withstand the test of time.

1. Growth-Oriented

Worst: Avoids change. Sticks to old methods. Resents or fears competition. Believes they've already "made it."

Below Average: Curious about growth but slow to act. Constantly gathering information but rarely implementing. Projects start, stall, then collect dust. Overwhelmed by ideas, underwhelmed by execution.

Good: Pursues new growth opportunities but experiences diminishing returns. Adds complexity without increasing capacity. Growth is linear, not exponential. Struggles to assign the right people to the right roles.

Best: Proactively seeks new learning, partnerships, and capabilities. Hires team members who scale capacity, not just support effort. Pursues exponential outcomes. Evolves both personally and professionally.

2. Coachable

Worst: Dismisses feedback. Believes most professionals are interchangeable. Reluctant to explore new tools, systems, or ideas.

Below Average: Pays for advice but overrides it with gut instinct. Acts first, then informs advisors after the fact, leaving them to clean up the damage.

Good: Values seasoned counsel but falls back into Rugged Individualism when it matters most. Starts strong but rarely follows through.

Best: Invites strategic input before making moves. Builds trust with advisors and seeks collaborative clarity. Asks probing questions that reveal hidden leverage. Understands that great advice is a multiplier—if used in real time.

3. Structurally Sound

Worst: Operates without legal or financial structures, or creates them haphazardly and ignores maintenance. Assumes they'll "fix it later."

Below Average: Sets up basic structures with help but neglects to maintain or scale them. Each new venture stands alone. No master plan. No coherence.

Good: It has a solid foundational structure that is maintained annually. However, it lacks optimization because professionals aren't coordinated or equipped for advanced strategies.

Best: Structures are pre-designed to evolve. Legal, tax, and financial teams collaborate proactively. The family enterprise is architected to seamlessly absorb future ventures, liquidity events, and transitions. Systems are stress-tested, updated, and aligned with purpose.

4. Tax-Aware

Worst: Unaware of obligations. Constantly behind. Pays penalties and interest. Delegates without oversight.

Below Average: Understands basic concepts but fears complexity. Asks for "simple," then wonders why the plan isn't working.

Good: Hires professionals to handle strategy but relies too heavily on CPAs without layering legal and liquidity tactics. Gets safe advice but not transformational outcomes.

Best: Designs tax strategy with an integrated team—minimizing income, capital gains, transfer, and self-employment taxes legally. Reviews plans consistently as goals and laws change. Understands the timing and character of income as planning levers.

5. Liquidity Conscious

Worst: No liquidity plan. Cash-strapped when it matters most.

Below Average: Reactive, not proactive. Doesn't plan for partnership buyouts, tax liabilities, or growth needs. Access to capital is slow, expensive, or both.

Good: Has liquidity for everyday needs but misses big opportunities. Could build internal cash systems but hasn't. Net worth grows; access doesn't.

Best: Builds tax-free liquidity structures designed to deploy capital with speed and control. Uses liquidity as a strategy, not just a cushion. Leverages internal cash systems to seize opportunities and defend against risk.

6. Collaboration-Ready

Worst: Operates in a vacuum. Believes only they can drive the outcome. Rejects help or tolerates it without engagement.

Below-average: The team occasionally seeks advice but rarely integrates it. Team lacks innovative thinking or a unified strategy.

Good: Collaborates internally but sees peers and competitors as threats, not potential allies. External team operates in silos.

Best: Builds environments where ideas, execution, and strategy sync. Converts competition into collaboration. Attracts the best minds by creating systems others want to be part of.

7. Risk Vigilant

Worst: Assets fully exposed. No protective structures in place, or the paperwork is outdated and nonfunctional. Doesn't know what they don't know.

Below Average: Covers basic risks. Misses the big ones. No plan for lawsuits, partner exits, cyber threats, or economic shocks. Assumes insurance alone is enough.

Good: Solid foundation: LLCs, corporate records, and insurance in place. Covers major risks. But the system is static, not adaptive.

Best: Uses multi-layered structures to protect wealth, business continuity, and personal liability. Maintains offense and defense strategies. Insurance, liquidity, and legal tools are pre-positioned for worst-case scenarios and used to gain a strategic advantage.

ACKNOWLEDGMENTS

They say writing a book is a solitary endeavor. Those people have never tried writing a book while running a successful 100+ year-old boutique law firm, leading a national consulting company, writing and recording podcasts, masterclasses, and webinars, introducing clients to advanced legal, tax, and financial strategies, keeping up with an ever-changing tax code, and trying to remember whether the cat litter box needs scooping.

The truth is, I didn't write this book alone. It wouldn't exist without the people who nudged, supported, educated, humored, and outright dragged me across the finish line.

First, to Kary Oberbrunner and his fantastic team at Igniting Souls Publishing, including Elizabeth Haller—thank you for helping bring this vision to life. This isn't just another legal and tax book, and from day one, you understood that. You saw it as it truly is: a blueprint for how entrepreneurs can structure their lives, wealth, and freedom. I kept asking, "Is this readable? Does it make sense? Am I losing people in legal/tax land?" And you kept reminding me that not only did it make sense, it mattered. Your belief in the uniqueness of this project made all the difference.

To my good friend, Susan Lipp, Editor-in-Chief of *Trusts & Estates* magazine, thank you for providing me a platform to serve not just clients but also the professionals who guide them. Your editorial vision and your insistence on clarity with substance gave me the space to write in a way that moves the needle, especially in a field known for its footnotes and density.

To Maria Reimer and Regina Sadoski, my right hands at Sheppard Law Firm and in The Freedom Practice®. You're the engine behind everything we do—spreading the message, supporting our firm's clients and our Freedom Practice member firms, planning and presenting at our Client Care, BluePrint, and Practice Xcelerator live events, and somehow keeping me on track. You make it look easy, and we all know it isn't.

To Michael B. Hill, my law partner of over twenty years and co-architect of what I genuinely believe is a premier Florida estate planning law firm. You work magic with automation and spreadsheets. Together, we've blended creativity and high-touch expertise with precision-built technology systems in a way that leaves the silk-stocking firms wondering how we do it. Here's the secret: we genuinely care, and our backstage processes—supporting our unique front-stage client experiences—execute better.

To Liam Ladia, my behind-the-scenes tech master—thank you for web design, podcast production, branding, IT, digital vendor wrangling, these book graphics, and at least five other things I probably don't even know you do. Your creativity, good humor, and *yes-we-can* energy have taken our digital game to a new level.

To my friend and colleague Alan Gassman, who proves that technical brilliance and tax humor—yes, tax humor—can coexist. Your Thursday reports, Leimberg posts, and uncanny ability to make 643(f)(1) feel like a punchline have inspired me more than you know. You showed me that being technically precise and entertaining aren't mutually exclusive.

To my former coach and good friend, Jan Mohamed, who has made the impossible look routine more times than I can count. You don't just "do insurance." You architect liquidity, solve the unsolvable, and save my clients bundles in the process. Your team—including Tammy Albitz and the sharp minds at Higginbotham Insurance Group, including Brian

Jung—deserves a standing ovation for the magic behind the illustrations and solutions brought to life in this book.

To Gary Klaben, who opened the door to how a family office operates. This badass former Army Ranger commander gave me valuable insights into financial maneuvering and client empowerment that planted seeds for many of the strategies found in these pages. And yes, you also gave me the nudge (read: push) to include some of the most thoughtful financial chapters. Consider this your victory lap.

To Alex Gertsburg, whose family emigrated from Moldova when he was a young boy and who exhibits classic immigrant drive in everything he does. Your legal work in liability identification and protection helps clients sleep better at night, and it has pushed me to think deeper about how liability fits into entrepreneurial strategy. You've raised the bar on what real legal strategy looks like.

To Dan Sullivan and the team at Strategic Coach—Babs Smith, Stephanie Song, and Shannon Waller—thank you for guiding me to reframe my career from that of a technician to that of an entrepreneur. Dan, you've said I'm one of your best clients over the past 20+ years—a "slow learner who writes checks." I'll take it as a compliment because you were right. You helped me unlock a bigger future.

Most importantly, to my family—first to our children, who, though grown, remain at the center of Patti's and my world:

To Gabi and our son-in-law Benji Bernstein, who live and thrive in the New York City suburbs after living in Manhattan. We don't see you as often as we'd like (though we enjoy pretending we're locals—Patti *is* from Brooklyn, after all). Gabi, your creativity, research, and marketing eye continually show me how to message with purpose. And Benji, your AI platform for estate planners, CPAs, and financial advisors, is redefining what's possible in our industry. I'm proud to call you family—and sometimes collaborators.

To Courtney and our son-in-law Philip Smith. Courtney, you've been our empathetic child—ever since you were a kid—and now you live it out every day as a pediatric physical therapist helping children in need. You remind me that true legacy isn't just wealth; it's compassion. And Philip, you are a dedicated and hard-working man for those without limbs and other prosthetic needs, and may be the only Jewish guy I know who can rebuild a car like it's a Lego set. Your talents and heart are one-of-a-kind.

And to our youngest, Madison Sage Hersch, who is crushing it in dental school. Not only are you earning your DMD from our shared alma mater—the University of Florida—but you're going the extra mile and getting your PhD as well. Whether you go into research or private practice, one thing's clear: you're going to be an extraordinary dentist. And your future is blindingly bright. (And for sure, I'll trust you with my teeth!)

To my father, Joel W. Hersch, who guided me to consider graduate paths in accounting and law, knowing that those skills would lead to an understanding of the entrepreneurial frameworks necessary for success. And for introducing me to Alan Gassman, who changed the course of my career. And to my mother, Phyllis K. Hersch z"l, who passed from leukemia in 2016—you were tough as nails but also a little goofy. That mix? I carry it proudly.

And finally, to my wife Patti, who has put up with me—drafting trusts, calling clients, chasing rabbits down holes, writing books (this is my seventh), working weekends and late nights at my home computer—for more than thirty-eight years. That alone deserves a medal of honor, or at the very least, a spa day, a shopping spree at Anthropologie, and a waterfront lunch of blackened grouper and a cold drink at Nervous Nellie's. You've been my constant, my compass, and the quiet force behind everything that's ever worked in my life—including this book. Whether it's dinner and music at Mills River Brewery near our mountain home in Asheville or a lazy Sunday boating through Florida's waterways—it all reminds me why I do this. I couldn't do it without you. I wouldn't want to.

To all of you: I love you and thank you.

You didn't just help me write a book. You helped me build something that, I hope, will ripple far beyond these pages.

To your bigger future.

ABOUT THE AUTHOR

Craig R. Hersch is a nationally recognized estate planning attorney, author, and practice development expert. He is the Senior Partner at the Sheppard Law Firm in Fort Myers, Florida. A Florida Bar Board Certified Wills, Trusts & Estates attorney and CPA, he has pioneered several trademarked processes within his estate planning and administration practice, including The Family Estate & Legacy Program™ and The Estate Settlement Program™.

As the creator of The Freedom Practice™, Hersch coaches estate planning attorneys nationwide, helping them enhance client service and distinguish themselves in an increasingly competitive legal marketplace. His expertise is regularly featured in Trusts & Estates Magazine, where he serves on the editorial advisory board.

Hersch is a prolific author with numerous books designed to educate clients and legal professionals. He has published professional articles in The Practical Tax Lawyer, The Florida Bar Journal, and Trusts & Estates Magazine. Beyond his legal practice, Hersch has an entrepreneurial background as a founding shareholder and director of a Florida private, state-chartered trust company, which, after eighteen years, was sold to a regional bank.

Hersch is a sought-after speaker and educator, delivering high-energy, insightful presentations that break down complex estate planning, tax, and business succession strategies into practical, real-world solutions. Whether speaking to attorneys looking to modernize their firms, CPAs, or financial professionals navigating the evolving estate planning landscape, Hersch delivers high-impact sessions that inspire professionals to elevate their approach.

Craig enjoys adventure travel, road biking, swimming, boating, white water rafting, and hiking. He divides his time between Fort Myers and Asheville. He and his wife, Patti, have been married for over thirty-five years. Together, they have three amazing daughters and two wonderful sons-in-law: Gabrielle Hersch Bernstein (married to Benji), Courtney Hersch Smith (married to Philip), and Madison.

PERPETUAL WEALTH™ INSIGHTS: THE BLOG FOR ENTREPRENEURS WHO REFUSE TO PLAY SMALL

STOP PLAYING DEFENSE WITH YOUR WEALTH.

YOU BUILT IT. NOW LEARN HOW TO STRUCTURE IT TO PROTECT IT—AND GROW IT. THE PERPETUAL WEALTH™ BLOG DELIVERS SHARP, USABLE INSIGHTS FOR ENTREPRENEURS READY TO OUTSMART TAXES, TAME LEGAL RISK, AND TAKE BACK CONTROL. NO FLUFF. JUST STRAIGHT-TALK STRATEGY.

PerpetualWealth.Law/Blog

THE PERPETUAL WEALTH™ PODCAST: CONVERSATIONS WITH THE RULE REWRITERS

NO FLUFF. NO BS. JUST SHARP CONVERSATIONS WITH THE LEGAL ARCHITECTS, TAX TACTICIANS, AND FREEDOM DESIGNERS WHO ARE REWRITING THE RULES OF SUCCESS. IF YOU'RE SCALING A BUSINESS AND WANT TO SCALE YOUR THINKING TOO—THIS PODCAST IS YOUR PLAYBOOK.

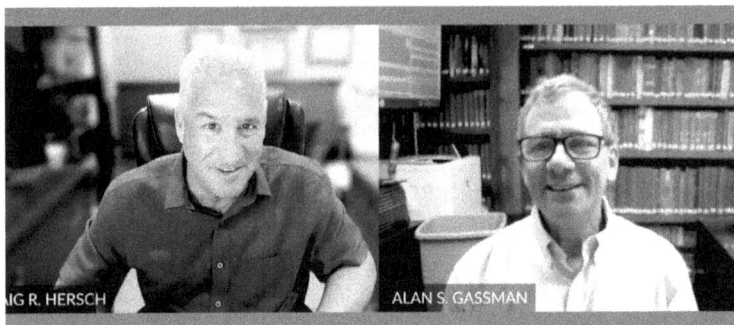

IG R. HERSCH   ALAN S. GASSMAN

PerpetualWealth.Law/Podcast

THIS BOOK IS PROTECTED INTELLECTUAL PROPERTY

Instant IP[IP]

The author of this book values Intellectual Property. The book you just read is protected by Instant IP[IP], a proprietary process, which integrates blockchain technology giving Intellectual Property "Global Protection." By creating a "Time-Stamped" smart contract that can never be tampered with or changed, we establish "First Use" that tracks back to the author.

Instant IP[IP] functions much like a Pre-Patent since it provides an immutable "First Use" of the Intellectual Property. This is achieved through our proprietary process of leveraging blockchain technology and smart contracts. As a result, proving "First Use" is simple through a global and verifiable smart contract. By protecting intellectual property with blockchain technology and smart contracts, we establish a "First to File" event.

Protected by Instant IP[IP]

LEARN MORE AT INSTANTIP.TODAY

www.ingramcontent.com/pod-product-compliance
Lightning Source LLC
Chambersburg PA
CBHW071541210326
41597CB00019B/3073